PELICAN BOOKS

ROMAN MYTHS

Michael Grant has been successively Chancellor's
Medallist, Fellow of Trinity College, Cambridge,
Professor of Humanity at Edinburgh University, first
Vice-Chancellor of Khartoum University, and President
and Vice-Chancellor of the Queen's University of Belfast.
Until 1966 he was President of the Virgil Society. He
has also translated Tacitus' *Annals of Imperial Rome*,
Cicero's *Selected Works*, *Murder Trials*, *Selected
Political Speeches* and philosophical essays (*On
the Good Life*) for the Penguin Classics; his other books
include *The World of Rome* (1960), *Myths of the Greeks
and Romans* (1962), *The Civilizations of Europe* (1965),
Gladiators (1967), *Roman Literature* (the last two
available in Pelicans), *The Climax of Rome* (1968), *The
Ancient Mediterranean. Julius Caesar* (1969), *The Ancient
Historians*, *The Roman Forum*, *Nero* (1970), *Cities
of Vesuvius*, *Herod the Great* and *Roman Myths* (1971),
Cleopatra (1972), *The Jews in the Roman World* (1973).
He has also compiled two Pelican anthologies:
Roman Readings (revised edition 1967), and *Greek
Literature in Translation* (1973).

MICHAEL GRANT

ROMAN MYTHS

PENGUIN BOOKS

Penguin Books Ltd, Harmondsworth,
Middlesex, England
Penguin Books Australia Ltd, Ringwood,
Victoria, Australia

First published by Weidenfeld & Nicolson 1971
Revised edition published in Pelican Books 1973

Copyright © Michael Grant Publications Ltd 1971, 1973

Made and printed in Great Britain by
Richard Clay (The Chaucer Press) Ltd,
Bungay, Suffolk
Set in Linotype Pilgrim

To My Mother

CONTENTS

PLATES

MAPS

ACKNOWLEDGEMENTS

The author and publishers would like to thank the following for supplying photographs for this book: Bibliothèque Nationale, Paris, plates 1, 7, 24 and 28; British Museum, 4, 6, 11, 12, 14 and 16; Werner Forman, 13, 15 and 17; Fototeca Unione, Rome, 26; John Freeman, 4, 6, 8, 11, 12, 14, 16, 18, 22, 25 and 28; Mansell Collection, 2, 5, 9, 10, 23 and 27; Palazzo Torlonia, 19, 20, 21; Warburg Institute, 3.

The author and publishers also wish to acknowledge the following for granting permission to quote from copyright sources: Cambridge University Press for L. P. Wilkinson, *Ovid Recalled*; Centaur Press Ltd for A. E. Watts, *The Poems of Sextus Propertius*; Faber & Faber Ltd and Random House Inc. for W. H. Auden, *Collected Shorter Poems 1927–1957*, 'Secondary Epic'; and Faber & Faber and Harcourt Brace Jovanovich for T. S. Eliot, *Collected Poems 1909–1962*, 'Choruses from the Rock, VIII'; Heinemann Ltd and Harvard University Press, The Loeb Classical Library, for *Cicero: De Senectute, De Amicitia, De Divinatione* (W. A. Falconer), *Florus and Nepos* (E. S. Forster and J. C. Rolfe), *Dionysius of Halicarnassus, Roman Antiquities* (E. Cary), vols. I and III, *Livy* (B. O. Foster), vols. I and III, *Diodorus Siculus* (C. H. Oldfather), *Varro: De Lingua Latina* (R. G. Kent); The Hogarth Press Ltd for C. Day Lewis, *The Eclogues, Georgics and Aeneid of Virgil*; Macmillan for Sir Edward Marsh, *The Odes of Horace*, and A. H. M. Jones (ed.), *A History of Rome through the Fifth Century*, vol. II, 'The Empire'; Mentor and the Viking Press Inc. for H. Gregory, *Ovid: The Metamorphoses*; James Michie (publ. Rupert Hart Davis), *Odes of Horace*, and Simpkin Marshall for S. G. Tremenheere, *The Elegies of Propertius*.

INTRODUCTION

The myths of ancient Rome are a unique success-story. So exciting and heart-warming did these heroic fictions, or partial fictions, appear to the Romans that they stimulated and inspired them for generation after generation, and have gone on inspiring the writers and artists of Europe ever since. They have therefore played a vigorous and integral part in western civilization.

And yet these myths – I will discuss a more exact definition of the term later on[1] – did not come up from among the ordinary people, as it has often been believed that a decent, respectable myth should.[2] They were produced, instead, by a whole series of different pressures coming, roughly speaking, from above: a fact which some people today may find rather disagreeable and which I shall discuss further in the final chapter. At this preliminary point, it is enough to stress that the unconscious, or much more often conscious, process of imposition of these mythical stories was so skilfully organized that it apparently did nothing to weaken the impact they made on the people of Rome: the absence of any popular origin did not seem to matter. The extent of this impact can be appreciated when one considers that throughout many centuries of their history the Romans found it necessary to change the myths, to give them a new slant or to add something to them or take something away, at very frequent intervals, sometimes as often as every few years or even every few months, as new topical or sectional situations and attitudes arose. Indeed, for similar reasons, there were often several versions of the same myth being actively canvassed at one and the same time, although it may well have been a story concerned with events supposed to have happened a thousand years ago.

One is reminded of the modern dictatorships which belabour the subscribers to their national encyclopaedias with revised texts of the historical sections every time there is a change of personnel and opinion at the top; though ancient regimes were nothing like so monolithic, and the possibilities of variation were much greater. Or it is rather as if the members of every new government in Britain attached the highest possible priority, as soon as it had taken up office, to putting forward a restatement of the myths relating to King Canute and King Arthur to suit the views of its members.

The difference clearly was that the Roman myths must have been favourite talking-points, as Canute and Arthur are not. When the ruling classes of Britain encouraged their women to retire from the dining-room after dinner so that their husbands could sit and drink port, it was said that the men usually discussed sex in England, and in Ireland (sometimes) theology. It seems pretty certain that, in similar circumstances, leading Romans talked about their myths. And they induced the poorer elements of society to think about them as well. These humbler people, no doubt, enjoyed the good stories, though they got some of the 'messages' as well. But as for their more sophisticated compatriots, these continually weighed and reweighed the personages who figured in the myths, adding and subtracting partisan nuances all the time. It must have been rather like the fashionable vicissitudes which modern critics impose on the reputations of past writers: 'the literary chit-chat which makes the reputations of poets boom and crash in an imaginary stock exchange'.[3] But in this case it was Aeneas, Romulus, or Camillus whose prestige moved up or down as fashions changed.

This means that the Roman mythology occupies a very special position among the mythologies of the world, because to a considerable extent we can watch it being built up. It is true that there are large and tantalizing gaps, especially at the beginning. But just to frown at Roman myths because they are 'artificial and literary' is to miss a great opportunity.[4] For that is precisely what is so interesting about them, and makes them a particularly rewarding subject of study : they were created artificially, in a piecemeal fashion, over a long period of time. This is likely to present difficulties for those who are chiefly interested in examining myths from the standpoint of their structure. Or perhaps it will mean that they do not consider the Roman stories real 'myths' at all, for precisely this reason, that they were only gradually put together over many hundreds of years.[5] But what is so remarkable about these stories is that, in spite of the enigmatic gaps, we can watch the process actually happening, and even sometimes say why. If only we could do the same for the North American Indians, or the Nigerians! Or if only we could get a view of the myths of Greece while they, too, were actually coming into being and unfolding! But we cannot. For at the time of our first encounters with Greek tales they are already very fully developed and mature (chapter 7, section 2).

It will therefore surely be worth while – not only to increase our knowledge of the Romans but also in order to touch upon matters of interest to comparative mythologists – if we take a closer look at the Roman myths and try to find out just how and when, and under the influence of what pressures and interests, their various components were assembled and inserted. If one understands the term 'Roman mythology' to signify the stories relating to the origins of Rome itself and its early, fabulous history, rather than those accounts of the Olympian gods which were imported with little or no adaptation, this general task has not, I think, recently been undertaken; though a host of important detailed contributions is written and published every year – and this massive body of research makes it all the more necessary to embark on a new survey of the whole field.

Can I claim any originality in my attempt? Where the material is so extensive, this would be a rash claim to make. It is true, however, that I have found myself obliged to deviate from more or less accepted views at certain points. For example, unlike many other students, I regard the ancient opinion that Rome was 'founded' in the eighth century B.C. as pure fiction. I also feel that recent research makes it desirable to emphasize the Etruscan factor a good deal more, and the Sabine factor rather less, than is customary in summaries of Roman mythology.[6] Nor do they usually say as much as I shall about the great Roman families – brief though my comments will necessarily be. There is, of course, nothing at all original, as far as more specialized studies are concerned, about the supposition that these families played a major part in establishing and adjusting the myths. But I have tried to detect their specific interventions more frequently than general studies of the Roman myths are accustomed to do, and I have added a little about the designs of family interest, still all too imperfectly understood, that were engraved upon their coins by the Republican moneyers.

In order to deal with these matters, one must try to show a historian's awareness about the successive phases of Roman history and cultural history, at least until the reign of Augustus – and it would have been possible to continue to a later date still. Yet it is not history that one has to write. I am not referring here to the well-known difficulty of disentangling history from myth, though this question will often come up in the course of these pages.[7] Although Roman mythology has to be treated historically – that is to say, each of its component stories has to be examined throughout all the phases that moulded its development – the product that emerges is not what happened but what people, at different times, said or believed had happened. This might be called para-history. An analysis of Roman mythology is a para-history of Rome. To get an idea of a civilization, one needs history and para-history as well.

This book, then, does not duplicate my earlier volume, *Myths of the Greeks and Romans* (1962), at any point, or at most only to a very small extent. There my approach was different. I was considering classical mythology as a whole, with emphasis upon its influence on subsequent cultures; and I treated Roman myth as an appendage and variant of Greek myth. Provided that the process does not imply a contempt for the Roman aspects of the phenomenon, this attitude has something to be said for it, since there is a certain unity about the classical world. But ever since I wrote that book I have been wanting to attempt another sort of approach as well: to offer a much more detailed treatment of the Roman mythology, treating it as an entity in its own right, and seeking to explain how it acquired its very remarkable characteristics, and how and why it became such an enormously influential factor.

Certainly it owed a lot to the Greeks, and the two collections of myths possessed certain analogies – notably in the political sphere – that have been insufficiently emphasized.[8] Yet the total result somehow became quite individual and peculiar – just as Latin literature, as a whole, is dependent on the literature of Greece yet entirely different; and just as Greek literature, before that, had been dependent on material provided by the near and middle eastern peoples, yet wholly different again.

I want to thank Professor Moses Finley for his encouragement, and to Mr G. W. Robinson and Dr O. Skutsch for their advice. I am also very grateful to Mr Julian Shuckburgh, Mr Peter Hames and Miss Susan Phillpott for their editorial help, to their colleagues who have contributed to the production, to Mrs Pat Hodgson for collecting the illustrations, to Mrs Helen Stell for making valuable comments and to Mr Arthur Banks for making the maps.

Gattaiola, *1973*   MICHAEL GRANT

1   ROME AND ETRURIA
WITHOUT THEIR MYTHS

There were two early Romes, the Rome of the great myths and
the Rome that has now been uncovered by the archaeologists.
Roman 'history', in any recognizable sense of the word, does
not come for many years, though as time goes on the archaeological record is eked out by fragmentary independent evidence of a literary and historical nature.

To say that this archaeological Rome is Rome 'as it really was'
would be to draw a dubious distinction, since there was equal
validity, on a different plane, in the myths, which were so
potent in people's minds. Nevertheless it remains true that the
mythical Rome and the archaeological Rome are in most ways
distinct from one another. They sometimes coincide, but rather
rarely. Yet if we are to understand either one of them, we need
to know something about the other. The purpose of this book
is to try to explain the myths. It is therefore essential to say
something first about that other Rome, the Rome which developed solidly upon the ground.

From about 1600 B.C. new populations, practising cremation,
began to arrive in Italy from central Europe. Their culture was
of the Bronze Age, to use the classic but inadequate term.[1] Concentrating at localities in the Po valley, these settlers, representatives of the 'Apennine culture', also established important offshoots in metal-producing Etruria, now Tuscany, which lay to
the north of the river Tiber upon which Rome was later to be
built. And indeed people connected with these settlers left
traces inside Rome itself, where objects that belonged to them
have been discovered near the river on the site of the cattle-

market (chapter 3, section 1). It is possible, however, that the artefacts in question did not originate from precisely this part of Rome, but came instead from one of the Roman hills in the immediate vicinity.

Settlement at Rome was nothing new, since previous Copper Age inhabitants have also left the marks of their habitation, over a wide region of what later became the northern part of the city; and Stone Age remains, of far earlier date, have likewise been found within the area comprised by modern Rome.[2] But, from the point of view of subsequent history, special attention needs to be drawn to the Bronze Age settlers, because there is quite a chance that from their time onwards habitation has been continuous. There are gaps still to be filled, but it is a fair presumption that the Rome which exists today was founded by the middle of the second millennium B.C. It is also quite probable that the men and women who lived there at that time were already speaking the Indo-European speech which later became Latin and Italian.

In about 1200 B.C. the populations of this area just south of the Tiber, which was later called Latium and is now the southern part of Lazio, were apparently joined by further immigrants, people of mixed origins who engraved bronze in a skilful fashion somewhat reminiscent of the great Bronze Age civilization of Mycenae; and the culture of these newcomers displayed central European analogies as well. They were familiar with the use of iron.[3] The nucleus of the region where they settled was the Alban Mount, thirteen miles south-east of Rome. Its peak, Monte Cavo (3,115 feet), dominating a surrounding semicircle of hills, had ceased to be an active volcano in about the fourth millennium B.C. Its eruptions guaranteed the future prosperity of the area by covering the clay plain for miles around with layers of new soil containing phosphates and potash. By the time the Bronze Age was merging finally into the Iron Age – a transition which, at certain identifiable spots not too far away, can be attributed to *c.* 850 B.C. – the process of settlement in this area was nearing completion. In historical terms, these Indo-European-speaking lowlanders who looked after their herds on the Alban Mount, and then ceased to be nomadic and began to cultivate the soil, became the Latins, a loosely federated group of communities sharing the common sanctuary of Jupiter Latiaris on the mountain top. From their more or less isolated and defensible hill-spurs, the Latins controlled the seaward plain. But on the Apennine hill-tops in the interior they could see the villages of the independent Sabines. These were immigrants of unknown origin who had fused with unidentifiable earlier settlers. Like the Latins, they spoke an Indo-European Italic language, but theirs was a somewhat different one, Oscan.[4] Culturally speaking, they were less advanced than the Latins. But even the more advanced Latin Iron Age offers no particular hint that these insignificant little bands of people were destined for future greatness.

Their principal centre of habitation was Alba Longa (Castel Gandolfo), on the lip of the crater which is now Lake Albano. The earliest tombs in the necropolis beside the town seem to date from *c.* 1100 B.C. Alba Longa influenced the Latin communities round about, and there may be some truth in the tradition that a number of them were its offshoots. But from the seventh century onwards the lead began to pass to Aricia, a few miles further south across the lake, sixteen miles south-east of Rome, on the edge of a fertile depression; and Lavinium and Ardea, too, became powerful, though in myth rather than in fact.

Very soon, Latins began to transfer themselves from this Alban hill-fringe towards the site of the future capital of Italy. First of all, groups of shepherds, and farmers with light ploughs, gradually moved down onto the rolling scrub-covered table land of the Roman Campagna, scored by marshy valleys leading to the heavily wooded coast. Then they came to the Tiber.

Here they found the Seven Hills of Rome, sharply separated, flat-topped elevations ranging from a hundred to two hundred feet in height, and projecting towards the river; their distinct identities and characters were to play a rich part in Roman mythology. From north to south rose the Quirinal, Viminal, Esquiline and Caelian hills. Between them and the Tiber stood the steep and almost isolated Palatine. The precipitous Capitoline to the north-west, and the Aventine to the south, do not seem to have been settled until later. As regards the other hills, however, this was probably – as we have seen – no new foundation. They had been inhabited at an earlier date, and the Latins, when they arrived, may well have found inhabitants still on the spot. If so, the newcomers joined forces with them, whether by peaceful or other means we cannot tell. The villages on these hills had hitherto been separate – in some cases there were two or more hamlets on a single hill, occupying its different spurs – and separate for a time they remained.

The immigrants were pretty backward, but the geographical situation of these hills offered them remarkable opportunities for development. The spurs on which these Latins had now settled commanded the largest river in the peninsula; it was also the river with the widest drainage area. And so they were in a good position to control the salt route running from the central hills to the adjacent Tiber mouth, which could be reached along river banks which provided much easier routes than they do today. The land round about was fertile, and there was winter pasturage not far off.

The first Iron Age Roman cemeteries are attributable to these new settlers, or to their mixture with the populations that they already found upon the hill-tops. These oldest graves appear, as one would expect, to be slightly later than the earliest so far discovered at Alba Longa. A few years ago *c.* 800 B.C. was suggested as the date of the first Roman tombs, but this has been revised to *c.* 850, and a strong case, though it is not universally accepted, has been made out for the tenth century. At Villanova, the place near the later Bononia (Bologna) which has given its name to the major Italian Iron Age civilization, archaeologists have discovered objects of *c.* 900. But a firmer basis for comparison with Rome may be forthcoming when we are able to date early deposits at Italian maritime centres which possessed a prominent Bronze Age history, as we cannot at present.[5] Meanwhile the years 900–850 may be tentatively regarded as the period of Rome's new Iron Age phase.

By the early seventh century B.C. the villages on the Palatine, Esquiline and Caelian hills had coalesced. Perhaps at first this

was only for purposes of common worship; but, if so, full uni-
fication followed not long afterwards.[6] The Forum Romanum,
the depression between Palatine and Esquiline, was at first used
by the two communities as a cemetery, but then followed a
period during which this piece of ground was inhabited (c. 700).
By c. 650, if not earlier, tracks were converging on the cattle-
market on the Tiber. Half a century later, the Quirinal and
Viminal hills were incorporated in the town, with the Capitoline
joining them a generation or so afterwards.

Throughout this period, cultural developments ran roughly
parallel to those of the villages and embryonic towns of the
Alban Mount, and many analogies can be traced with other
parts of Latium too. For example, the Iron Age deposits on the
Palatine and in the Forum correspond to the Alban group,
whereas discoveries on the Esquiline display a relationship
(though not quite such a close one) to the communities of
southern Latium. It has often been asserted that the two forms
of burial found in early Rome, cremation (in urns) and inhumation (in oblong graves or trenches), correspond with the two
racial elements identified by the literary, mythological traditions, the Latins who allegedly settled on the Palatine and the
Sabines who supposedly made their homes on the Esquiline and
Quirinal (chapter 4, section 3). But this correspondence should
apparently be rejected. In the first place, the evidence regarding
the two sorts of rites that comes from other parts of Italy –
including a number of places where they are found, as at Rome,
side by side or even cutting into one another[7] – suggests powerfully that these divergent customs should be differentiated in
terms of the geographical rather than the racial origins of the
different elements in the population, which is not necessarily
the same thing. In other words, people tended to hang on to the
institutions of the regions they had come from, regardless of
the races they belonged to; so that there is no possibility today
of using burial rites as evidence justifying the identification of
any Sabine element at Rome. Secondly, distribution of the two
funeral customs inside Rome itself is uncomfortably complicated, much too complicated to admit of tidy racial answers.
The two forms of burial, heavily mixed in the Forum, are not

distributed neatly hill by hill. On the Esquiline, for example, though inhumation predominates, there is also cremation; and it is rather lame to explain this coexistence by suggesting that Sabines settled on one spur of the hill and Latins on the other. Nor does the Quirinal obey the pattern which would require it, according to the tradition, to be a Sabine centre. Indeed, although there were later inhumations on this hill, the earliest burial so far discovered on it is of cremation type. It is true that the archaeology of the Quirinal is still very little known. But neither there nor on the Esquiline nor anywhere else in Rome can one identify a distinct Sabine culture; and it does not seem very likely that one will prove identifiable in the future.

That is not to deny that the Sabines played a part in early Rome. Indeed, linguistic indications of their presence are clearly to be seen.[8] But this Sabine element was so completely merged, at an early date, that its specific contribution, or even its geographic location, can no longer be distinguished. And, in any event, there is little point in talking about race. In all Mediterranean or near eastern communities, races have always been deeply and inextricably mixed since the very beginnings of civilization, and indeed of human occupation. And Rome, too, from the very earliest times, was as racially mixed as any other place – there is that much truth in the myth of Romulus inviting outcasts from far and wide (chapter 4, section 2). The possibilities of the site attracted a varied collection of immigrants, and in due course the mixture assumed a more or less homogeneous appearance.

In the seventh century B.C., the population of the Roman hills had come to include not only shepherds and farmers but merchants and craftsmen as well. Signs of wealth and importance increased, and towards the end of the century there were revolutionary changes and improvements in the appearance of the city. The principal inspiration for this very much more advanced way of life came from the Etruscans. A century or two earlier these people or peoples, whose own name for themselves was the 'Rasenna', had gradually established a group of independent city-states in what is now southern Tuscany and northern Lazio, covering a territory of two hundred miles from the Tiber to the Arno and the Apennines. The specific qualities of their civilization are recognizable from *c.* 700 B.C. Its basis was the Italian Iron Age culture, which had developed out of the preceding Bronze Age of the same area. But the language of the Etruscans, though our understanding of it is notoriously limited, seems not to have been Indo-European. As for their culture, it was famous for the display of unmistakable eastern features. These include personal names; belief in revealed religion and in specific methods of divination; the construction of chamber-tombs of peculiar forms; Syrian, Anatolian and Mesopotamian artistic themes and techniques; large-scale iron-workings, which seem to owe extensive debts to Asia Minor and the regions to the east of it; and the existence, on the island of Lemnos, of inscriptions in a tongue which is evidently related to that of the Etruscans.

Eastern immigrants may conceivably have arrived on the shores of Etruria, as they arrived on many other Mediterranean coasts, during the very disturbed period of the twelfth and eleventh centuries B.C., the period mythically associated with the Fall of Troy. But if so, new arrivals at this period can scarcely explain the oriental features of Etruscan art, since this did not develop for another four hundred years. It is again possible, however, that a new set of immigrants appeared at this later period, in *c.* 800–650 B.C., as part of a phase of widespread exploration and colonization involving people of many different civilizations: Phoenicians, from Tyre and Sidon in what is now Lebanon; merchants from Carthage which the Phoenicians had founded in North Africa; Greeks from numerous cities of the Hellenic homeland and Asia Minor; and groups and individuals from many other parts of the near east.

Most, though not all, of the ancient authorities (not, however, Dionysius of Halicarnassus, chapter 2, section 1, and perhaps not the Etruscans of imperial date themselves) believed that this people had come from Lydia in Asia Minor. But whether such a group, presumably a conquering aristocracy, arrived from that or some other region of the near east or not – and this question will continue to be disputed – the oriental look of the art of the Etruscans is sufficiently explained by the fact that they were acquainted with the work of oriental artists. In the first place, by the end of the seventh century B.C., they were maintaining direct contact with Syrians, Anatolians, Assyrians, and above all with the Phoenicians[9] who were around the coasts of Sicily and Sardinia from at least the eighth century B.C. and possessed their own harbour facilities at Etruscan ports (chapter 3, section 3). These commercial contacts led to imitations and adaptations in the artistic field as well. But more important still was the Etruscans' indirect contact with eastern lands through the Greeks. For the designs on the Greek vases and other objects which were pouring into Etrutia (and into Latium too) during this period had been subject to powerful oriental influences: the epoch when the Etruscans experienced the maximum impact of Greece was its orientalizing age.

The principal intermediaries in these contacts with Etruria were the Greek colonies of 'Magna Graecia', the area of Hellenic settlements in south Italy and Sicily. The main wave of this Greek colonization, agricultural in purpose, had been preceded by certain Italian foundations, geographically remote from Greece, which seem to have been guided by commercial rather than agrarian considerations. For these intrepid colonists had their eye on the rich metals of Etruria; and so they too contrived to land on the coast of the Tyrrhenian Sea. But it was necessary for the new settlements to be planted well outside the area of Etruscan control, considerably south of Etruria itself. Early in the eighth century, therefore, the two towns of Chalcis and Eretria (on the island of Euboea north of Athens) collaborated with Aeolian Cyme, on the coast of Asia Minor, to send settlers to the island of Pithecusae (Aenaria, now Ischia), which lies just beyond the western extremity of the bay of Naples. By c. 750, however, volcanic eruptions made it necessary to evacuate Pithecusae, and one of the Euboean groups, the Chalcidian section, moved with the Cymaean settlers to the Italian mainland, where they founded the colony of Cumae two miles north of the bay. The town became powerful and prosperous, and maintained close contact with the nearest Etruscan city-states (though these were a hundred miles to the north, separated from Cumae by the whole of Latium). Some time during the seventh century B.C., for example, the Etruscans, in spite of the total difference between their language and that of the Greeks, adopted an alphabet of twenty-six letters which was probably derived, with necessary adjustments, from the Greek script of the Chalcidian settlers at Cumae.

But other Greek cities of southern Italy, too, even if they had been founded with a predominantly agricultural purpose, likewise had their contribution to make to the Hellenization of Etruria. Those which will be mentioned during the course of the present investigation include Croton (*c.* 710), a city at the edge of the Tarentine gulf which became the headquarters of a politico-religious brotherhood founded by the mystic and mathematician Pythagoras; Taras (Tarentum) itself, the Spartan foundation which inherited the Pythagorean community from Croton; Locri in the toe of the peninsula; and the great Sicilian city-state founded by the Corinthians at Syracuse, which, although farther away, could not fail to exert an effect over a wide area.

Such were the Hellenic centres from which 'ever-widening ripples of Greek fashion' spread northwards to familiarize the Etruscans with Hellenic art and thought.[10] And meanwhile Corinth on the Greek mainland, which had become the leading commercial emporium of the Mediterranean in *c.* 700 B.C., was flooding Etruria with its ceramics and other products.

Each Greek city maintained its own contacts with each individual Etruscan city. Traditionally there were twelve of the latter; the many others revealed by archaeology were mostly of subordinate importance. In spite of traditions that there had once been a single king over the whole country,[11] the major cities were fully independent of one another. Once a year, they sent delegates over their excellent roads to a joint gathering at the shrine of Voltumna, perhaps not far from Volsinii, which is probably the modern Orvieto. But the political initiatives this loose confederation sometimes attempted were generally ineffectual:[12] no doubt the Etruscan cities maintained a shifting pattern of alliances with each other, but they tended to act on their own. We have become accustomed, in dealing with relations between Greek city-states, not to say 'the Greeks', but to refer to Athenians, Spartans, Cumaeans, Tarentines, and so on, and it is desirable to form the same habit regarding the Etruscan cities. This complicates matters and introduces a whole new set of differentiations about which our knowledge is fragmentary, but the attempt must be made all the same. Its necessity is emphasized by a visit to Etruscan sites and museums, which shows clearly the highly individual character of each of these powerful units. As we shall see, their individuality plays a large part in determining the myths of Rome, the place which lay just across the Tiber – so close to the greatest cities of Etruria.

For during the seventh century B.C. the centre of Etruscan power increasingly passed from the northern regions of the country to these communities that lay upon its southern spurs and slopes. The oldest of all the cities of Etruria may have been Tarquinii, forty miles north-west of Rome on a stream-girt hill near the sea. Its abundant wealth is demonstrated by an early bronze industry, supreme until *c.* 650, and then, a century later, by splendidly painted cemeteries on neighbouring hills. A rival town nearby was Vulci, again not far from the coast, in what was in those days a fertile plain. Burials at Vulci start soon after 900 B.C. – before the date when a recognizable Etruscan culture can be said to exist. Two centuries later, huge numbers of Greek vases were imported; while the bronzework of the town, derived from the metalliferous Monti di Tolfa which lay to its south, was exported as far as Greece and central Europe. In the sixth century Vulci was powerful, and even later on, its paintings reveal a vigorous local epic tradition (chapter 5, section 2).

On the other, southern side of the Monti di Tolfa and the Monti Cimini which rise on their inland flank, lies a region of Etruria which these mountains somewhat isolate from other Etruscan territories, linking it rather with the river Tiber which borders it on the other side. This Etruria Tiberina, or Etruria Minor, contained two cities which were extremely close to Rome and exercised a profound influence upon its history, historiography and mythology. One of them was Caere (Cerveteri), which owed its prosperity to the metal-filled mountains to its north. From ancient beginnings Caere had risen by 600 B.C. to be the greatest and most outward-looking city in Etruria, and one of the most important centres of the Mediterranean world. Caere possessed several ports from which it policed the sea. They included Pyrgi (Santa Severa), where inscriptions on sheets of gold indicate the existence of a Phoenician community in *c.* 500 B.C. The ruler of the city, Thefarie Velianas, records a bilingual dedication to a Phoenician deity Astarte who is equated with Uni (Juno), a goddess of Etruria (cf. below, and note 20). The name of one of Caere's other harbour towns, Punicum, is equally suggestive; it was through the joint efforts of the Etruscans and the Carthaginian (Punic) descendants of the Phoenicians that Greek colonization, so powerful in southern Italy, was kept away from the Tuscan coast.[13] Yet among the approximately twenty-five thousand inhabitants of Caere there were also Greek residents, since this exceeded all other Etruscan cities in its interest in trade with Greece. It is not surprising that Herodotus, looking at the region from a Greek point of view, regards Caere and Etruria as interchangeable terms.[14] The Caeretans worshipped Greek gods and had a Treasury of their own at Delphi. The fact that Etruria, in its culture, was more than half Greek, was largely due to the people of Caere.

Caere was only fifteen miles north-west of Rome – and Veii only twelve. This was a little further inland than Caere; it stood on the edge of a volcanic plateau, with ravines descending on three sides. Although again a very ancient pre-Etruscan town, which during the Etruscan period continued, as excavations reveal, to show an unbroken rise, Veii began its greatest days soon after the climax of neighbouring Caere (*c.* 550 B.C.). Like Caere, Veii was strongly Hellenized. Its prosperity was based, first, upon remarkably well-developed agriculture, and, secondly, upon the control of the Tiber route, leading from the strategic crossing at Fidenae, above Rome,[15] to the river mouth and its deposits of salt. For a long time the domination of this route by Veii was unquestioned, but in the end the situation was bound to lead to a conflict of interests with the Romans.[16]

It was perhaps at the end of the sixth century B.C. that Caere and Veii began to lose something of their absolute superiority over Rome. They were suffering not only from the Roman threat but from a dangerous prevalence of piracy; and perhaps some of their principal sources of metal were becoming exhausted. Moreover, challenges were springing up from rival Etruscan cities inland. Of these the most notable and thrusting was Clusium (Chiusi), standing seventy miles from the coast on an isolated hill overlooking a Tiber tributary, the Clanis (Chiana). The stream ran through a fertile valley which provided a corridor through central Italy. Twice in the history and mythology of Rome the Clusians played a leading part, when they were at the height of their power (chapter 6, sections 1 and 2). But Clusium belonged to a different Etruria from the Hellenized, maritime Etruria Minor or Tiberina, and it is round the latter region that Roman mythology tended to concentrate. Caere and Veii are the cities which exercised a really decisive effect on Rome and its sagas.

To sum up, then, Etruscan Caere and Veii, the Greek colony of Cumae, Latin Alba Longa, Aricia, Lavinium and Ardea supply the major influences on Roman myths.

The various cities of Etruria expanded both northwards and southwards. Their northern expansion brought them to the valley of the river Padus (Po), and in a southerly direction they very soon coveted the rich lands of Campania which lay behind Cumae. In about 600 B.C. the important town of Capua, which lay inland from that colony, fell into their hands. Whether they arrived, on this and other occasions, by sea or land cannot be determined. If the former, perhaps Caere and Veii provided the guiding spirits, if the latter perhaps Clusium. But at all events the occupation of Campania by Etruscans inevitably implied their eventual absorption of the country which lay between Campania and themselves: which was Latium, the land of the Latins. The keypoint of this advance in Latium was probably Praeneste (Palestrina), east of Rome, where tombs show Etruscan characteristics from the mid-seventh century onwards. And then, but more slowly, Etruscan influences took over at Rome, as at other Latin towns.

Greek influences, too, began to be noticeable at Rome, at about the same time; and it is still hard to discover the relative extents to which these influences came from Cumae and other Greek cities of southern Italy (sometimes through Latian intermediaries such as Satricum [Borgo Montello])[17] or were imported by the Etruscans. There is, surely, a measure of truth in both versions – and the further possibility cannot be excluded that scattered migrant groups from Greece or troubled Asia Minor may have landed, not only in Etruria, but also on the coasts of Latium, during the years before and after 700 B.C.

It was not until two or three generations after that date that Rome witnessed the decisive steps which brought about its urbanization. A lot of things happened within a few years – mainly, we can now say, during the last quarter of the seventh century B.C. Increased wealth was displayed by a burial on the Esquiline, which reveals the remains of a chariot and armour. The Forum, which had briefly become an inhabited area after a long period as a cemetery, was converted during the years 625–575 B.C. into a pebble-floored meeting-place and market for the unified Roman hills. It is uncertain whether the beginnings of this development were due to the initiative of the Etruscans or to cultural advances which had taken place prior to their arrival. However, the transformation of purely domestic industrial arrangements into high-class professional handicraft indicates that, culturally speaking, Rome now became an Etruscan city. For finds datable to the second quarter of the sixth century B.C. include pieces of terracotta decorated with mythological scenes and designed for the external ornamentation of shrines which, to judge by the style of this art, must have been purely Etruscan in character. And, at the same time, some of the earliest shrines that have been excavated, dating from *c.* 580–60 B.C.,[18] contained vases of Athenian manufacture. They are of the black-figure variety which Athens, succeeding Corinth as the leading commercial Greek state, was importing not only into Rome but also, in very large quantities, into Etruria – while importing, at the same time, the craftsmen who could fabricate similar products locally. (There are also strong reasons for believing that Rome possessed harbour facilities for Phoenician traders, like other Etruscan cities such as Caere.)

It is quite evident that Rome had been conquered by an army belonging to one of the powerful Etruscan city-states – or perhaps belonging to more than one of them, acting for the time being in unison. There was nothing surprising about this, since the same fate had befallen the other towns of Latium. Moreover, in Rome's case, very special temptations were offered by its proximity both to Etruria itself and to the salt supplies of the Tiber mouth.

And then for a hundred or a hundred and fifty years – spanning the sixth century B.C., with possible overlaps at either end – the city remained under Etruscan control, and became one of the Etruscan city-states. Roman architecture, and architectural fittings, were wholly Etruscan in character. So was Roman engineering, and so was Roman agriculture. Etruscan, again, were many elements that persisted in the religion and ceremonial of the Romans, and the names of some of their leading families, and very probably their alphabet, which somewhat resembled the writing of Cumae but is likely to have been brought to Rome not direct from Cumae but by intermediaries: that is to say, by the Etruscans.

But, although brief Etruscan *graffiti* occur, the language mainly spoken by the Romans, to judge from inscriptions going back to *c.* 525, was Latin. So perhaps Rome was never quite as Etruscan as Caere and Veii. A closer parallel would be a town like Falerii (Città Castellana), twenty-eight miles north of Rome on the other side of the Tiber. For this, again, was a frontier post of the same sort of hybrid culture. But the transformation of places like Falerii and Rome into cities of the traditional Mediterranean type was the work of the Etruscans, who in each case established control over the non-Etruscan native populations.

There was a tradition that by the end of the sixth century Rome contained a major Etruscan shrine, the temple of Jupiter, Juno and Minerva on the Capitol; and excavation seems to confirm the reports, since the traces of a large early building can be seen. It is true that its date is not universally agreed, but its ascription to the years before 500 remains probable. If this estimate is correct, it was one of the largest temples in Italy at the time, and Rome must already have been quite an important city, controlling a substantial strip of Latium. There are good archaeological reasons for accepting the tradition that it was governed by kings, described by the word *rex* like the *raj* of the Aryan invaders of India and the *rig* of the Goidelic Celts. This conclusion is confirmed by a number of pieces of evidence, not all incontestable in detail but cumulatively convincing. For the word appears in a Forum inscription which seems earlier than 500 B.C.;[19] a building nearby, supposed to have been the king's palace, was called the *Regia*; there are certain suggestive formulations in the calendar; and in later days there still survived a priest bearing the title of king (the *rex sacrorum*). There were also early monarchies in other Etruscan cities. By the end of the fifth century they had mostly given way to Republics, and since Rome, in later times, had become a Republic, the same transformation must have occurred there. How and when the process took place, gradually or otherwise, has been endlessly disputed, but the possibility of an interim transitional period – perhaps comprising a number of disturbances and reversals of fortune – is now canvassed afresh after the discovery, already mentioned, of a ruler of Caere of about 500 B.C. who is described, in the Phoenician part of his bilingual inscription, as *melek*, king, but in Etruscan apparently as *zilath*, chief magistrate.[20]

At all events at some stage before or after 500 B.C. the government of Rome became Republican. The early Republic was dominated by the aristocratic Roman families, among which the six recognized as the greatest (the *gentes maiores*) were the Valerii, Fabii, Cornelii, Claudii, Aemilii and Manlii. All these families, and a number of others too, played a dominant part both in the course of events and in the creation and presentation of the Roman myths.

At this time Rome was beginning, dimly, to emerge into the light of non-Roman history. For one of the rulers of Cumae, Aristodemus the Effeminate, who was alleged to have fulfilled a significant role in Rome's affairs, is a historical figure, though also the subject of many a legend. Before seizing autocratic power (*c.* 504–480), he had twice repelled Etruscan attacks upon Cumae – assisted by Aricia which had by now replaced Alba Longa as the principal power in Latium. The result was that the influence of the Etruscans declined in Campania, and declined in Latium too. However, Aristodemus himself subsequently gave their cause a new lease of life. For he seems to have concluded that the true interests of Cumae did not lie with its Greek neighbours as much as with certain of the principal maritime states of southern Etruria, namely Tarquinii and Caere, and Etruscanized Rome; and to all these cities he apparently provided important supplies of grain.

Nevertheless, the pressure of the Etruscans upon Cumae continued. But the conflict did not turn out in their favour, for, in 474 B.C., outside the Cumaean port, a battle against King Hiero I of Syracuse resulted in the elimination of Etruscan seapower. From that time onwards, the maritime cities of Etruria Minor were not in a position to play such a prominent part in Italian inter-city affairs, and Rome tended to go its own way more and more.

But this brief appearance of the Etruscans and Romans on the sidelines of recorded international history is followed by another century, or longer, in which history and archaeology are once again eclipsed by myth. At Rome, during the first half of the fifth century, almost the only events that are at all firmly fixed are the dates of a number of temples[21] and of certain chief magistrates (chapter 6, section 1). The Republican city-state was locked in two prolonged struggles, which were both highly productive of mythology. One was the conflict of poor against rich (plebeians against patricians) which ended after two long centuries in an ingenious compromise such as the more sophisticated Greeks had never been able to achieve. The other long-drawn-out Roman struggle was a national one, against the external enemies which compassed about the little state on every side. They were Sabines, Latins, Etruscans; the Aequi, who fortified Mount Algido at the extremity of the Alban Mount and penetrated as far as Praeneste and Tusculum, near the modern Frascati; and the Volsci who, descending from central Italy in the sixth century, had moved up westwards from the Liris (Garigliano) valley, making the seaport of Antium (Anzio) their principal base.

The details of this constant fighting are obscure and repetitive, but laden with heroic saga. The Romans won everywhere in the end. The siege of Veii, the most sensational event in the recurrent Etrurian wars,[22] is a historical fact attributable to the early years of the fourth century B.C.; though, paradoxically, this full emergence of Rome on the stage of history is accompanied by an exceptional proliferation of myth (chapter 6, section 2). So is the attack by the Gauls (settlers in northern Italy) which followed soon afterwards. It resulted in a grave Roman defeat on the river Allia, and a brief enemy occupation of Rome, with the possible but unlikely exception of the Capitol (390–87). But the Romans recovered quickly, and pressed on towards their final conquest of their own neighbours the Latins (338), followed by a settlement which, like the adjustment of Rome's internal problems, was far more skilful and satisfactory, in its calculated generosity, than anything that had ever happened in the Greek world. Subsequently, by reducing the Samnite hillmen, Rome extended its control over most of central Italy (c. 290), comprising a confederacy of 50,000 square miles.

Further food for new myths, and for the adjustment of existing ones, was provided by the events that followed thereafter. These included a treaty with the chief Greek town of south Italy, Tarentum (Taras), in the latter part of the third century B.C.;[23] the first serious encounter with the Greek mainland, in the shape of an invasion by King Pyrrhus of Epirus (282–76); and the three Punic Wars (264–146) against Carthage, whose maritime empire, notably in Spain, had made conflict with the equally ambitious Romans inevitable. The First Punic War acquainted the Romans with the culture of Syracuse and led them to annex the rest of Sicily, and in the Second War (218–201) their endurance triumphantly survived a desperate trial during the long invasion of Hannibal. Rome had now become an imperial state, to which the further annexation of Africa (Tunisia) and Asia (western Asia Minor) brought enormous additional riches (196–33).

But internally a new struggle was developing, and it coloured a great deal of Roman mythology, seeming to many, rather mistakenly, a revival of the long-finished strife between the patricians and plebeians. During the third century B.C. there had been a move towards a more democratic society, but in the end a new dominant nobility had crystallized. The ultimately successful conduct of the Hannibalic war by the chief council of the Republic, the senate – which was in the hands of this élite – confirmed the controlling position of its members as the ruling class. But two young aristocratic reformers, Tiberius and Gaius Sempronius Gracchus, precipitated a challenge to the senate's stagnant policies. It cost both of them their lives (133, 122), and promoted a sharp division in the state. This took two forms, a disagreement between senators and knights (the class next below them, including men with strong business interests), and a hostile confrontation of *optimates* with *populares*, the *optimates* – in this distinction between embryonic political groupings – being conservatives who supported the senate's dominant role and the *populares* seeking to appeal over the heads of the senators to the Assembly, which was officially the sovereign, law-making body but had usually hitherto bowed to the senate's 'advisory' powers.

The deepening strife and an Italian revolt (91–87) led to autocracy. The dictator Sulla, after routing the *populares* who supported the political heirs of Marius, tried to put the clock back by forcibly re-establishing senatorial rule (81–79 B.C.). But after his abdication and death, conflicts continued, and amid deepening chaos two further aspirants to domination, Pompey and Julius Caesar, came to blows in a terrible civil war (49). The victory and autocracy of Caesar led to a fresh series of adjustments in the national mythology; and so, once again, did the triumph of his grand-nephew Octavian over Antony and Cleopatra (30). Octavian changed his name to Augustus (27), and the long line of Roman emperors had begun.

This new regime was as interested as ever in retaining and, if necessary, bending the mythological traditions. Its installation is also a decisive moment as far as the present book is concerned, because it was at this point, during the reign of Augustus, that there emerged the authors to whom we owe a very large proportion of our knowledge of the myths. Those writing in Greek included the prose writers Dionysius of Halicarnassus (Bodrum in Turkey) and, somewhat less important for our purpose, Diodorus of Agyrium in Sicily. At the head of the Latin authorities are a historian and a poet, Livy of Patavium (Padua) and Virgil of Mantua. Both of them were supremely talented; whereas the two Greeks wrote very boringly – unlike a later Greek, Plutarch, who applies considerable charm to his own summings-up, in biographic form, of the mythical material.

The reason, however, why we owe such a vast proportion of our knowledge to these five, artistic and inartistic alike, is an accidental one. It is because the works by the vast number of previous writers who were their sources have survived only in fragments or not at all. Nevertheless, they had written a great deal about Roman mythology. That is to say, its creation took place long before the time of Dionysius, Diodorus, Livy and Virgil. It is now our task, a difficult one owing to the disappearance of almost all the material, to try to trace how these successive developments occurred, and how they led up to the literary climax under Augustus.

2 SOURCES OF INFORMATION

I THE GREEK SOURCES

Let us first consider the Greek writers whose works, though now largely lost, can be seen to have contributed to the creation of the Roman mythical tradition.

From Cumae and other Greek settlements on the west coast of Italy, Hellenic works of art and other objects poured into Rome, directly or through the Etruscans, from an early date. Such Greek importations included numerous vases, and these and their imitations made by copyists in Italian towns helped to familiarize the Romans with Greek mythology. Furthermore, there was a specific Cumaean mythological tradition. Like other Greek settlements, Cumae cherished stories relating to its foundation, and may well have possessed its own city Chronicle. There was also a biography of the historical but partly legendary figure of the first identifiable Cumaean ruler, Aristodemus the Effeminate (chapter 1), who was depicted as paying a dreadful penalty for his luxurious habits. Since this literature has entirely disappeared, it would be useless to try to determine the extent to which it influenced our existing mythological tradition – though Plutarch, for one, seems to have been affected by the interpretations it offered. But the importance of the Cumaean sources, however dimly we now apprehend them, lies precisely in the fact that they were *external* to the Roman tradition. For such foreign authorities – reflecting un-canonical points of view, and consequently either suppressed at Rome or only surviving owing to some chance – no doubt played a much greater part than we can now realize in forming the variant unorthodox threads which comprise such an interesting feature of Roman mythology.

Later in the fifth century B.C. a Sicilian historian, Antiochus of Syracuse, apparently turned his attention from his native isle to the mainland, writing not only a *Sicilian History* but a treatise on Italy.[1] At the same period Hellanicus of Lesbos carried on the story of mythical Troy to the alleged events that followed after its fall, bringing Aeneas and Odysseus westwards as far as Latium and Rome (chapter 3, section 3). According to Dionysius, however, the first Greek author 'to touch on the early period of the Romans', that is to say to give closer attention to their mythological origins, was Hieronymus of Cardia (c. 350–260), who was regarded as a writer of learning and integrity. Like many of the other authors summarized here, he has left no surviving works, though portions of what he wrote may well have been retained anonymously in our tradition. The same is manifestly true of Timaeus of Tauromenium in Sicily (c. 356–260 B.C.), whose attractively written *Histories* (now represented only by fragments) offered a mass of historical, ethnographical, miraculous and pietistic information. Though the main stimulus behind Timaeus' work was the strife within his own island, he also contributed an account of early Rome and the myths that were now clustering round its beginnings. Writing on the eve of the First Punic War, he may have been the first historian to take a real interest in Rome and its creation and early development.

The poet Lycophron, a Euboean who became the adoptive son of an Italian Greek from Rhegium (Reggio in Calabria), was perhaps drawing on Timaeus when, in his surviving poem the *Alexandra*, he offered a cryptic, retrospective prophecy of the emergence of the Romans upon the world scene.[2] Heraclides Ponticus, still in the fourth century, is said to have declared that Rome was a Greek city.[3] And then we have a reference to a certain Diocles of Peparethus, who, at some time before 200, wrote about the origins of Rome. We do not know who he was or where he obtained his information; perhaps he got it on the spot, and then added his own Greek trimmings for Hellenic consumption.[4]

The first Romans to compose accounts of their native city and its earliest times, Fabius Pictor and Cincius Alimentus, likewise wrote in Greek, but they were Roman senators imbued with native as well as foreign traditions (section 3). Then, early in the first century B.C., there was a Greek vogue for scholarly mythological romances, represented, for example, by the novels of Dionysius Scytobrachion of Alexandria, who drew his material from the Trojan War and other such subjects.[5] And meanwhile a remarkable polymath, Posidonius of Apamea (*c*. 135–50 B.C.), was writing *Histories* which, although they concentrated on the contemporary scene, are relevant to the mythical period because of their emphasis on Rome's divinely appointed imperial mission.

Posidonius' voluminous works are only extant in fragments. But when we come to the Augustan writer, Dionysius of Halicarnassus, the first ten of the twenty 'books' or volumes of his *Roman Antiquities* have survived (in addition to small portions of subsequent books). Begun in 30 and completed in 7 B.C., the work was regarded by Dionysius as his masterpiece, though it is intolerably longwinded and manages to make even the great fascination of the Roman myths wane into prolix dimness. However, the charge that the *Roman Antiquities* are a slavish panegyric of Rome, intended to persuade its Greek subjects to acquiesce, is not quite fair. On the other hand, it is equally off the mark to interpret Dionysius as an opponent of the regime of the emperor Augustus. Living, as he did, at Rome, he was in close contact and sympathy for over twenty years with its political and intellectual leadership. Dionysius was a passionate admirer of the Romans and of their history and mythology. But he was also a deeply patriotic Greek. He felt profoundly, and made it his business to explain, that the Roman tradition served the fame not only of the Romans but of the Greeks; and, although he echoes Posidonius in his emphasis on a single, Roman-controlled world state, his account of Rome's origins strikes a very unfamiliar note (at least as far as surviving literature is concerned), because it interprets every single early ingredient in the city – each successive body of new arrivals and immigrants – as being thoroughly and completely Greek: and this theme pervades the entire work.

Nor did the pro-Roman feeling of Dionysius exclude all criticism of the Roman people he loved so well. The dictator Sulla, for example, is violently attacked, although it is left undetermined whether his brutal acts may or may not have been necessary.[6] And the disloyal, extravagant Roman leaders whom Dionysius had himself known are more than once contrasted with the ancients – though this was welcome enough to Augustus' reforming spirit, and welcome enough also to Dionysius' aristocratic friends, since it showed the need for the revival of their role as guardians of the tradition, a revival which Augustus too (though keeping a close eye on them) meticulously encouraged. Dionysius' writings were intended to interest Romans as well as Greeks; otherwise he would not have commented so carefully on Roman legal technicalities, such as the procedures for liberating slaves.

For the benefit of Romans and Greeks alike, he was for ever discerning antique examples of Roman virtue, and decking them out in the manner of the rhetorical schools. He also possessed quite a bit of curiosity for ethnological details, some of them derived, no doubt, from the antiquarians who flourished during the first century B.C. In his frequent attention to mythological points, Dionysius understands, to some extent, what constitutes a myth, doing his best to omit this type of material except when he feels it is necessary to his noble story, and believing that he can rationalize every such feat of the imagination into respectability.[7] He takes a lot of trouble to collate the various opinions of his predecessors; but to contribute any helpful comment or criticism himself is usually beyond him.

Diodorus 'Siculus', from Agyrium in Sicily, was an older contemporary of Dionysius who lived until at least 21 B.C. and wrote a World History (*Bibliotheke*) in forty books from the earliest times to 54 B.C. He began with a general survey of the institutions of all the most important parts of the civilized world, culminating in Greece and other countries of Europe and including extensive references to their mythical prehistory. This survey filled six books, of which the first five and fragments of the sixth have come down to us. 'A stupid, credulous, posing old ass' he was called by Thomas Babington Macaulay. Diodorus certainly gets very confused. Yet he has also taken over some interesting material, for example from the romancer Dionysius Scytobrachion and from mythological handbooks,[8] a form of literature which is only known to us, at first hand, from much later examples.[9] And Diodorus used a large number of other authorities too.[10]

The *Roman Questions* of Plutarch of Chaeronea, who lived into the third decade of the second century A.D., contain numerous references to Roman mythology, and his *Lives* of Romulus, Numa, Valerius Poplicola, Coriolanus and Camillus are mines of information on the subject. Like Dionysius of Halicarnassus, Plutarch is aware of the difference between prosaic actuality and myth, and believes, wrongly, that he can convert the latter into the former by snipping away the most obviously imaginative tales; though his stories of Rome's foundation, he says – and this too had been said before – should not be treated with complete incredulity, since so great a city must surely go back to divine origins. Plutarch derived most of his numerous anecdotes from collections of this sort of material, and he has also studied the more emotional Greek historians of the third and second centuries B.C. He quotes no less than 250 Greek authors, including 80 who are otherwise unknown; and he has read quite a lot of Latin as well. His biography of Romulus is particularly rich in the names of authorities (chapter 4, note 73), which show what a vast amount of research he was prepared to devote to mythical themes of this kind.

2 THE ETRUSCAN SOURCES

Although voluminous works written about Roman mythology by Plutarch and his Augustan predecessors have survived, the sources these writers used are often thoroughly obscure, since the equally vast works of their forerunners have only come down to us in fragments, if that. With regard to Etruscan literature we are in a very much worse position still: because none of it has come down to us at all, either in the originals (which in any case we could not have understood) or in translations.

But there is no doubt whatever that this Etruscan material dealt extensively with the subjects of Roman myth. For enough of it has survived, in the form of the visual arts, to make this clear, and there are tell-tale references to such literature scattered about in our Greek and Latin sources. Sometimes there is an Etruscan basis for stories that passed into the canonical Roman tradition. But on other occasions we have managed to retain Etruscan renderings which differ markedly from this tradition and in due course, like other such extraneous versions, became extruded from it, only surviving fortuitously (cf. section 1 above). When the cities of Etruria, and in particular Veii, succumbed to the Romans, the Etruscan versions of events, and the heroic myths founded upon them, were largely suppressed by the conqueror; and then they only rose to the surface again, in minute and accidental quantities, at the whim of some later annalist or antiquarian. According to one modern view the suppression was deliberate. And in such a surmise there is this degree of truth, that at the time when the first Roman historians were composing their works the wars against the Etruscans had only ended in living memory, with the fall of their last bastion Volsinii (264 B.C.; chapter 1, note 22). So their story and mythology reaches us through hostile eyes, and the possibility that the Romans patriotically and intentionally stamped out a certain amount of pro-Etruscan material cannot be excluded. But much of the suppression was just part of the natural course of events; and it was encouraged by the extremely alien nature of the Etruscan language.

There was therefore, in later Rome, a good deal of vagueness about the Etruscans, due to ignorance. But it still left room for fairly extensive literary references, since, after all, they had not only been enemies but close neighbours and, at one time, the occupying power. Relations with Etruria in the fourth century B.C. – both historical and mythical – at the time when the siege of Veii brought enforced contact, were a subject about which Roman writers had particularly much to say. And the occasion also influenced the attitude they adopted towards remoter epochs still. For their desire to give the struggle with Veii portentous dignity caused them to 'promote' many of the happenings or supposed happenings of those years to the much more distant past (cf. chapter 6, note 63).

Reference has been made to the enormous number of Greek vases displaying mythological designs which flooded into Etruria or were copied and reproduced in that country. The Etruscans 'lived more naturally in the absolute',[11] felt a great devotion to myths, and must have drawn on Greek writings as well as Greek ceramics for their extraordinarily wide knowledge of Greek mythology. Already in the sixth century B.C., if not earlier, this whole Hellenic corpus of stories was exerting a powerful influence on their culture. However, like the Romans in later times, they were by no means just slavish imitators of Greek civilization. They absorbed it and utilized it to make something new and individual.

This is perceptible in the works of art, depicting mythological themes, that were created in Etruria itself, whether by natives or Greeks. Some of the vases made at Caere, for example – apparently by a Greek from the coast of Asia Minor – show odd and seemingly original scenes. It is true that in certain cases the originality may be an illusion, due only to the fact that the artist was working from Greek models that happen not to have survived.[12] But in other cases the deviations are specifically Etruscan. Our chief sources of knowledge for the mythology of the Etruscans are the designs incised on their bronze mirrors, and it is clear enough that these often alter the Greek myths by the introduction of Etruscan peculiarities. Sometimes the Etruscan artists just misunderstood the Greek myths – the names inscribed on the vases do not always correspond with the figures they are intended to represent – and sometimes they deliberately changed them. For example, gods mix less with the world of men, for the Greek idea of heroes, half way between gods and men, was alien to the Etruscans (cf. chapter 3, section 1). There are also numerous burlesques. Furthermore, the Etruscans made the Greek tradition lopsided by concentrating upon the themes that interested themselves. For example, they displayed an increasing interest in Underworld stories and their horrors. This tendency, in visual art, became accentuated from the fourth century onwards; it may have been the reaction of a conquered nation.

But there were also Books of the Dead, *Libri Acheruntici*, which might well date from an earlier period. We knew little or nothing about what they contained, but it is possible that they had already been written down as early as the fifth century B.C. Furthermore, Veii had its own prophetic books, *Libri Fatales*,[13] which are particularly relevant to our present theme since they clearly contained mythological material, exploiting past events and tales with retrospective 'forecasts', as prophecies so often do. Moreover, there were stories about the seer Tarchies (possibly Tages), who was said to have taught divination to Tarchon, the mythical founder of Tarquinii and bearer of the same name as Rome's royal house the Tarquins (Tarchna) (chapter 3, section 3; chapter 5, section 2). There were also sagas of the prophecies delivered by the clairvoyant Vegoia (or Begoe) to Arruns Veltumnus, apparently a priest or prince of Clusium, whose first name recurs often in Roman myth. These Libri Vegoici were well known at Rome during the first century B.C., to the generation or two that immediately preceded our surviving mythographical corpus. For at that time these and other Etruscan religious works were translated into Latin (or loosely adapted, with infusions of Greek philosophy) by a certain Tarquitius Priscus, belonging to a family of which several successive generations flourished at Rome. They were Etruscans, for their name is a by-form of Tarquinius, being equated in inscriptions with Tarchna. Another influential Etruscan antiquarian was Lucius Tarutius Firmanus (chapter 4, section 2), and Gaius Fonteius Capito (section 3 below), though not Etruscan himself, also played a part.

One of a number of other writers about this *Etrusca disciplina*, during the same first century B.C., was Aulus Caecina, a friend of Cicero and of the antiquarian Varro. Caecina, who came from Etruscan Volaterrae (Volterra), possessed some repute as an author. A surviving fragment of his work attributes the establishment of Virgil's birthplace Mantua and other cities of north Italy (Cisalpine Gaul) to Tarchon, who was also the mythical founder of Tarquinii. But there was nothing new about the acquisition of such learning by Romans, because the historian Livy, writing of the year 310 B.C. (chapter 6, note 76), remarks that it was the custom, at that time, for Roman boys to be well schooled in Etruscan literature. A youth who took this sort of course will naturally have been familiar with the attitudes of the Etruscans to mythology, and knew of their versions of the Greek myths and their deviant interpretations of the myths of their Roman neighbours.

Family archives, no doubt containing mythical early material, were preserved in Etruria; and its aristocratic houses were proud of their genealogical trees.[14] The Etruscan city-states also cherished their own patriotic records, for we learn, more or less by chance, of their national or civic traditions of epic character, which are quite independent of the surviving Latin and Greek literary traditions and have narrowly escaped being squeezed out of existence by them. For example the François Tomb at Vulci was covered with wall-paintings depicting sagas which relate to Rome but deviate entirely from any of the canonical Roman versions (chapter 5, section 2). These paintings, like a few random passages from the surviving Greek and Latin literatures, depict great Etruscan heroes, Mastarna and the brothers Vibenna. It has been quite reasonably deducted that their deeds were sung by bards in Etruria, and that this early, oral poetry was perhaps written down in a literature which has not come down to us. Very probably this Etruscan folklore also included renderings of Greek epics, models for the variant versions of the same epics which appear in Etruscan visual art.

We happen to know the name of an Etruscan playwright, who wrote tragic dramas in his own language, perhaps during the later second century B.C.[15] He was a certain Volnius. His plays referred, on occasion, to Roman institutions, but apart from such insertions, and apart from whatever specifically Etruscan touches he may have chosen to add, it appears likely that the tragedies of Volnius to some extent took the form of adaptations from Greek originals. Nevertheless, the additional existence of a thoroughly independent Etruscan tradition, such as was revealed by the Vulci tomb, is confirmed by the discovery of a series of commemorative inscriptions (*elogia*) from the Forum of Tarquinii. These inscriptions, although written in Latin and belonging, in their present form, to a date not earlier than A.D. 40, insist strongly on local tradition, telling of the city's founder Tarchon and going on to speak of a series of events or alleged events in Tarquinian history, which are totally lacking in any known Roman records. These supposed happenings, which seem to be attributed to the fifth century B.C., include the dispatch of an Etruscan army to Sicily attributed to a certain Vel ... (?) the son of Lars who is described as the first Etruscan to lead a military expedition overseas, and a battle in which a leader from Norchia (near Tarquinii) defeated Caere, Arretium and another community which may be Latin.[16]

Such ancient traditions of Etruria, historical and mythical alike, were set down not only in inscriptions but in Etruscan history books as well; and it is the total disappearance of these historical works which is our severest handicap when we attempt to reconstruct Roman mythology. In the first century B.C. they were no doubt drawn upon by the Etruscan writers who adapted their national material for Roman study, such as Tarquitius Priscus and Caecina. But the Etruscan corpus was also known to a number of the Latin writers whose work will be discussed in the next section. One of them, no doubt, was the historian Licinius Macer, whose family name is Etruscan (Lecne).[17] And the antiquarians were well versed in this category of material. The greatest of them all, Varro, knew of 'Etruscan histories', and so evidently did his Augustan successor Verrius Flaccus (cf. below, and note 54), whose lost works included a book of studies of Etruria.

But the period in which the Etruscan historiography, consulted by these authorities, had chiefly flourished is uncertain. It certainly went back as far as the second century B.C., and a recent theory has argued strongly and plausibly for its attribution to the fourth century, a seminal period for Roman myth. At all events, the memory of this Etruscan contribution was conserved and revived in the time of Varro – and, later on, people were not allowed to forget it under Augustus. This was partly because a blue-blooded Etruscan, Gaius Maecenas of Arretium (Arezzo), was immensely powerful at that emperor's court. For Maecenas was very proud of his Etruscan origins, and particularly of his descent from the great house of the Cilnii, to which Rome had once given aid in about 300 B.C.[18] The interest of Maecenas in such matters could not fail to exercise an effect, since not only was he an author himself – his writings included a tragedy on the theme of Prometheus – but he was one of the most remarkable literary patrons of all time; and his protégé Virgil, who is likely to have been partly Etruscan himself, has a lot of important things to say about the mythology of Etruria (chapter 3, section 3). After 23 B.C., however, Maecenas lost some ground with Augustus: although the two men were not necessarily estranged,[19] the power of the Etruscan was no longer as great as it had been. Maecenas had his Roman enemies, and the treatment of the myths by his contemporaries, if we understood its implications more fully, would no doubt be seen to reflect both friendly and unfriendly attitudes towards Maecenas, just as for generations past it had reflected friendly and unfriendly attitudes towards the Etruscans in general. The theme could be pursued into the reign of Tiberius, whose principal adviser Lucius Aelius Sejanus was a product of Volsinii.

In the days of Maecenas, Virgil and Augustus, Dionysius of Halicarnassus intended to compose an Etruscan history.[20] It did not materialize, but the learned emperor Claudius, whose first wife, Plautia Urgulanilla, was of Etruscan descent, wrote a work of this kind in twenty 'books'.[21] Its non-survival is a disastrous handicap to our knowledge of Roman mythology: we can deduce as much from a remarkable reference he once made, in a speech, to a deviant Etruscan tradition (chapter 5, section 2, note 86).

3 THE ROMAN SOURCES

And so both Greece and Etruria made their own contributions to the Roman mythology, the former largely lost and the latter entirely lost, but each important, and the Etruscan contribution evidently much more important than is generally appreciated. Obviously, however, the native, Latin contribution of Rome itself was the most important of all. As in Greek literature, it is the Augustans who are chiefly extant – Livy and Virgil. Of the works of their Latin predecessors in the mythological field only fragments, more or less diminutive, have survived.

The antique Roman sources are obscure and controversial. Ancient rituals, with which myths sometimes got linked (chapter 7, section 1), are recorded in festival calendars. These have come down to us in a form that is as late as the first century B.C., when many of the oldest feast days and religious seasons had lost their former prominence. Nevertheless, the calendars include some material dating back to regal times.[22] For religious events such as these annual rituals, sometimes with mythical appendages, were the only kind of happening that stood a good chance of exact preservation in the Roman memory. The archivists of the temples, and the members of the various priestly boards and corporations, were all able to see to this. All Roman temples, for example, had the year and day when they were vowed, and the year and day when they were dedicated, handed down from generation to generation.[23]

And 'from the earliest period of the city each Chief Priest used to commit to writing all the events of his year of office, and record them on a white surface, and post up the placard at his house' (the Regia).[24] These Priestly Chronicles (*tabulae pontificum*), wiped clean and reinscribed each year, contained a list of annual festivals, interspersed (in the spaces between the festivals) with a record of the daily events at which ceremonial action had been taken – including for instance treaties, and including also occasions on which the gods were alleged to have signified their displeasure so that measures had to be taken to conciliate them.[25] Probably a certain amount of this traditional lore survived the Gallic sack (390–87),[26] though this is much disputed. Thereafter – at the hand of some unknown historical and mythological investigator – the material was adapted to archive form when the Board of Priests was reorganized in *c.* 300.[27]

Dionysius of Halicarnassus assures us that historians made

some use of such records,[28] though the extent of this consultation, in any individual case, is unprovable; and in any case
surely it was all too often sketchy. But the Priestly Chronicles
played a vital part in the claims of political groups and families,
which were determined to twist alleged events to their own
favour even when these events were supposed to have happened
six or seven hundred years previously. That is to say, if and
when any political or family issue was involved – and the whole
of Roman religion, together with the myths attached to it, was
inextricably bound up with such issues – the Chronicles could
be tampered with and adjusted. Among the great houses, suspicion falls particularly on the Fabii and Cornelii. For the former
provided three Chief Priests in succession during the critical
period of the Italian wars of the fourth century B.C., whereas
the Cornelii, with six out of the twenty-three known Chief
Priests of Republican times – and a cherished tradition of maintaining their own family festivals and customs – were even
better placed to falsify records and reshape myths. And such
opportunities were rarely missed.

At some date or other the names of the principal state
officials of every year, from the supposed beginning of the
Republic, were added to these Chronicles – perhaps quite early
on, though the title 'consul', which they apply even to the first
of these officials, did not exist so early (chapter 6, section 1).
However, according to a plausible recent theory, 37 of the 122
consular pairs before 386 B.C. are fictitious.[29] For, in addition to
whatever tamperings may have occurred at earlier dates, these
lists or Fasti, as they have come down to us, are the products
of a process of adjustment in *c.* 12 B.C., presumably undertaken on the initiative of Augustus himself who had just been
elected Chief Priest. They may therefore be described as the
official version, or legend, of the Augustan regime – a legend
assisted by the antiquarian researches of Varro and Atticus and
many others, including the emperor's own learned freedman
Verrius Flaccus (see below, and note 54).

Any ancient researcher on this subject had carefully preserved Roman family records to draw upon.[30] They have not
survived, but we can be sure that they were influential in the

creation of the national mythology – as they were in Etruria, and in Greece too, where until the fifth century B.C. the survival of older traditions was almost entirely due to the initiative of royal and noble families (chapter 7, section 2). Such archives, at Rome, contained not only family history, but also a variety of statistical details which earlier members of the house had collected in the course of their official duties. However, we hardly need the reminders of Cicero and Livy that these records also gave full scope for an enormous amount of loyal mendacity, resulting in the embroidery of many old myths and the creation of new ones.[31] For one thing, it was so often regarded as essential to set back as many heroic events as possible to the most venerable antiquity that could be achieved (cf. last section); and the fact that any given family was likely to use the same names for generation after generation made this temptingly easy. Nor was this practice restricted to the Romans, since alleged central Italian (Samnite) personages of the fourth and third centuries B.C. are given names suspiciously like those of authentic Samnite leaders in the Social (Marsian) War (91–87 B.C.).

Myths also gathered readily round the marked Roman attentiveness to ancestors and funerals. Waxen images of the dead were borne by mourners at the head of the bier, and then set up in the reception-rooms of houses. Brief records of the men's careers were added, and highly laudatory epitaphs. A considerable crop of these, relating to the Cornelii, has come down to us, including specimens inscribed at the end of the third century B.C. and relating to men who had lived earlier in the same century.[32] Formal eulogistic orations and poems were also delivered at funerals, at first as part of the private family rites of patrician houses, and later in the form of public addresses. We know of such a speech in praise of Lucius Caecilius Metellus, a hero of the First Punic War (d. 221 B.C.).[33] It was believed that the custom had originated no less than three centuries earlier;[34] that may be an exaggeration, but the practice was certainly antique. There is also a suggestion that these sagas were perpetuated by songs sung at banquets,[35] and it is indeed possible that such songs were sung, in early days, and exerted some influence on the development of the mythical corpus. But, if so, it seems on the whole unlikely that this influence was very substantial.

Nevertheless, somehow or other, round about the fourth century B.C., the mythological corpus gradually evolved. At this decisive point, our knowledge is wholly deficient. We cannot tell how many of their traditions the Romans of those years derived from earlier times. In any society, oral traditions rarely go beyond the third generation, unless a practice or belief – or a family interest – is involved.[36] But at Rome, in some cases, involvements of such kinds did exist, so that at least a little of their mythology is likely to have seeped through to the people of the fourth century B.C. from more ancient epochs.

Again, however, we are at a loss when we come to the persons who first knocked this material into some sort of shape. For we have no idea who they were. They must surely be credited with a lively proliferation of ideas, formed amid sharp, dramatic tugs of war between one great family and another, and between the various political and religious interests. The process was getting on for canonical completion during the external wars of the third century B.C.; that is a reason for supposing it to have been already well under way during the fourth. Mythical novels, remarked Hermann Broch, come into being at periods of dislocation. And it was evidently during those disturbed, exciting years before 300, when the Romans were locked in the struggle which would make them the leading power in Italy, and were becoming increasingly conscious of the historical and mythical pasts of their Greek neighbours in the south of the peninsula, that they decided to give themselves an official past. The initiative did not come from the people; this was no popular upsurge of myth. It came from the top, from intellectuals and specialists who formed part of the ruling class.

Perhaps Appius Claudius the Blind, who was still swaying the decisions of the senate in his old age (279–8 B.C.), had been the first Roman to realize the importance of the written word, and, indeed, the first Latin prose-writer on his own account;[37] he may well also have taken a hand in formulating the mythology of Rome. Not long afterwards, its historiography, with mythical accretions, began to assume definite form as a reply to the

Sicilian Greeks who were hostile to Rome during the First Punic War (264–61 B.C.), notably writers such as Philinus of Agrigentum who made it his aim to justify the war-aims of the Carthaginians. In the Second Punic War (218–201) the Romans increasingly felt the need for a specifically Roman tradition, and Rome joined the ranks of the other non-Greek, 'barbarian', peoples who were writing histories of their own in order to make themselves independent of Greek historical traditions which did not seem to do them justice.

Such peoples, paradoxically, had to use the far-reaching Greek language to secure their historiographical independence from Greece; and so, at first, did the Romans. Their first identifiable writer about their own history and mythology was Quintus Fabius Pictor, who, though he wrote in Greek,[38] was a Roman senator of the great Fabian house, a living illustration of the surmise that the tradition was created from above.[39] Writing not only for Greeks and possibly Carthaginians, but for Romans as well, he established the long-lived custom by which his leading compatriots, members of the senate, were regarded as the proper people to compose Roman history. Born in *c.* 260, Pictor had fought against the Gauls. Then, after Rome's disastrous defeat at Cannae in the Second Punic War, he was sent on a mission to the Delphic oracle (216). He wrote a history of his own city which, like other histories composed by Romans for many years to come, has only survived in exiguous fragments. But we know enough about it to see that it went right back to the mythical beginnings of the city, and indeed further back still. We cannot tell for certain whether he wrote on these themes soon after his return from Delphi or later, after the war was over (201). Pictor's interest in mythology was no doubt all the keener because he held a Roman priesthood. That may have been why he was chosen to go to Delphi; or he may have been selected because he knew the literature and mentality of the Greeks. This knowledge enhanced his importance as a historian and mythographer. So did his family's very close connections with Etruria and its literary traditions (chapter 6, note 76).

Pictor played a vital part in the evolution of the Roman mythical canon. To attribute its almost entire creation to him, as has recently been attempted,[40] is to go too far, but he clearly did a great deal to cast it into shape. For one thing, being a Roman senator, he took a powerfully nationalistic line, endeavouring to replace all pro-Carthaginian or otherwise unfavourable versions from Greek sources by a securely pro-Roman interpretation. For this reason an outstanding Greek historian of the next generation, Polybius, though he used and praised Pictor, warned readers against his chauvinistic distortions, even though, he said, they stopped short of deliberate falsehood.[41] Secondly, and as an almost inevitable corollary, Pictor enveloped the whole of the Roman past, myths and all, with a sympathetic attitude to his own senatorial class – which was now winning, or had won, new prestige by its ultimately successful conduct of the war against Hannibal. Thirdly, Pictor supported the Fabii of the past against other families, especially the Claudii whom they hated. For example he was in a position to boost Quintus Fabius Rullianus who (perhaps in association with Pictor's parents) had opposed the liberal reforms of Appius Claudius the Blind; and a partly legendary Appius Claudius of the fifth century B.C. could also be denigrated (chapter 6, section 1, note 47).

It is uncertain whether Pictor used the Roman, 'annalistic' method – employing a year-by-year treatment based on the annual lists of consuls in the Fasti – or whether he adopted the looser, episodic, structure employed by Greek historians. Perhaps he blended the two methods. But he certainly imitated the exciting, romantic, tragic style of presentation favoured by a dominant contemporary school of Greek historians,[42] and this vivid method was one of his greatest contributions to the growth of the Roman mythology. Though hurrying somewhat, apparently, over Rome's origins, he dwelt skilfully upon the more colourful stories, such as that of the actual foundation of the city (chapter 4, section 2).

We do not know whether Pictor wrote before or after the Campanian poet Cnaeus Naevius (c. 270–201 B.C.); perhaps be-

fore, since Naevius' attack on a member of the Claudian family
(Publius Claudius Pulcher) seems to be indebted to the historian.
Naevius performed a pioneer task by the composition of an
epic on the First Punic War, the *Bellum Poenicum*. The sixty-
five lines that survive include passages, perhaps digressions, relating to Rome's mythological beginnings, notably an important
though cryptic reference to Aeneas (chapter 3, section 4). Greek
mythology was already being popularized by the production of
Greek plays adopted for the Roman stage. But Naevius also
took a decisive new step by writing some tragedies about
Roman historical and mythological subjects, the *Clastidium* (relating to Rome's crowning victory over the Gauls, 222 B.C.), and
a play on the theme of the national founder, or more probably
two, entitled *The Wolf* and *Romulus*.

Ennius of Rudiae in Calabria (239–169 B.C.) wrote another
tragedy of the same type, the *Sabinae* about Romulus' Rape of
the Sabine Women[43] (chapter 4, section 3). It is lost, but 550 lines
of his epic poem *The Annals* survive, recounting the story of
Rome from its mythical beginnings down to a couple of years
before he himself died. Although the poem as a whole, as its
title indicates, is arranged according to the 'annalistic' pattern
based on the consular Fasti, its first three books dealt with the
mythical and regal period before the time when Fasti or consuls
or the Republic had existed. Ennius' *Annals* set out to display
an unending irresistible forward move by the Roman nation:
and all the time he hammers home the message that this ascent
depended on heroes from the mighty families of Rome, Fabii
Maximi and Claudii Marcelli. Used as a school book for two
centuries, and still revered in later times for its fine archaic
ruggedness, Ennius' epic did a great deal to infuse the Roman
mythology with romantic grandeur and magnificence. Yet, as
his prose work the *Euhemerus* shows, he held quite advanced
views on supernatural matters, for Euhemerus of Messene
(c. 280 B.C.) claimed that the gods had originally been human
beings, and Ennius supported him in this rationalizing tendency.[44] By doing so, he stimulated new ideas and interpretations of mythology which could, it is true, be employed
subversively but could also be mobilized in the interests of

patriotic piety, for example in connection with Hercules and Romulus (chapter 3, section 1; chapter 4, section 2).

An equally important reshaping of the myths came from Ennius' contemporary Cato the elder, born of peasant stock at Tusculum, near the modern Frascati. His *Origins* in seven books, of which fragments survive, were in fact a history of Rome – written in Latin prose, not the Greek of Fabius Pictor – from the beginning down to the year of Cato's death (149 B.C.). Although, like other men of his day, Cato disliked the intrusion of Greek decadence into Rome,[45] the title of his work is reminiscent of the 'Foundations' of Greek cities, and he went out of his way to link the beginnings of Rome with the best of Greece. How far he consulted and preserved Etruscan traditions we do not know, but he certainly incorporated a number of Etruscan threads into his story.

Cato's attitude to Roman tradition was ambivalent. For example, he scoffed at the trivialities of the Priestly Chronicles, and yet adopted their year-by-year chronology, while blending it with a Greek method of arrangements by subjects. He also extolled the history and mythology of Rome by stressing that, in contrast to Greek states, the city owed its national success not to a few individuals but to the genius of a host of different people extending throughout many centuries. He carried this attitude to the length of suppressing the names of great Roman commanders altogether; and he blamed earlier writers for glorifying their own families. Yet he himself was by no means unaware that his career had been launched by the Fabii and made by the Valerii,[46] who were enemies, like himself, of the dominant Cornelii Scipiones; and his upbringing in the Sabine country of the Valerian and Fabian houses helped to promote the huge part played by the Sabines in Roman mythology (chapter 4, section 3). Furthermore, as a man of Tusculum, he was very conscious that his story was the story of Italy as well as of Rome. For this reason, whereas Book 1 of the *Origins* deals with the preliminaries of Rome's foundation, followed by the Kings, the second and third books describe the mythical foundations of other Italian cities.[47]

Cato mocked a contemporary historian, Aulus Postumius

Albinus (consul in 151 B.C.), for continuing to write history in Greek, as well as a poem about Aenea, Albinus had a high opinion of himself, and no doubt favoured the numerous Postumii who had studded early Republican history. Cato's influence was more apparent in the Latin writings of the 'old annalists', Lucius Cassius Hemina (still alive in 146) and Lucius Calpurnius Piso Frugi (consul 133). In their systematic reconstructions of the Roman past, both these writers displayed a great interest in myth. Hemina shared Cato's absorption in origins. As for Piso, though Cicero regarded his style as bald, he was very fond of anecdotes; he even professed to know some of the table-talk of Romulus. He may also have been largely responsible for the genealogy later claimed by his own Calpurnian family, which had risen to great prominence during his lifetime and became famous for the antiquity of its lineage (chapter 5, section 1). Piso also did a lot to convert Roman history and mythology into a series of ethical lessons (chapter 7, section 2), praising ancient simplicity and honesty and allowing his account to mirror, in topical fashion, his own switch from 'popular' politics to 'optimate' conservatism. This topicality is apparent, for example, in the way in which he reviles a legendary would-be democratic tyrant of the fifth century B.C. (Spurius Maelius) and a low-born legal popularizer of the fourth (Cnaeus Flavius).[48]

Meanwhile Lucius Accius, who lived from 170 to at least 90 B.C. and later became known as the greatest of Roman tragic poets, was writing dramas on Roman historical and mythological themes, the *Aeneadae* or *Decius* on the self-immolation of the second Publius Decius Mus at the battle of Sentinum (295 B.C.; chapter 6, section 3, note 104), and the *Brutus* on the supposed founder of the Republic (chapter 6, section 1). The latter, Lucius Junius Brutus, though he had lived, if he lived at all, more than three centuries earlier, was extolled in honour of the poet's own patron Decimus Junius Brutus Callaicus (consul 138 B.C.). Roman tragedy was an élite taste, but it was the Roman élite who were responsible for the shaping of the nation's myths.

They were given a vigorous and permanent new stimulus by the publication of the *Annales Maximi* in eighty books. This compilation incorporated the Priestly Chronicles, which had hitherto been erased every year and then reissued; and material from other archives was added. The *Annales Maximi* set out the principal national events year by year, right back to the beginnings of Rome. Indeed, the fourth book had still not got as far as Romulus;[49] someone must have put in a great deal of antiquarian research on the mythical preliminaries. Perhaps it was the sponsor of the project himself, who was Publius Mucius Scaevola, chief priest from 130 to 115 B.C., a great believer in the salutary national value of religion and mythology as a means for keeping the Roman populace quiet and obedient (chapter 7, section 2). This work of reconstruction provided yet another occasion to infuse the tradition with political biases. In this case the bias was particularly likely to be conservative, because Scaevola, like Lucius Piso, turned from 'popular' to 'optimate', praising the assassination of the democratic reformer Tiberius Gracchus whom as consul he had supported (133 B.C.).

The opportunity was also no doubt taken to import mythological additions from Greek sources. Much, or at least some, of the lore contained in the *Annales Maximi*, Roman and Greek alike, had probably been available earlier to any senator who wished to write history, if he was prepared to make the effort to track it down. But now this material was far more accessible, and attracted correspondingly greater interest. Cnaeus Gellius was a writer on history and myth who must have started work before the publication of the *Annales Maximi*, but clearly he had access to them, at least in draft form. Together with the rhetorical methods that were now coming into use, they enabled him to write at great length, depicting the Roman past on an unprecedentedly broad canvas: one or more of his books had been completed before the Rape of the Sabines was reached, and Book III brought the regal period to an end. Gellius was careless, and indulged in strong likes and dislikes, but Dionysius of Halicarnassus (section 1 above) found him congenial.

The publication of the *Annales Maximi* meant that the basic framework of Roman history and myth was now accepted; and future writers on early times had to try to find novel approaches. The political strife between *optimates* and *populares*, cast back to a distance of anything up to six centuries, was one answer. For this struggle was convulsing the Roman state during the later second and first centuries B.C., and the historians of that period were only too glad to employ the mythical past in order to display their own current partisanship – for example on the side of the optimate Sulla against the *populares* who were the followers of Marius, or vice versa.

A striking example was the pro-Sullan Valerius Antias, who infused his highly patriotic treatment of the old stories with a sharply topical tinge, in addition to perpetrating many exaggerations and distortions in favour of the great family of the Valerii who had made him their protégé.

In spite of his Sullan sympathies, Antias the historian was always eager to show how his mythical ancestors had worked to help the poor as well as their own class. Furthermore, some of the men of unknown families who had risen to the political surface during the Sullan convulsions are taken up by Antias, who insinuates their names and families into the supposed happenings of the past. Indeed, he even inserted an ancestor for himself way back in the third century B.C., a fictitious officer whom he called Lucius Valerius Antias. The historian's cognomen, which he thus endowed with respectability, reflects his origin from Antium (Anzio), a town which had been illtreated by Marius, but in compensation, it would appear, received more than its share of attention from Antias as his account moved on through the centuries. He endeavoured to give plausibility to some of his feats of invention by offering bogus exact statistics; and Livy makes fun of this. Yet such imaginative flights, however disastrous to history, gave a fresh novelty to many of the myths, which Antias refurbished at length with a rhetorical vigour that represented the highest point of literary achievement attained, up to that time, by a writer of Latin prose.[50]

Gaius Licinius Macer, who killed himself in 66 B.C., was yet another writer of a history of Rome from the earliest times; and again his history is lost, apart from certain fragments which offer useful clues. He resembled Antias in his unscrupulous exaltation of the great family whose name he bore – and to which he really belonged: the house of the Licinii, which had produced splendid soldiers and orators, often with the Fabii as their allies. But Macer differed sharply from Antias because his politics, reacting back from a brief last-minute conversion to the almighty Sulla, became 'popular', anti-Sullan, rationalist and anti-clerical. This meant that although, being an aristocratic Roman with knowledge of practical affairs, he made use of the works of his senatorial predecessors, his version of the conflict between the Orders in the fifth and fourth centuries B.C., while no less anachronistic and topical than the accounts of any of his predecessors, has a democratic instead of a conservative twist.

Furthermore, Macer claimed to be using a hitherto unemployed source for his knowledge of the past. This was a collection of books written on linen (*Libri Lintei*), a technique attested among the Etruscans, from whom Macer was distantly descended (see section 2 above). These records which, according to one recent theory, originated from notes jotted by officials on their linen clothing, allegedly contained antique lists of annual state officials, and perhaps included records about other matters also. The mysterious Linen Books, stated to have been preserved in the temple of Juno Moneta, need not be dismissed as sheer forgeries fabricated by Macer. Yet it is not very likely that they went back to the fourth century B.C., as he believed they did; they may not have been more than a hundred years old. At all events, they injected into the dim past new versions and points of view which, even at this relatively late date, prevented the mythological canon from crystallizing completely.

The Linen Books were also used, with less confidence, by another historian, Aelius Tubero, who likewise wrote about myths. Praised by Dionysius of Halicarnassus (section 1 above) as shrewd and careful[51] – though his archaic style came in for some criticism – this author was either Lucius Tubero, a friend of the orator Cicero, or less probably Lucius' son Quintus. And Cicero himself, in his work *On the State* (Book II), has left us our earliest surviving account of the Roman kings; while his closest friend Atticus composed a *Liber Annalis* which attempted the chronology of 700 years of Rome's story in one book, 300 of them more or less mythical.[52] Atticus also drew up the pedigrees (with indications of offices held) of the Claudii Marcelli, Fabii and Aemilii, a study which was no doubt found very useful by the learned editors who were more or less unscrupulously 'editing' the Fasti under Augustus.

The work of Atticus was part of a great wave of antiquarianism which persisted during the first century B.C., influencing Macer, Tubero, and other authors of the time, and enormously stimulating interest in Roman mythology. The leading figure of the movement was the most learned and versatile writer of his age, Marcus Terentius Varro (116–27 B.C.).[53] Although certain of his works have survived, it was writings that are now lost – his *Human and Divine Antiquities* (dedicated to the antiquarian-minded Julius Caesar), *On the Life of the Roman People* (a social history), and particularly *On the Roman Nation* (*De Gente Populi Romani*) – which chiefly fertilized the study of the myths. Varro was also at pains to emphasize, and exaggerate, the Sabine element in the mythological tradition – in pursuance of the same tendency in Cato the elder – for he had probably been born at Sabine Reate, now Rieti (cf. chapter 4, section 3). The influence of Tusculum (near Frascati), on the other hand, was stressed by the learned diviner and astrologer Gaius Fonteius Capito (consul, 33 B.C.), whose family (chapter 6, note 45) came from that place.

These researches continued actively into the reign of Augustus, when the tutor of his grandsons Verrius Flaccus, whom we have seen as an Etruscan expert (section 2 above), wrote on many antiquarian subjects. He reconstructed the Fasti of the town of Praeneste (Palestrina), and very probably took an active hand in the tendentious new Augustan edition of the Fasti of Rome itself.[54] Meanwhile Augustus' confidant Marcus Valerius Messalla Corvinus not only objected strongly when inferior Valerii sought to graft themselves onto his family tree but, observing with equal disapproval similar frauds affecting the Cornelii, provided fresh fuel for the mythological tradition by compiling in his old age a treatise *On Families*.[55] And meanwhile another of Augustus' friends Gaius Asinius Pollio – who was also a friend of Virgil and Horace – was apparently writing, among much else, legendary stories of the deaths of the early kings. His bias was probably different from Messalla's. It is likely to have taken an Italian rather than a Roman form, since Pollio's grandfather had been a rebel leader who fell in the Social (Marsian) War.[56]

The outstanding Augustan prose writer on the mythology of early Rome was Titus Livius of Patavium (Padua), who lived from 64 or 59 B.C. to A.D. 12 or 17. His great work took the story of Rome from mythical times down to 9 B.C. Although 107 of his 142 'books' are lost, the first ten, comprising the period dealt with by the myths, are among those that survive. They cover the same field as the first part of Dionysius' work, but much more briefly and attractively. For although Livy himself probably regarded the portion of his work dealing with recent affairs as his most important achievement, his telling of the myths is incomparably effective, and has contributed very greatly to the part which they have played in the subsequent culture of Europe. For Livy writes wonderful, colourful Latin, and has learnt and improved upon all the lessons he has learnt from the tragic, pathetic and horrific schools of Greek historical writing. Each myth is selectively rearranged so that it becomes a drama in itself, with its own heroes or heroines and villains.

Livy is a moralist – a man who sees political and social and economic change in terms of ethics. He wants to lead men away from evil towards good by showing the nature and conse-quences of both courses of action. Above all else, he is a national and nationalistic moralist. 'No state has ever possessed more abundant greatness, higher principles, and nobler examples than Rome;'[57] and he sets out to illustrate these assertions in edifying detail, drawing upon the whole mythological corpus to supply paragons of patriotic virtue or vice. Once found, they are em-ployed to show the decisive impact of ethical qualities and considerations upon the long-drawn-out perils and trials from which Rome emerged as the ruler of the western world.

Like Dionysius and Plutarch, but with greater conviction, Livy tries to tidy up many of the myths by excising their more fantastic and supernatural features, in the hope and belief that what emerges from this operation will be non-mythical. For there is a strong rationalizing streak in his character; and this impels him to reshape the myths in the hope of making sense of them in human terms.

However, he remains extremely well aware of the mythical character of his early material, and he often reminds us of this.[58] Like his contemporaries, he feels that if a people as great as the Romans feel inclined to endow themselves with supernatural origins, such stories are well worth recording. Another reason why he dwells on these tales is because they are linked with venerable Roman religious rituals, sites and institutions (cf. chapter 7, section 1). For although Livy's attitude to divine interventions in history was equivocal, ranging from guarded belief to a high degree of scepticism,[59] he possessed in full measure all the antiquarian spirit of his age, combined with a deep feeling for the ancient, national religion – which indeed, in its public ceremonials, was sometimes quite as theatrical as Livy's own techniques. And so he never missed an opportunity to stress antique religious observances, and link them with the traditional mythology.

He himself, in the preface to his work, quotes other reasons, too, for dwelling on these prehistoric, mythical times. Not only, he remarked, were they a *safer* field than contemporary history, but he found them a relief from the depressing degeneracy of his own age. Some modern critics have felt surprised that a devoted Augustan, such as Livy clearly shows himself to be, should have made such observations when Augustus had recently become sole ruler and was busy introducing some of the main features of his reformist regime. But there is no real contradiction. It was correctly Augustan to look back in shame and horror at the two decades of violence and anarchy which Rome had just experienced; and indeed the main purpose of the emperor's social and religious reorganization was precisely to ensure that such a situation should never be allowed to recur. Nevertheless, it still remains a little strange that Livy's preface, written in *c.* 27–25 B.C. – between four and six years after the emperor's decisive triumph over Antony and Cleopatra at Actium – offers no indication that the decline has been halted as yet. One can understand why Augustus, after reading Livy's account of the civil wars (a section of his work that has not come down to us), commented half-jokingly on the independent nature of his treatment.[60] Yet the emperor himself chose to dress his autocracy in the guise of a Restored Republic. It was therefore politically possible, and legitimate, to look back at the legendary beginnings of the Republic as a glorious Golden Age, and that is what Livy did (see chapter 6, section 1). But Rome must be invested with even greater antiquity than that, and so he enthusiastically ranges still farther into the past, passionately and romantically tracing back the ancestral virtues to the earliest possible mythical and quasi-mythical times.

Like most people of his age, Livy deeply admired Augustus for having rescued the Roman world from prolonged civil war. He also welcomed the antique Republican screen that the emperor threw over his regime; the society which produced Livy, at Patavium, was thoroughly traditional and puritanical in character. These two trends, Augustanism and conservatism, are constantly reflected in his treatment of the myths of early Rome.

But his treatment, in many respects, mirrors the views not so much of himself as of his predecessors, for he used a variety of sources. And obviously, since he wrote such an immense amount, he employed these authorities very uncritically, often reproducing their points of view and propagandist distortions without adding or subtracting very much on his own account and indeed without displaying any consciousness of the biased character of the statements he reproduced.[61] This applies particularly to the political and family prejudices of the authors whom he is citing, since Livy, whose life was quiet and secluded, remained ignorant of power politics and was very rarely on his guard against the topical rivalries which these earlier writers, who were far more aware of such matters, had thrown back into the alleged situations of the past.

For example, though he may not have consulted Fabius Pictor directly,[62] he quotes him on a number of occasions; and it is because of Pictor that he takes an unfavourable view of early Claudii, a family whom the Fabii hated. Indeed, this element in Livy's history may provide one of the reasons why he decided to terminate it at 9 B.C. (unless death was what caused him to end at that point). He had evidently not been deterred by the elevation of a Marcus Claudius Marcellus to became Augustus' son-in-law. But then, although Marcellus died in 23 B.C., yet another Claudius became a major political phenomenon, Tiberius, the stepson of Augustus. It appears that Livy, in books that are now missing, had praised the generalship of Tiberius. However, the relations of the latter with the emperor had now taken on strains which made it embarrassing to continue to praise him; while the traditional denigration of the Claudii would strike an even more jarring note, since Tiberius and his family, after all, were evidently not done for.

But Livy's main sources were the annalists of the first century B.C. They had been singularly unscrupulous in their infusions of contemporary political circumstances into mythical times; and Livy's uncritical methods placed him completely at their mercy. For instance, the surviving portions of his *History* quote Valerius Antias nearly forty times, and apparently follow him for long stretches. Antias is one of those who are responsible for Livy's patriotic view that all Roman wars and dealings are just and honourable; and the same source is largely responsible for his idealization of the senate and abuse of democrats and of agrarian reforms. On Sulla, however, Livy also made use of a modifying source and viewpoint, admiring his revival of the ancient system yet deploring his cruelty. This critical element, together with the pro-plebeian elements in Livy's early books, may come from Macer, whom Livy also quotes for consular names, referring to Macer's use of the Linen Books.[63] Tubero, too, was consulted, and use was made of his antiquarian researches.[64] It is curious that there is no trace of consultation of Varro; for it is in the surviving part of Livy's work, referring to the mythical period, that one would have expected to find it. And Livy's incursions into mythology much resembled those of Varro in one important purpose that they served, for they provided a stimulus to Augustus' programme of religious and moral reforms.[65]

The other principal Latin authority for our knowledge of the Roman myths is the poet Virgil (70–19 B.C.), whose *Aeneid* is one of the most influential books ever written. The story of

Aeneas which it tells will be the subject of the next chapter. Here it will only be observed that Virgil and Livy, though independent of one another, used much the same material in much the same spirit, though with differences of emphasis. They seem to have acquired this common poetical and mythological outlook at about the same time, during the years immediately following the crowning victory of Actium. At first, Livy was the pioneer, for he had finished Book 1 before Virgil, apparently, had started the *Aeneid* and while he was still engaged in his preceding work, the *Georgics* which sang the praises of Italy. But after Virgil had died in 19 B.C., leaving the *Aeneid* very nearly complete, it was then Livy who came to owe a great deal to Virgil. And so too, although they were profoundly different in their methods, did Propertius, Horace and Ovid, who continued to write their poetry under Augustus and devoted a lot of attention to mythological themes.[66]

3 AENEAS

I GREECE AND ROME: EVANDER AND HERCULES

Dionysius of Halicarnassus was determined to see the origins of
Rome as wholly Greek in every respect (chapter 2, section 1), in
pursuance of his conception of a single Graeco-Roman world in
which the Greeks inaugurated civilization and the Romans
then began to exercise their divinely inspired rule. The idea of
Rome as a Greek foundation was as old as the fourth century
B.C., when it was promoted by Heraclides of Pontus; and the
theory had been subsequently revived two centuries later. But
it was Dionysius who gave it exceptional emphasis, over and
over again. 'One will find no nation that is more Greek than
Rome':[1] and it even seems to him that there were no less than
two Greek foundations of Rome in the dim, distant days *before*
the arrival of the Trojan Aeneas – who is himself declared to be
a Greek, since that is what the Trojans, too, were said by
Dionysius to be. The first of these alleged pre-Aenean foundations is a vague story about two tribes of Greek origin, the
Pelasgians and Aborigines, which supposedly united to build the
first Rome.[2] But the second tale is a detailed and characteristic
myth.

Soon after, another Greek expedition landed in this part of Italy,
having migrated from Pallanteum, a town of Arcadia, about the
sixtieth year before the Trojan war, as the Romans themselves say.
This colony had for its leader Evander, who is said to have been
the son of Hermes and of a local nymph of the Arcadians. The
Greeks call her Themis and say that she was inspired, but the writers
of the early history of Rome call her, in the native language,
Carmenta. The nymph's name would be in Greek *Thespiodos* or
'prophetic singer'; for the Romans call songs *carmina*, and they

agree that this woman, possessed by divine inspiration, foretold to the people in song the things that would come to pass.

This expedition was not sent out by the common consent of the nation, but, a sedition having arisen among the people, the faction which was defeated left the country of their own accord. It chanced that the kingdom of the Aborigines had been inherited at that time by Faunus, a descendant of Mars, it is said, a man of prudence as well as energy, whom the Romans in their sacrifices and songs honour as one of the gods of their country. This man received the Arcadians, who were but few in number, with great friendship and gave them as much of his own land as they desired. And the Arcadians, as Themis by inspiration kept advising them, chose a hill not far from the Tiber, which is now near the middle of the city of Rome, and by this hill built a small village sufficient for the complement of the two ships in which they had come from Greece. Yet this village was ordained by fate to excel in the course of time all other cities, whether Greek or barbarian, not only in its size, but also in the majesty of its empire and in every other form of prosperity, and to be celebrated above them all as long as mortality shall endure. They named the town Pallanteum after their mother-city in Arcadia; now, however, the Romans call it Palatium, time having obscured the correct form, and this name has given occasion to many to suggest absurd etymologies.

But some writers, among them Polybius of Megalopolis, relate that the town was named Pallas, a lad who died there; they say that he was the son of Hercules and Lavinia, the daughter of Evander, and that his maternal grandfather raised a tomb to him on the hill and called the place Pallanteum, after the lad. But I have never seen any tomb of Pallas at Rome nor have I heard of any drink-offerings being made in his honour, nor been able to discover anything else of that nature, although this family has not been left unremembered or without those honours with which divine beings are worshipped by men. For I have learned that public sacrifices are performed yearly by the Romans to Evander and to Carmenta in the same manner as to the other heroes and minor deities; and I have seen two altars that were erected, one to Carmenta under the Capitoline hill near the Porta Carmentalis, and the other to Evander by another hill, called the Aventine, not far from the Porta Trigemina; but I know of nothing of this kind that is done in honour of Pallas.

As for the Arcadians, when they had joined in a single settlement at the foot of the hill, they proceeded to adorn their town with all the buildings to which they had been accustomed at home and to erect temples. And first they built a temple to the Lycaean Pan by the direction of Themis (for to the Arcadians Pan is the most ancient and the most honoured of all the gods), when they had found a suitable site for the purpose. This place the Romans call the Lupercal, but we should call it *Lykaion* or 'Lycaeum'. Now, it is true, since the district about the sacred precinct has been united with the city, it has become difficult to make out by conjecture the ancient nature of the place. Nevertheless, at first, we are told, there was a large cave under the hill overarched by a dense wood; deep springs issued from beneath the rocks, and the glen adjoining the cliffs was shaded by thick and lofty trees. In this place they raised an altar to the god and performed their traditional sacrifice, which the Romans have continued to offer up to this day in the month of February, after the winter solstice, without altering anything in the rites then performed.[3]

Augustus restored the Lupercal, adorning it with a statue of his stepson who was victorious in Germany, Nero Drusus (died 9 B.C.).

Virgil, too, has the same story to tell, for the Arcadian Evander is already ruling over Rome when Aeneas arrives there:

> Arcadians, a people descended from Pallas, followers now
> Of king Evander in peace and war, having chosen a site
> Within this country, have built a township on the hills
> And named it Pallanteum after their ancestor, Pallas.[4]

But Virgil, as will be noted, although he makes Evander provide a hospitable reception to Aeneas – and uses him as a device to point out to his guest the future glories of Rome – does not, like Dionysius, regard Rome as directly stemming from a series of Greek immigrations. His attitude to the Greeks is much more complex, and the founder of historic Rome is descended from Aeneas who has been, at his native Troy, a principal enemy of the Greeks (section 2).

Nevertheless, Virgil places Evander in pre-Aenean Rome. As a hypothetical contemporary of Aeneas, Evander, if he ever existed, would have been living round about 1240 B.C. As we saw in the first chapter, Rome may very well have been in existence at that time, and the story of the arrival of Evander, or for that matter of Aeneas, could conceivably mirror some immigration that genuinely took place in those troubled times. But this must remain wholly conjectural.

Evander, in Greek religion, was a minor god in the circle of Pan, worshipped in the land of Arcadia in the Peloponnese, and especially at the small town of Pallanteum. He owes his importation into Roman myth, which believed him to be the monarch of the Palatine Hill, to a wholly false derivation of Palatine from Pallanteum. Dionysius speaks of 'absurd etymologies' invented to explain the word 'Palatine', and there are many of them – the real origin of the word remains uncertain[5] – but his own explanation is as baseless as any. As he points out, the link with Pallanteum was thought to be confirmed by the grotto of the Lupercal on the Palatine. For 'Lupercal' was held to originate from *lupus*, wolf, and so the name of the grotto was thought to be derived from the Arcadian festival of Zeus Lycaeus, whose title (like the name of Mount Lycaeon nearby) seemed to come from the Greek word *lukos*, which meant wolf. It is quite probable, though not certain, that 'Lupercal' is derived from *lupus*, and that the extremely ancient and bizarre annual festival which was associated with the Lupercal at Rome had originally been conducted by wolf-men (the later Luperci) impersonating wolves so as to exercise a magic control over these scourges of the countryside. It is also true that, at least by the fourth century B.C., the cult of Zeus Lycaeus was associated with wolves, whatever the real derivation of the word Lycaeus may have been.[6] However, the link between the Arcadian and Roman localities was not an authentic one, and probably only came into existence in the years before or after 300 B.C.

Since Mount Lycaeon was the home of the Greek God Pan, Evander was, in certain Roman quarters, identified with that god – or rather with the Italian deity who (in pursuance of a regular policy of equating Greek and native divinities) was equated with Pan. This was a god of forests, agriculture and oracles called Faunus, who was given a connection with the festival of the Lupercalia. Dionysius describes Faunus as a precursor of Evander, but they were also sometimes identified; and indeed it is conceivable that Evander owes his name and part of his story to this association. For Faunus' name appeared, perhaps rightly, to come from *favere*, to favour, and thus to mean 'the kindly one', like the name of Evander, who is 'the good man' in Greek (*eu, anēr*). And that, perhaps, is how Evander was made into the kindly host of Aeneas. Or his name may instead mean 'strong man', in punning relation to the name of Rome, *rhomē*, which is the Greek word for strength.

The Arcadians were sometimes known as 'Proselenoi', meaning that their race was more ancient than the moon.[7] This was a tribute to the religiosity of Arcadia, which contained so many myths and cults. Knowledge of the country first impinged upon the outside world in the fourth century B.C., when the foundation of its confederacy and its new city of Megalopolis made it into a political force. In due course, knowledge of this new entity came to the Romans, as they gradually formed outside contacts. And since the rustic people of Arcadia were believed to have competed in ancient singing contests, the land gained a special place in the affections of poets, who came to make it the background for the Pan pipes of pastoral verse. And for Virgil in particular, whose *Eclogues* depicts shepherds of Arcadia, it has been suggested that the peace and security symbolized by the name satisfied a profound inner need.

Dionysius explains the reason why Evander's mythical mother Themis (otherwise known as Nicostrate) was identified with Carmenta.[8] It was because she was a prophetess, and *carmen* signifies song or prophecy. This is yet another improbable piece of etymology, though perhaps better than the rival theory deriving the Italian name from *carens mente*, witless, because she used to go out of her mind when uttering her oracles. The true explanation of the name Carmenta is unknown. She was an Italian deity of prophecy, water and childbirth; and sometimes she was said to have taught the natives how to write – though this achievement was also attributed to Evander, and to Hercules as well (see next paragraph). There were taboos on leather in connection with her worship, though this is one of the many aspects of her cult of which we know nothing.

*

The whole myth of Evander exemplifies with curious thorough-
ness the way in which writers, tentatively attributable to the
fourth century B.C. and later, repeatedly tried to link Greek and
Roman observances with one another until finally, by the time
of Augustus, a fully-fashioned story had emerged. And then, in
the hands of Virgil, the story helped to create one of the master-
pieces of literature, the eighth book of the *Aeneid* in which
Evander and Aeneas meet. When the Trojan comes to the holy
site, Evander informs his guest that he has arrived in time for
an annual feast: a feast that is celebrated in honour of an
earlier visitor, Hercules, who, according to some versions, had
married Evander's daughter Lavinia[9] (more usually regarded as
the wife of Aeneas, section 3 below), and had taught the
Arcadian colonists letters.[10] And then Virgil makes Evander
describe the heroic deed of Hercules which the festival was
instituted to commemorate.

Hunger being satisfied, the desire for eating checked now,
King Evander began:

These solemn ceremonies,
This ritual feast, this altar hallowed by deity were not
Imposed on us by some fanciful heresy regardless
Of older gods. We keep up these rites, Aeneas, in honour
Of one who saved us from cruel danger and well deserves them.
Look at that scarp up there, that overhanging rock face!
See the wide scatter of boulders! How desolate stands the mountain
Abode, with the crags that have toppled down, gigantic debris!
Once a cavern was there, deeply recessed in the hill-side,
Impervious to the sun's rays: its occupant was a half-human,
Horrible creature, Cacus; its floor was for ever warm with
New-spilt blood, and nailed to its insolent doors you could see
Men's heads hung up, their faces pallid, ghastly, decaying.
This ogre was the son of Vulcan; as he moved
In titan bulk, he breathed out his father's deadly flame.
But to us too, in our longing that help would some day come,
Time brought deliverance, aid divine. For the great avenger
Hercules came, in the glory of having slain and despoiled
Triform Geryon; victorious, he drove this way
His great bulls, and his herds were thronged by our marshy river.
Cacus, beside himself with lunatic greed, so that nothing
Crooked or criminal should remain undared, unattempted,

Rustled four bulls of surpassing build out of the steadings,
And with them as many heifers, very fine creatures. These,
To ensure that they left no tracks pointing the way they had gone,
He dragged by their tails backwards into his cave, reversing
The trail, and hid his plunder deep in the sunless rock there.
A searcher would find no clues leading him to the cave.
Well, when the time had come for Hercules to move on
His herds from the pasturage they had cropped down, as he was
  going,
His oxen plaintively mooed at leaving the place, our hills
And woods all rang with the lowings of the departing herd.
Just then one of the heifers, coralled within that desolate
Cavern, bellowed in answer, betraying Cacus' plot.
Then, bitterly galled, the son of Alcides erupted in furious
Anger: seizing his weapons, his heavily-knotted club,
He made hot-foot for the top of that mountain, right up there.
Then did our folk for the first time see Cacus thoroughly frightened,
With panic in his eyes: he was off in a flash and running
Towards his cave like the wind; fear gave wings to his feet.
Now he had shut himself in there by breaking the iron chains,
His father's handiwork, which held a huge rock poised,
So that it fell, blocking and reinforcing the entrance
Like a portcullis: next moment Hercules, wild with rage,
Was there, looking this way and that to find a possible way in,
Grinding his teeth. Three times all over Mount Aventine
He scoured in furious anger; three times he vainly went for
That rock barricade; three times sank down in the valley, ex-
  hausted.
There stood a tapering needle of flint, sheer upon all sides,
Which soared up out of the cave's roof, dizzily high to view –
A convenient place for carrion birds to lodge their nests in.
This pinnacle leaned from the ridge at an angle over the stream
To its left: Hercules threw his whole weight against its right side,
Shook it, wrenching it loose from its deep-rooted base; then sud-
  denly
Pushed: at that push a crack like thunder rang through the wide
  sky,
The river-banks leapt apart, the river recoiled in terror.
But the den of Cacus, his whole great castle, unroofed, was now
Visible, the dark cavern revealed to its inmost depths.
It was as if the earth, violently fissured and yawning
Right to its depths, should uncover the regions of hell, the spectral

Domain unloved by the gods, and you could peer into the abyss
From above and see the ghosts there flinch at the gush of daylight.
As Cacus, caught in his rocky chamber, startled and shocked
By the unexpected torrent of light, was uncouthly roaring,
Hercules showered down arrows upon him, then anything
That would do to pelt him with – boughs and immense boulders.
Cacus, seeing no other escape from his predicament,
Belched a great cloud of smoke (you may well be amazed at this part of
The story), so that a smoke-screen went rolling over his lair,
Blotting out everything from sight, and the cave was all one
Thick, black, fog-bound night, shot through with glares of flame.
Hercules lost all restraint in his fury at this: he hurled himself
Down through the fire with a headlong leap, to the point where the smoke
Rolled thickest and billowed about the huge cave in eddying black clouds.
He laid hands on the ogre, who vainly was vomiting flame
Through the mirk, got a quick hold, knotted him double, and throttled him
So that his eyes started, a haemorrhage came in his dry throat.
At once the doors were torn open and the dark den exposed,
Bringing to light the cattle which Cacus had stolen, the loot
He'd had to disgorge, while his own grotesque carcase was dragged
Out by the heels. Our people could never be done with gazing
At the bestial creature – his terrible eyes, his face, the bristling
Hair on his breast, the extinct volcano of his gullet.
Since then these rites have been practised, this day kept holy by grateful
Posterity, headed by its founder, Potitius, and by
The Pinarian family, wardens of the worship of Hercules.
This altar, which he himself set up in the grove here, always
Shall be for us, in name and in truth, the Ara Maxima.[11]

This grandiose Virgilian set-piece followed a briefer account by
Livy, who dealt with the story in a similar fashion but omitted
the fabulous fire and smoke. And another account, in the same
vein, but longer and more pedestrian, was supplied by Dionysius.

There are any number of different renderings of the Cacus
story and as many different interpretations of the figure of
Cacus himself. The main surprise is that although Cacus is often

bad – in one version he is a villainous slave of Evander – he is sometimes good. His badness seems to be derived from the fictitious equation of his name with *kakos*, the Greek for 'bad', which established him as the counterpart to Evander the good. But Diodorus follows an entirely different version according to which 'Cacius' is a benevolent pillar of the local community who welcomed Hercules to the future site of Rome.[12]

This is somewhat closer to the Etruscan version of Cacus, which represented him as a youth with the beauty of Apollo, an inspired singer and seer whom Hercules killed. A mirror from Etruscanized Praeneste, the modern Palestrina, shows Cacus playing the lyre while a small Artile, identified with Arruns the hero of Clusium, intones responses; and what the Praenestines said about Cacus carried weight, because Cacus was identified (on dubious but not impossible etymological grounds) with Caeculus the supposed originator of the family of the Caecilii which often dominated Rome during the later centuries of the Republic (chapter 5, section 2; cf. note 72). From a number of Etruscan and Etruscanized towns, too, come artistic representations of two Etruscan heroes, the brothers Vibenna (chapter 5, section 2), attacking Cacus in a sacred wood.[13] This theme of the capture of a divine seer, to force him to make useful disclosures, occurs elsewhere in Etruscan lore and was very widespread in Mediterranean folk tales. Virgil inherits and reproduces similar stories relating both to Silenus (with whom Cacus was sometimes associated) and to Proteus, who tried to elude capture by changes of shape. A Roman historian of the second century B.C., Cnaeus Gellius (chapter 2, section 3), relates Cacus to the mythical founder of Tarquinii, Tarchon. Cacus, he said, had come from Asia Minor to Tarchon, was imprisoned, escaped, invaded Campania, and was put to death by Hercules in defence of the Greeks.[14] These sagas form a sort of bridge between Cacus the good and Cacus the bad.

The interest of the Romans in the story derived chiefly from the fact that there were Steps of Cacus (Scalae Caci) on the Palatine hill; and this was just the sort of site which, according to a well-known custom, the mythologists made it their business to try to explain (chapter 7, section 1). The steps presumably formed one of the approaches to the primitive village on the Palatine hill, connecting one of its two spurs (the Cermalus, where Evander's home was believed to have been situated) with the valley between the Palatine and Aventine, in which the Circus Maximus was later built. Virgil surprisingly transfers Cacus' cave to the Aventine – this may have been his own idea, designed to remove all violent associations from the Palatine hill, which was an area of special sanctity since it was held to have been the site of the first Roman city founded by Romulus (chapter 4, section 2).

It was on the Palatine, too, that the Steps of Cacus were to be seen. The real reason why they bore this name was because Cacus was an ancient fire-divinity of this hill, believed, as Virgil says, to be the son of the fire-god Vulcan (Hephaestus). This relation with fire made it easier for Cacus to fluctuate between benevolence and malevolence, and caused him, in the latter capacity, to be regarded as a force of darkness and the Underworld.[15] His cave represents that darkness, and Hercules' recovery of his cattle is a successful attempt to break the power of death and release the dead.

Cacus, as fire-god, was associated with Caca, the two powers forming a pair of divinities such as early Italian religion tended to favour. Caca, the power of the flame, was perhaps a predecessor or even a synonym of the great goddess Vesta, who had once possessed a fire-shrine in the Palatine village in the days before her round temple was built on the edge of the Forum below. When Greek ideas led the Romans to find genealogies and stories for their deities, Caca was made into Cacus' sister, and it was said that she fell in love with Hercules and betrayed her brother into his hands by revealing the place where he was hidden.[16]

In an old native version of the story, preserved by the antiquarian Verrius Flaccus, the conqueror of Cacus bore the name not of Hercules but of Garanus or Geranes or Recaranus. The name seems to be connected with Geryon (Geryones),[17] a monster whose destruction, in the version of Virgil and others, Hercules had undertaken just before coming to Rome. Geryon was known to the Etruscans, who called him Gerun, and he was also revered as an oracular god at Livy's home-town Patavium.

Hercules' exploit in recovering his cattle from Cacus seems an obvious imitation of the Greek story describing Heracles' seizure of the cattle of Geryon. The point is elaborated by one of Virgil's younger fellow-poets under Augustus, Propertius of Asisium (Assisi), in one of a series of antiquarian poems. For Geryon had been a monster of three bodies or sometimes three heads, and Propertius attributes three separate throats to Cacus as well.

> For Cacus who was native there
> And raided from a dreaded lair –
> A monster with three separate throats
> That bellowed out three separate notes –
> Dragged off the cattle by their tails
> To hide his theft by baffling trails.[18]

The hero who has to confront a triple enemy is a well-known figure in Indo-European mythology, whom we shall encounter again in the saga of Horatius and the Curiatii (chapter 5, section 1). As for the general theme of combats with monsters and dragons, such stories, often connected with religious rituals (chapter 7, section 1), can be found in the folklore of numerous countries.[19] They go back at least as far as the Sumerians, whose heroes Gilgamesh and Enkidu cut off the head of the giant Huwawa – a tale which may have helped to shape the myths of Heracles–Hercules.[20] The latter came to Pallanteum while driving Geryon's cattle back home to Argos from Erytheia, the land of Sunset Glow to which Evander was said to have accompanied him; at some stage this western country was identified with Spain. In the Greek art of the seventh century B.C., Heracles had been the most popular of all the heroes, and in the sixth and fifth centuries there was no lack of poets to sing his praises.[21] Stesichorus, who was born in Italy and lived in Sicily until his death a few years before the middle of the sixth century B.C., was particularly interested in Heracles' western expedition, about which he wrote a *Geryonid*. Timaeus, too (d. 260), wrote of the hero's passage through Campania. The cult of Heracles was very widespread in Greek southern Italy, notably at Croton, Locri and Poseidonia (Paestum).[22]

But the Virgilian and Livian versions of the encounter between Hercules and Cacus are very far from mere adaptations
of the Geryon myth, in which, indeed, many of the features
included in the Cacus story had not occurred. Possibly both the
Roman writers go back to a second-century version by Ennius.
Historians of the same century likewise offered accounts, but
before that the myth is very likely to have attracted the interest
of Fabius Pictor (chapter 2, section 3), since the Fabii considered
themselves descendants of Hercules.

But there must also have been an important Etruscan contribution, though details of its transmission are now irrecover-
able. The Etruscan conception of Cacus has already been discussed, but Hercules, too, under the name of Hercle, was
particularly popular among the people of Etruria, in whose
art he became a well-known figure during the sixth century B.C.
Indeed, he was popular all over Italy, as Dionysius records.
This was largely because he was honoured as a patron of
merchants and trading enterprises and commercial agreements,
in view of his prolonged and successful journeys and his powers
to avert evil.[23] However, as so often happened, the mythology
of the Etruscan Hercules differs from the canonical Greek form
(chapter 2, section 2). For his representations in Etruria tend to
immobilize and deify him without always paying regard to his
myths,[24] owing to the inability or unwillingness of the Etruscans
to follow the Greek conception of heroes half-way to gods.[25]
Their own Hercules was not only the god of merchants but a
helper on warlike expeditions; at Rome, too, he came to be
known as the Unconquerable and the Conqueror. In Etruria he
was also the deity of water, springs and the sea, and presided
over fertility and the Underworld. The Underworld was the
realm of Cacus, symbolized by his cave, and the recurrence of
the cave in Virgil's and Livy's story is likely enough to represent
an echo, direct or indirect, of an Etruscan source. There were also
deviant Etruscan versions, half-suppressed, which flattered the
early power of Etruria by claiming that none but Hercules had
been able to free the Romans from paying a tithe to the Etruscans, which was why henceforward they paid it to him instead.[26]

However, it was not Etruria but Greece which supposedly gave Rome its enormously important cult of Hercules at the Greatest Altar, the Ara Maxima. This altar was just within the borders of the original Palatine village, on the edge of the Tiber cattle-market (Forum Boarium), and the worship of Hercules there served to bring the market under the auspices of a god of wide international renown. But this step was evidently taken for the special benefit of traders from Greek south Italy. For there was stress on the fact that whereas Romulus, after his foundation of Rome, employed the Latin ritual of Alba Longa for the worship of all other gods, he instead instituted Greek rites for Hercules, whose cult was alleged to be, and perhaps really was, the earliest foreign worship to be introduced in the city. The employment of this form of ritual, still practised in historical times, was cited to support the argument that Rome was of Greek origin.[27]

What it may instead signify, however, is that worship of Hercules was *reconstructed* on Greek lines, at an early but none the less secondary stage: its character may well not have been Greek at first. We might well have suspected, in view of the popularity of Hercules in Etruria, that his worship at Rome had originally been Etruscan. But it is, in fact, very probable that the altar was established in the first place by merchants who were not Etruscans but Phoenicians. For these traders, in about the seventh century B.C., possessed a settlement and anchorage on the Tiber front of Rome, just as they had in Caere's ports Pyrgi and Punicum (chapter 1),[28] and at harbour towns in other parts of the Mediterranean. And it was the custom of the Phoenicians, at such maritime centres, to establish the worship of their god Melqart, who was identified with Hercules. The assumption of a Phoenician origin for the altar explains various oriental taboos associated with its cult, such as the exclusion of women.[29]

But then in the sixth or fifth century B.C. the Etruscan presence at Rome, which had favoured this Phoenician link, was gradually removed, and it must have been at the same time that the worship of Hercules was reorganized according to Greek practices, borrowed from southern Italy.[30] There may, however, have survived a certain Etruscan aura, associating elements of the Cacus story with the cult, and these associations were fastened upon when the usual etymological speculations came into play and invented what seemed to be appropriate connections. The Virgilian tradition tells how Hercules was able to discover where his cattle were because he heard one of the heifers shut in the cave bellowing. Now, on the Palatine side of the cattle market beside the Ara Maxima was a town-gate, the Porta Mugonia, which suggested to Varro the word *mugire*, to bellow. Presumably it had originally been given this name (if this etymology is correct) because the cattle market was no near, but the myth of Hercules and Cacus provided a more attractive explanation. Cnaeus Gellius also indicated that Hercules' discovery of the cattle is the reason why there was an altar nearby dedicated to Jupiter Inventor,[31] a forlorn attempt to explain a term of which the real meaning, as so often, was lost in the mists of time.

As for the altar of Hercules himself, the tradition held that its guardians were two families, the Pinarii and Potitii. This indicates that at first, or at least after the reconstruction of the cult in the sixth or fifth century B.C., it was a privately organized affair. The Pinarii, one of whose members, according to Diodorus, had welcomed Hercules to the site of Rome, are probably authentic. For otherwise it is difficult to see why they should have been mentioned, since they were a pretty obscure family in historical times – though it was something that people of such an ancient name still survived at all.[32] And they were still *just* worth mentioning, because a Lucius Pinarius Scarpus was a nephew and secondary heir of Julius Caesar; his coins show that he effected a timely desertion from the cause of Antony to that of Octavian.[33] As for the Potitii, however, they do not seem to have been a family at all. They were grouped with the Pinarii owing to a relic of the Phoenician origins of the cult, which had been handed down though its explanation was forgotten. For they are apparently a priestly order of 'the possessed' (*potiti*, *katochoi*), like the priests of Semitic cults.[34]

The first known appearance of Hercules in Roman state cult was dated to 399 B.C. In 312 the worship was nationalized and entrusted to state slaves, mainly, perhaps, because of the decline of the Pinarian family, but also, it may be, because of trends of opinion, encouraged by the remarkable Appius Claudius the Blind, who wanted to alter the emphasis of Roman religion by popularizing other more mystical elements of Greek thought instead (see chapter 5, section 1).

The persistence of the Cacus story in later Roman times was partly due to its philosophical implications. All combat myths, from the earliest civilizations onwards, had stood for the conflict of good against evil, and this was particularly applicable to the successful struggle of Augustus against the hostile forces which were held to stand for anarchy. Indeed, in more general terms, the triumphs of Augustus were readily comparable, in the eyes of his supporters, to the Labours which Hercules had successfully carried out. Besides, according to the theory of Euhemerus which Ennius had helped to make fashionable at Rome (chapter 2, section 3), Hercules was one of those rare human beings whose great deeds upon earth had caused them, after death, to be elevated to the ranks of the immortal gods. The same transformation was ascribed to Rome's founder Romulus (chapter 4, section 2), and the idea was in everyone's minds when Julius Caesar – who in his youth had composed a eulogy of Hercules – was likewise, after his murder in 44 B.C., declared a god of the Roman state. It was obvious that the same destiny was in store for Augustus, and meanwhile, like others before him, he was often deified in private practice and complimentary poetry. The parallel between Augustus and Hercules is explicitly stressed by Horace.[35] And Virgil and Livy, too, although their methods do not permit them to make the direct comparison, showed that they did not fail, any more than their contemporaries, to have it in mind.

2 GREECE AND ROME: AENEAS

The *Aeneid* possesses a deep complexity which it would take many lifetimes to unravel. No summary can do justice to any part of the poem. Yet a summary is desirable all the same, so as to enumerate some of the many myths, of different epochs, that were woven into its fabric.

The story of the *Aeneid*, then, may be briefly described as follows.

From Aeneas came the Latin race, the lords of Alba Longa, and the lofty city of Rome. When Troy was captured by the Greeks, he contrived, with the help of the goddess Venus his mother, to escape from the burning city, carrying his father Anchises on his shoulders and leading his son Ascanius by his side. And so he set sail to find a new land where he and his surviving fellow-Trojans could try to settle. With him, too, were the household gods of Troy, destined like himself for this new home. After spending a short time in Thrace, he went on his way and put in at the island of Delos, where he was bidden by the oracle of Apollo to go to 'the land of his forefathers'. Reminded by his father that Teucer, ancestor of the Trojan royal house, had come from Crete, he sailed on to that island. But his household gods (Penates), appearing in a vision, told him that Dardanus' original home had been Italy, and that this was the country to which he must go. (Dardanus was said to have been born at the Etruscan town Corythus, which may be Cortona). Arriving in Epirus upon the eastern Adriatic coast, Aeneas learned from the Trojan Helenus, who was now the ruler of that land, that, when he reached Italian soil, he must look for a place where he should see a white sow with thirty young. And on his way towards the place where he was to settle, which lay somewhere on the farther coast of Italy, he must visit the Sibyl at Cumae, who would tell him more.

Next he landed in Sicily, where he was welcomed by his kinsman Acestes, ruling at Drepanum (Trapani), near Eryx where Aeneas' mother Venus had her shrine; and at Drepanum his father Anchises died. In the following year Aeneas left the island, but the goddess Juno, who had constantly pursued him with her hatred during the journey, sent a sudden storm which drove him onto the African coast, near the site of Carthage. Here he and his men were hospitably received by Dido, who was the foundress of that city. But Venus caused her to fall deeply in love with Aeneas; and he responded to her love, which was consummated when a storm drove them to take shelter in a cave. For Venus had persuaded Juno to consent to the match. But now Jupiter sent a warning to Aeneas that it was not his destiny to remain in Africa, and that he must leave Dido and go. Aeneas planned a secret departure, but the queen discovered his intention and desperately begged him to stay. He refused, because he must obey the orders of the gods. And so she killed herself.

With her funeral pyre before his eyes, Aeneas sailed away. Calling in at Sicily for the second time, he celebrated the anniversary of his father's death by holding funeral games at Drepanum. While these celebrations were taking place, the women-folk of his Trojan companions, at Juno's instigation, set fire to four of his ships. But he himself, leaving the older and weaker of his followers behind as settlers, moved on to the mainland of Italy.

And now comes the turning-point of the *Aeneid*, Book VI in which he describes Aeneas' descent to the Underworld. The Trojan pilot Palinurus, sleeping at the helm, fell overboard and was drowned. But Aeneas landed in Italy, and sought out the Sibyl at Cumae, sitting in her rock-hewn cavern beneath the Temple of Apollo. She bade him arm himself with the Golden Bough, and they went down to the Underworld together. There Aeneas encountered Dido, who turned away from him in silence. But then he came upon his father Anchises, who disclosed to him the future glories of Rome, reaching their climax with the rule of Augustus.

Rejoining his comrades, Aeneas coasted along to Caieta, and then onwards to a landing-place at the mouth of the Tiber. During the following night, the river god appeared to him in a dream, and asserted that the prophecy he had received in Epirus was about to be fulfilled. For the god of the Tiber declared to him that on the following morning he would see the sow with thirty young in the place which was to be his future home, and so he did, on the site of the future Lavinium.[36]

Then Aeneas entered into friendly relations with Latinus, the aged king of the Aborigines who ruled at Laurentum nearby; and Latinus, warned by an oracle that his daughter Lavinia should wed a man from a foreign land, promised that she should be given in marriage to Aeneas. But Juno incited Turnus of Ardea, prince of the tribe of the Rutulians, to stir up strife; his supporters were able to claim that the oracle referred to himself, since his princedom was separate and therefore foreign, and his family had originated from Greek Mycenae. Latinus supported Aeneas but his queen Amata was bitterly opposed to him, and when Aeneas' son Ascanius unknowingly killed a pet stag, the old man was powerless to check the hostile leadership of Turnus. Virgil lists thirteen Italian chieftains who rallied against Aeneas, including Camilla, the heroic maiden who led the Volscian people, and above all Mezentius, the exiled and hated king of Etruscan Caere. But the reigning monarch of Etruria, Tarchon, who had been warned that he would only prevail over Mezentius by accepting a foreigner as his leader, took the other side and backed Aeneas; and so did other Etruscans, including Arruns.

And now Aeneas, again in accordance with the instructions he had received in his dream, visited the Greek king Evander, who was ruling over the Palatine hill; and it was now that Evander told him how Hercules, too, had come to the place in former days, and had slain the monstrous Cacus (section 1 above). Evander promised Aeneas help, gave him his own son Pallas as a comrade. And then, as they left the Palatine together, the goddess Venus appeared to them and bestowed upon Aeneas the armour her husband Vulcan had made for him, including a shield engraved with a prophetic series of scenes from Roman history, culminating in Augustus' triumph at Actium.

Then war broke out. Turnus attacked the camp of the Trojans, and set their ships on fire. But at the request of the goddess Cybele, from whose holy mountain of Ida beside Troy the timbers of the vessels had come, Neptune transformed them into nymphs of the sea. On the following day Turnus renewed the attack, and even broke inside the ramparts, but he was cut off and only extricated himself with difficulty. Faced by a conflict between Juno and Venus, Jupiter decreed that the issue must be left to Fate.

As the fighting continued, the young son of Evander, Pallas, was slain by Turnus, but Aeneas killed the Etruscan Mezentius. After the dead had been buried under truce, many other warriors fell on either side, including the Volscian chieftainess Camilla who was cut down by Aeneas' Etruscan ally Arruns. And now Turnus, who had previously refused single combat with Aeneas as a solution for the war, decided to accept the challenge, brushing aside the dissuasions of Latinus and Amata; and Amata, who had been wrongly informed that Turnus was already dead, hanged herself. Jupiter conciliated Juno with a decree that Trojans and Latins should unite with one another and form one nation; yet the two heroes fought, and Turnus was struck down. As he died, he begged that his body might be returned to his old father. His conqueror might have weakened. But then he saw on his vanquished enemy's body the bright-studded belt of Evander's son Pallas whom Turnus had slain. And so, with a shout of vengeance, Aeneas struck the fatal blow.

According to Virgil, Evander had ties of kinship with his Trojan visitor Aeneas. Their families were related, possessing Atlas as a common ancestor; and in his youth Evander had entertained Aeneas' father Anchises in Arcadia, from which he had later been driven out by their common enemies the people of Argos (the Mycenae of Agamemnon, the commander against Troy). Dionysius, however, goes much farther in uniting Evander and Aeneas, for in pursuit of his determination to make Rome's origins wholly Greek he persistently declares that Aeneas, too, was Greek, since Troy had been a Greek city. Virgil, on the other hand (probably going back to Cato) brings about a more balanced amalgamation of the two rival traditions of the Greek and Trojan origins of Rome: for whereas Evander remains a Greek, Aeneas the Trojan is not represented as Greek at all.

Yet Virgil, too, in his own way, was extremely eager to reconcile Rome with the Greek world, and thus to end the bad old mutual suspicions and dislikes between west and east.[37] Moreover, his feeling on this subject was precisely in accordance with imperial policy. For one of the chief aims of Augustus, also, was to unify the two halves of the empire, which had almost split apart under the stresses of his conflict with Antony. But Virgil's approach to this delicate question did not involve Dionysius' wholesale hellenization of the alleged past, for it involved no shying away from former Graeco-Roman enmities, only recently resolved by the death of Cleopatra. Hence the advantage of having Aeneas as a hero. For, granted that his story came within the Greek tradition – which cultural respectability required – he had been an enemy of Greece; though one of his major Greek foes, Diomedes, who had come to Apulia, was now his friend.

Virgil again symbolizes the reconciliation with Greece by locating the most solemn and decisive event of the *Aeneid* at Cumae (Cyme), the Greek town on the Campanian coast which had made such exceptional contributions to Rome's knowledge of Hellenic culture (chapter 1). For it was here that Aeneas descended to the Underworld. Odysseus in the *Odyssey*, too, had made a similar journey to the ghosts beyond the stream of Ocean,[38] but this central Book VI of the *Aeneid* is far more heavily loaded with meaning. For one thing, the place where the hero goes beneath the earth is the necromantic shrine of the Greek Apollo. It was this very cult of Apollo, the brilliant Hellenic civilizer, which Augustus exalted as his token of the reconciliation between the worlds of Greece and Rome.

And so, in the Cumaean grotto of Apollo, Aeneas sought out the god's prophetess, the Sibyl.

> There's a huge cave hollowed out from the flank of
>   Cumae's hill;
> A hundred wide approaches it has, a hundred mouths
> From which there issue a hundred voices, the Sibyl's
>   answers.[39]

Then, in the company of the Sibyl, Aeneas descended into the Underworld. This was the decisive happening. He had gone down to the Underworld as a wanderer and immigrant; his wanderings symbolized the trials of the soul. And now, after this supreme trial among the dead, he returned to the light as the mature man of destiny whose future Italian homeland, preg-

nant with the history of days to come, was ready for his occupation.[40]

The name of Aeneas was associated with Campania, and even
possibly with Cumae, from an early stage of Greek literature.[41]
As for the Roman writers, it appears likely that Naevius brought
him and his fellow-Trojans to consult the Sibyl, before a storm
blew them off their course and took them to Africa.[42] Fabius
Pictor attributed a prophetic dream to Aeneas,[43] and Virgil, like
Cicero before him,[44] but with far more intricate profundity, saw
how to expand this theme into the prophetic experiences of
the hero in the Underworld. These insights into the future are
coupled with disclosures about the mysteries of the universe,
which Virgil has derived from a vast and many-sided blend
of Greek religious writing, Platonic and Stoic philosophy,
mythology and folklore drawn from a multitude of different
sources.[45]

At an early date people in western Asia Minor had known of
verses supposed to be the inspired utterances of *Sibyllai*,
prophetesses whose name is of uncertain origin.[46] Then similar
ideas had come to Greece. Gradually the Sibyls became localized
at various centres, of which the most prominent in western
lands was the oracle at Cumae. Pre-Greek in origin, the oracle
now became associated with Apollo, the Greek god of all
diviners. Cumae's Sibylline books, which seem to have contained not only oracular pronouncements but a mixture of
Greek and Etruscan sacred rules for warding off menacing prodigies, were believed to have passed into the hands of Rome at
the time of Etruscan rule (chapter 5, section 2), and were lodged
in the Capitoline Temple of Jupiter. But in about the fifth century B.C., the period in which the worship of Apollo was
thought to have been installed in the city, the Romans imitated
Greek practice by declaring the god to be the patron of these
Books. And, indeed, it was probably from Cumae that the cult
of Apollo had come to Rome, though he was also well known
in Etruria and other parts of Italy. In 399 B.C., it was afterwards
said, the Sibylline Books ordered the Romans to perform novel
rituals. It was not, however, until the Second Punic War that
the Books, and the worship of Apollo, achieved real impor-

tance at Rome, absorbing a variety of prophetic writings and exercising a profound effect on religion.

And then Augustus had the Books copied, that is to say edited to suit the requirements of the regime. This was done in 18 B.C., the very year after Virgil had brought the *Aeneid* nearly to completion and had died. The urns containing the Books are shown on a coin of Augustus beneath a figure of his patron-god Apollo.[47] For it was to his new Temple of Apollo on the Palatine, the religious centre of the new order, that these records were now transferred.

Both before and after his descent to the Underworld, Aeneas was believed to have paid visits to Sicily. The stories of his presence in the island were greatly expanded in the third century B.C. when, as we saw above, Greek writers were paying attention to his Italian and Roman exploits. However, the association of Aeneas with Sicily was older than that, being part and parcel of his links with a great many Mediterranean regions. Like the myths connecting him with the mainland of Italy, the stories of Aeneas' immigration to Sicily might possibly represent dim echoes of real visits by navigators from the eastern Mediterranean towards the end of the troubled second millennium B.C., such as were recorded by Thucydides.[48] The story that Aeneas came to Sicily may conceivably have been told by the poet Stesichorus, who lived in the island (see below, note 70). The existence of a large non-Greek population in the island encouraged the supposition that there had been a Trojan settlement. Moreover, there was a priestly tribe of the Aeneadae in Sicily, and many local sites cherished Aenean connections.

Then, during the later fifth century B.C., the Syracusan historian Antiochus was ready to bring the Romans themselves under Sicilian auspices, writing of a mythical figure called Sicelus who had been at Rome in pre-Trojan times. In other words, he envisaged an original Sicilian foundation of the city. So by his time the point had been reached of alleging, not only a Trojan landing in Sicily, but a direct link between Sicily and the origins of Rome.

Shortly after 300 B.C., the Romans began to direct more serious

attention than before to the Greater Greece of southern Italy
and Sicily. At this point, too, they started utilizing their alleged
common possession of Trojan descent as a means of seeking
closer ties with these Greek communities, in the hope that they
could thereby counteract the power of Carthage in western
Sicily. But very soon, too, the same mythological corpus was
used not only by and for the Romans but against them. For
when Pyrrhus, king of Epirus, in response to an appeal by the
city of Tarentum (Taras), invaded southern Italy and Sicily in
281, he reminded everyone that he – supposedly the descendant
of Achilles[49] – was waging a second Trojan War, against Rome
which was a colony of Troy; and that this new Graeco-Trojan
conflict would have the same result as the first. In fact, it did
not. But the point had been made that these mythological pretensions, to which all parties had become so deeply attached,
were two-edged.

During the First Punic War Rome returned vigorously to the
mythological charge. The matter came up when the Sicilian
town of Segesta sided with Rome against the Carthaginians
(263–2). For the new alliance was proclaimed by the Romans
to be a natural consequence of the Trojan origins they shared
with Segesta – which had a temple Aeneas was said to have
founded. The First Punic War was the theme of the poet Naevius
(c. 270–201), and although the fragmentary nature of his *Punic
War* makes it impossible to be certain on this point, his introduction of the Aeneas myth seems to have been linked with
Segesta's defection to Rome – or perhaps with the subsequent
campaigns that were fought near the place two years later.
Drepanum (Trapani), the focal point of Virgil's narrative, was
captured in the course of the fighting. After the war was over,
Sicily increased its claim to incorporation in the mythology of
the Romans when they annexed most of the island and made it
into their first overseas province. And meanwhile, at the same
period, Rome was utilizing its claim to Trojan origin in order to
justify interferences in the Greek east. The Seleucid king of
Syria was requested to free the inhabitants of the Troy region,
the Troad, from taxation,[50] and in 238 Rome responded to an
appeal from a people in western Greece, the Acarnanians, on

the grounds that Acarnania had been the only part of Greece which had not taken part in the Trojan War.[51] Such debating points were evidently considered very well worth while.

In the Second Punic War the Sicilian connection was vigorously revived. Much of the fighting in the north of the island went on in the neighbourhood of a former dependency of Segesta, Mount Eryx (Monte San Giuliano), which possessed an altar of Aphrodite Aeneas – the most famous shrine in the island – and used Drepanum as its port. Profiting by the supposed common link with Aeneas, the Romans proceeded to offer honours on their own account to his mother Aphrodite, under the name of Venus Erycina, actually going so far as to introduce her cult into their own city and build her a temple there (217). To take over the cult of Eryx in this way was an act of boldness characteristic of the political sleight of hand which exemplified the whole Roman exploitation of religion and mythology.

The goddess at Eryx had originally been Astarte – a Phoenician divinity, like Melqart who preceded Hercules at Rome (section 1 above). In the early times of the Greek colonization of Sicily, she had been identified with Aphrodite. Then Aphrodite, in her turn, became equated with Venus – perhaps only after Rome had got to know the Sicilian shrine.[52] The name of this Italian goddess comes from *venus*, charm or blooming nature, or possibly from *venia*, the grace of the gods. In the days before her identification with Aphrodite, she had already been personified as a deity, at Rome's Latin neighbour Lavinium (section 3 below). This evolution had probably taken place by at least the first century B.C., and therefore it may well have been Lavinium which passed on the knowledge of the goddess to Rome. But it needed the Punic Wars to give her cult there a real boost. And the politically significant shrine at Eryx, combined with the assertion in the *Iliad* that Aphrodite was the mother of Aeneas, provided all the stimulus that the astute Roman propagandists needed.

That is to say, Virgil's emphasis on Sicily is a poetic reflection of the national experience of the Romans during the years before 200 B.C. In the following century, they found a new field for the exploitation of their alleged Trojan ancestry in the Greek east. The Roman 'liberator' of Greece, Flamininus, was duly compared with Aeneas, and high Roman officials paid special, highly publicized visits to Troy, like Alexander the Great before them.[53] When Macedonia succumbed to Rome, it was pointed out that Troy had at last taken its revenge upon the northern Greeks such as Achilles, who had once brought about its destruction.[54] But then, during the first century B.C., fresh reasons for an interest in the story came crowding in thick and fast. The dictator Lucius Sulla, a member of the house of the Cornelii who were one of Rome's six greatest patrician families, called himself Epaphroditus,[55] claiming – in the eastern provinces at least – that he enjoyed the special patronage of Aeneas' mother Aphrodite (Venus). And above all the patrician Julian house asserted its descent from the same goddess and her Trojan son. The assertion had already been put forward on coins issued a generation before 100 B.C., as well as after that date, by moneyers belonging to this ancient family, when it was beginning to recover from prolonged eclipse.[56]

And then the same claim was specifically reiterated by Julius Caesar in public orations.[57] His coins showed the traditional scene of Aeneas rescuing his father Anchises from Troy;[58] and Venus, who had been raised to lofty philosophical heights by the contemporary poet Lucretius, became the central divine figure in his religious policy, hailed as Mother (Genetrix). Caesar, profoundly antiquarian by interest and temperament, visited Troy himself, like so many others before him, and his alleged Trojan descent was naturally stressed by the professional experts of the day. Varro in particular (chapter 2, section 3), who had abandoned his enmity towards Caesar in order to accept the dictator's offer of the headship of Rome's public library, took pains to bring out many of the national and religious implications of the wanderings of Aeneas, including, it may well be, their dynastic, Julian significance.

And then, after Caesar's death, emphasis on the descent of the Julii from Aeneas played a very prominent part indeed in the official publicity of the dictator's adoptive son Octavian, later to become Augustus. The coin-type of Aeneas and Anchises reappeared as early as *c.* 42 B.C. to announce Octavian's own dynastic claims.[59] Later on, the theme persists on the great monuments of the Augustan regime. The Altar of Peace showed a sacrificial scene presided over by Aeneas, balancing another relief which depicted a sacrifice by Augustus himself. And then in his own new Forum, the Temple of Mars the Avenger – sponsor of the emperor's vengeance upon the assassins of Caesar – was flanked on one side by heroes of the Monarchy and Republic, but on the other by ancestors of the Julian house, with Aeneas at their head.[60]

Before the Altar of Peace and Forum of Augustus were built, Virgil had written his *Aeneid*, which propounded the same messages. There is no longer any need, today, to stress the fact that Virgil was not just a propagandist for Augustus. His achievement was infinitely more subtle than that – to take only a single example, he showed a deep feeling for the weakness and weariness of human flesh and blood, a theme for which, obviously, there was no place in Augustan publicity. But, even if Aeneas is by no means the exact replica of Augustus, he is, just as obviously, meant to be the emperor's forerunner, and it is not too much to say that Virgil selected him as his hero because the Julian house were supposed to be his descendants. With this ancestral emphasis, the tendency to interpret Aeneas as the man of Roman destiny *par excellence*, a tendency already increasingly perceptible during the past two centuries, achieves its climax.

Everything that Virgil says, every one of his unequalled dramatic resources, is mobilized to stress and illustrate the continuity between that mythical time and his own day, to make recent events the culmination of the mythic-historical process, and to display the indissoluble connection between the men he was writing for and the heroes he was writing about. This note is struck very clearly by a speech of Jupiter at the outset of the work.[61] Romans often oscillated between a belief in their own permanence and a feeling of anxiety that this was not really so comfortably assured after all. Jupiter, through Virgil, reassures them by his prophecy that a thousand years of myth and history are reaching their climax in the imperial mission of Augustan Rome.

This technique, which permeates every page of the *Aeneid*, caused pain to W. H. Auden.

> No, Virgil, no:
> Not even the first of the Romans can learn
> His Roman history in the future tense,
> Not even to serve your political turn;
> Hindsight as foresight makes no sense.[62]

But the overwhelming influence of the Roman mythology on Rome and on Europe shows that others have felt differently.

The methods by which Virgil achieved this supremely Roman effect are permeated and saturated by the tradition of Greece, or rather, to an overwhelming extent, of Homer. The Roman poet is that strange paradox: his *Aeneid* is utterly un-Homeric, and yet in ten thousand ways it depends on Homer, re-enacts and preserves his work, so that 'the most excellent way to an understanding of Virgil is by comparison with Homer'.[63]

In the *Iliad*, Aeneas had been one of the greatest Trojan heroes, so strongly (though briefly) exalted that it has even been conjectured that Homer belonged to a local Aenead priesthood. Homer's duel of Aeneas with Achilles anticipates the later duel between Achilles and Hector, and shows that the hero is within that same peerless class. He is rescued from the perilous battle-field by a god – no humiliation, for this happened to the best of heroes. The god who rescues him is Poseidon (Neptune). Usually, Poseidon is not so friendly to the Trojans; but now he has wider aims in view. For he prefaces his action with a prophecy. Aeneas had been charged with the ambitious desire to become king of the Trojans,[64] and at this point the god declares:

> On great Aeneas shall devolve the reign,
> And sons succeeding sons the lasting line sustain.

Or, rather, to add prosaic exactness to that version of Alexander Pope:

And now in truth shall mighty Aeneas be king among the Trojans,
and his sons who shall be born in days to come.[65]

This shows why some divine intervention in the conflict, to put
an end to his duel with Achilles, was a mythical and literary
necessity. Homer knew that Aeneas was destined to escape, and
so he had to protect him from fatal involvement in battle.
Aeneas was unique among the Trojans in that he had a future
as well as a past.

The dating of the composition of the *Iliad* is a notorious
problem, but it is reasonable to suppose that most of the work
was completed in Ionia during the eighth century B.C. It does,
however, remain possible, and has been argued again lately, that
Poseidon's prophecy was an addition inserted at a later date by
a poet at some Greek court whose masters claimed descent from
Aeneas. After all, it was not only the Romans who for patriotic
reasons adjusted their myths. The Greeks had constantly adjusted theirs too (chapter 7, section 2). For example, they had
inserted passages in the *Iliad*: Solon and Pisistratus, in sixth-
century Athens, were both accused of this sort of falsification.[66]
So it cannot be determined whether Poseidon's prophecy belongs
to the years after 800 B.C., or was introduced into the poem at
some subsequent date – perhaps after 600. For it was not far
from the latter date that Acusilaus of Argos was maintaining
that the Trojan War had been instigated by Aphrodite (Venus)
with the sole object of establishing Aeneas in power. In later
centuries, the Romans shamelessly rewrote the prophecy so as
to make it assert that Aeneas should be king not over the Trojans but 'over everyone'.[67]

In any case, however, the lines of Christopher Marlowe are
very relevant:

> Many tales go of that city's fall,
> And scarcely do agree upon one point.

And, in particular, there was a strange and rich variety of
opinion about what Aeneas really did during the fall of Troy,
and what happened to him afterwards. For one thing there was
a persistent tradition, at least from the fourth century B.C. and
presumably earlier, that he had been *allowed* by the Greeks to

leave Troy, since he had been pro-Greek, had been in fact a traitor – betraying his city, according to some versions, because he hated the Trojan prince Paris who had caused the war by seizing Helen; so that, in consequence, Aeneas had worked persistently for peace.[68] A similar story of his treachery was actually still retained in the writings of a learned Roman consul of 102 B.C., Quintus Lutatius Catulus.[69] This shows how, at quite a late date, the version soon to be given undying form by Virgil was still far from securing general, canonical acceptance.

There was also a difference of opinion about where Aeneas went. The poet of the *Iliad* seemed to imply that he was to remain in the region of Troy, and so did the epic poet Arctinus (who supposedly wrote in the eighth century B.C.). And so again, three centuries later, did the tragic poet Sophocles – a point which reminds us how ignorant we are of Virgil's debts to dramatists and epic poets whose works have come down to us in incomplete form or not at all. On the other hand a surviving piece of sculpture may provide evidence for a belief in the western migration of Aeneas at a date considerably preceding the time of Sophocles. This is the relief known as the Tabula Iliaca in the Capitoline Museum at Rome. It was probably made in about the last quarter of the first century B.C. – the period which saw the publication of the *Aeneid*. The scenes that it depicts, however, come from the ancient Greek epic cycle. Among them are two representations which are explicitly stated, by an accompanying inscription, to have been derived from *The Sack of Troy* (*Iliupersis*) by the Greek poet Stesichorus, who wrote in the early or middle sixth century B.C.[70] Aeneas is shown leaving Troy with his father and son and with his trumpeter Misenus, and the inscription asserts that he is leaving 'for Hesperia' – the land of the west, a word which later came to be used for Italy or Spain, and in the context of this relief, in view of the absence of a tradition of Spanish travel for Aeneas, has been thought to mean Italy or Sicily. But the word is not, as far as we know, found until a date three hundred years later than Stesichorus. That means very little, it is true, when so much of the literature of the period is lost. Nevertheless, we cannot be sure that the engraver of the inscription was right to suggest that Stesichorus had indicated this particular destination for Aeneas – or indeed a western destination at all.

However, it became customary, probably before 300 B.C., to believe that the end of the Trojan war had brought some of its military leaders to Italy: though these are normally identified as Greeks, Philoctetes, Epeius, Diomedes, and particularly Odysseus (Ulysses). This variety confirms the conclusion – already suggested by the persistence of an unfavourable tradition about Aeneas – that his nomination by Virgil as the official ancestor of Rome was by no means the matter of course, and foregone conclusion, that it has seemed in retrospect. For the stories of the Trojan war had produced other possible founders of Rome as well, not Trojans but Greeks. Moreover, as these variant traditions went on to assert, it had been Diomedes, or Diomedes and Odysseus – this is the version Virgil prefers – who had brought the sacred Palladium to Italy, the image of Pallas Athene (Minerva) which was revered, from about the third century B.C. onwards, as an essential part of the Romans' claim to a Trojan past, symbolizing their domination and permanence.[71]

By far the most powerful rival of Aeneas as Italian founder, at least from the time of a passage in our text of Hesiod's *Theogony* (which may not be earlier than the sixth century B.C.),[72] was Odysseus. Italy was crammed with mythical accounts of his presence, in which Etruria, where he is called Utuste, plays a very full part.[73] In the late fifth century B.C. Hellanicus described his arrival in Latium in the company of Aeneas. Together, he declared, the two heroes founded Rome.[74] But Hellanicus had also wanted to make room for an alternative tradition about a foundress named Rhomē (chapter 4, section 1), and so he recorded that what made Aeneas stay and found Rome was the burning of his ships by Rhomē on the Italian coast – a version reflected in Virgil's story that some women burnt Aeneas' ships in Sicily. Hellanicus' ascription of joint founder-roles to Aeneas and Odysseus gained an influential following. His pupils and later Greek writers kept on reverting to the theme, in one form or another, adding new facets to the myth as Rome formed new, dramatic links with the Greek world in the course of the third century B.C. Timaeus of

Tauromenium (d. 260 B.C.) was particularly prominent in this field.

But such developments gradually exalted Aeneas at the expense of Odysseus; and Timaeus' follower Lycophron, though he still associates the two heroes, already places Odysseus in a subordinate role. By the third century B.C., Odysseus' claims had begun to fade. As a Greek, a casual wanderer and discredited exile, he was not very suitable to be the ancestor of the noble Roman people. Virgil is deeply conscious of his indebtedness to the wanderings of Odysseus for his own account of those of Aeneas, and indeed it has often been pointed out that whereas the second half of the *Aeneid* is an *Iliad*, the first half is an *Odyssey*, culminating in the descent to the Underworld which directly echoes the similar journey of Odysseus to the shades of the dead. Nevertheless, there is also a contrast: Aeneas is passing on to a new life instead of returning to his old one. And so Odysseus' claims to be regarded as a founder of Rome began to seem inappropriate and out of date in comparison with those of Aeneas.

There were a number of places in the Balkans where Aeneas was venerated as a god, or a hero, or the founder of cults in honour of his mother Aphrodite, including Aeneia in Macedonia which displays the hero with Anchises on coins of about 500 B.C.[75] Under the stimulus of the Homeric prophecy of his escape from Troy, it seemed natural to suppose he had come to Thrace, Macedonia and Epirus, and the tissue of local temple-legends and other traditions in these regions was in due course woven together to make a single more or less consistent story. Indeed, it is possible that this was the route by which the Aeneas myth reached Italy. However, that is not a necessary assumption since Etruria and other Italian regions were open to Greek influences through direct channels, without requiring the supposition of intermediaries in more northerly Balkan territories.[76]

A study of the art of the later sixth and early fifth century B.C. indicates that this was the period in which a preoccupation with Aeneas burst strongly upon the Etruscans. They may have known about him earlier, but there was a sudden and strong interest in c. 525–470. This was displayed by the frequent and widespread reduplication of the scene of the hero leaving Troy with his father Anchises on his shoulders. More or less simultaneously, very many Greek vases found in Etruscan and Etruscanized towns depict this same incident, and so do numerous terracotta statuettes from Veii, and gems and scarabs from various parts of Etruria.[77]

In the same way as Dionysius of Halicarnassus regarded each alleged successive new migration of the Greek into Italy as a 'Return', because there had been Greeks there before, so it came to be supposed that Aeneas' arrival in Etruria was a 'Return', because Dardanus, the mythical founder of Troy, was said to have come there originally from Etruscan territory, where he was credited with the foundation of Corythus.[78] Aeneas, too, was regarded by the Etruscans as one of their city-founders, for the art of some of the cities in the southern part of their country – those with the easiest access to Rome – suggests that they venerated him in this capacity.

Why there was such a strong effervescence of interest at this particular time we cannot yet say; perhaps future researchers will throw some light on the question. Some of the vases found in Etruscan territory displaying Aeneas are of Greek origin, and indicate that the Greeks, too, had become interested in him. But the fact that they selected this particular theme for the designs of the vases they were importing into Etruria may well have been a reflection of a special interest on the part of their Etruscan clients rather than of themselves. Moreover since this was a period during which, in spite of all those trading connections, there were wars between the Etruscans and Greeks, it is possible that the former deliberately fastened on Aeneas as a non-Greek or anti-Greek element in the Hellenic tradition, in order to stress their kinship with the mythical enemies of the Greeks. If so, the Greek importers dealing with Etruria were evidently prepared to go along with this idea.

The situation became reflected in the literary tradition in a variety of ways. Tyrrhenus, the founder of the Etruscan people, was allocated a number of different Greek parents, including Heracles. A Tyrrhenus was also, in some quarters, considered one of the leaders of the people of Latium against Aeneas. On the other hand, a fourth-century Greek writer Alcimus recorded that Aeneas married a woman called Tyrrhenia. She was sometimes considered the daughter of a king of Mysia, in the neighbourhood of Troy.[79]

It is difficult to read the *Aeneid* without feeling that Virgil was very specially interested in the Etruscans and the part they could be made to play in the story of Aeneas and in the foundation of Rome. Lately, almost the opposite has been claimed: that the role of the Etruscans is less specific than one would have thought, in the light of Roman interest and knowledge. But there were many reasons – past and present suppressions of deviant Etruscan traditions, and past and present antipathies – why Virgil should omit to cross the 't's and dot the 'i's too meticulously, preferring to write in larger symbolic terms. In any case, this was in accordance with his general practice. But it also harmonized well with what was surely his intention, to establish a spiritual reconciliation between the conflicting Roman and Etruscan pasts. That is what he was doing for the Roman and Greek traditions, and a Roman-Etruscan unity, in the spirit of his friend and patron Maecenas, was likewise part of his plan.

As in his Greek reconciliation (section 2 above), no attempt is made to gloss over old conflicts with the Etruscans. On the contrary, Aeneas is given a terrible Etruscan enemy in Mezentius, the exiled king of Caere. Many of the incidents in Aeneas' fight against Mezentius were inspired by the Romans' traumatic war with Veii (though Virgil does not specify the comparison) at the beginning of the fourth century B.C., which represented the most important and dramatic stage in their long-drawn-out strife with the Etruscans (chapter 6, section 2).

Like Mezentius, Veii was defeated 'by Fate', and, like him again, it had first been isolated among its own people, for when Veii's final reckoning with the Romans arrived, the city gained hardly any support from other Etruscan communities.

There were various stories about Mezentius. One, cited by the elder Cato who brought him firmly into the Roman mythical cycle, indicated that he tried to impose on all Latins the humiliating obligation to deliver wine – a reflection of the time when Etruscans were seeking to impose their domination in the area (section 1 above).[80] Indeed, the whole tale of Mezentius reflects that epoch of Etruscan aggression and may constitute a recollection of it, however dim; while his brutality could be regarded as recalling a particular incident in the sixth century B.C. when the people of his city Caere were said to have stoned Greek prisoners of war (Phocaeans) to death after their capture off Alalia in Corsica (535). Mezentius is the despiser of the gods, *contemptor divom*, blasphemer and violator of divine laws, in deliberate contrast to the Etruscans as a whole, who were regarded as the most religious of all peoples.[81]

According to one variant of the story, Mezentius was not such a bad man after all: after his defeat in single combat by Aeneas' son Ascanius, he became a firm friend of the Trojans. But Virgil prefers that Mezentius should remain wicked, so that he can be contrasted with his friendly Etruscan counterpart Tarchon, who is the firm ally of Aeneas. Thus Mezentius and Tarchon together symbolize the two faces of Etruria's historic relationship with Rome. Perhaps the role of Tarchon – such as it is, for it is not worked out beyond the symbolical level – was Virgil's own invention, since Tarchon was the mythical founder of his own city Mantua (section 2 above): though his welcome to the immigrant Aeneas had already been hinted at by the poet Lycophron, who made him the companion of the immigrant Odysseus.[82] Tarchon was described as the son or brother of Tyrrhenus the mythical founder of the Etruscan nation, who, after arriving in his new homeland, had, according to one tradition current in Etruria, placed Tarchon in charge of the colonization of the area. Above all, however, the latter was the founder of the city of Tarquinii, which the Etruscans called Tarchuna or Tarchna after him, unless it was he who derived his name and mythical existence from the city.

But there were inscriptions of this same house of the Tarchna at Caere as well, ranging from the fifth to the third century B.C. This Caeretan branch of the family did not, in this case, make 'Tarquinius' the Latin equivalent of its name, but instead employed the by-form Tarquitius, the name of the expert who interpreted Etruscan lore to the Romans (chapter 2, section 3). And it was said that Tarchon was taught divination by Tages, a childlike seer of divine wisdom who was unearthed by a peasant in the fields near Tarquinii and revealed the Etruscan lore to the twelve leaders of the cities of Etruria. An Etruscan mirror at Florence shows a certain Tarchies, who may or may not be the same as Tages, examining a liver for omens while Tarchon looks on (chapter 2, section 2).

Besides Tarchon, Virgil assigns to Aeneas another Etruscan ally named Arruns. The name constantly recurs in Romano-Etruscan relations. It had a connection with priesthood and divination, and its memory was no doubt kept alive by a rich and powerful Lucius Arruntius. He was a man of religious and historical interests, who was one of the commanders of the victorious fleet at Actium and became consul in 22 B.C.; his family were given patrician rank, though little had been heard of them before. Arruntius had been born in the Volscian town of Atina, but his name could clearly be linked with the Etruscan Arruns, and this aspect of the family's tradition may explain why Virgil pits the Arruns of the *Aeneid* in combat with the Volscian Amazon Camilla (see section 2 above).

Virgil himself, who refers so often, in his own allusive way, to Etruscan matters, came from a town, Mantua, which was partly of Etruscan origin. It was one of the colonies which the Etruscans had founded beyond the Apennines, and, as the poet points out, it was from Etruria that the place drew its strength.[83] And he himself manifestly possessed strong Etruscan connections, strong enough for a late writer, relying on sources we are unable to identify, actually to describe him as the Etruscan bard or seer, *vates Etruscus*.[84] Fruitless though it usually is to speculate on the racial origins of ancient writers – since their antecedents are unlikely to have attracted enough notice to be recorded – it is worth pointing out that the name of Virgil's mother, Magia, may be Etruscan, that his family name Vergilius is more commonly found in Etruria than anywhere else, and that his last name (cognomen) Maro may be linked with the Etruscan title *maru*.[85] In other words, Virgil may very well have been an Etruscan. But in any case the cumulative significance of these points is fairly strong. They make it clear how Virgil could have been in a position to possess special knowledge of Etruscan affairs. And they suggest, also, that his choice of the Aeneas theme was to some extent inspired by its extreme popularity in Etruria.

The question how and when the knowledge of Aeneas came to the territories that lay to Etruria's south, those of Latium and Rome, cannot be answered with certainty. But probably the answer is ready to hand : since he was a highly favoured mythological figure in southern Etruria towards the end of the sixth century B.C., it was inevitable that he should be known at the same time in Latium, which was under Etruscan control (chapter 1); so that stories about his deeds which were circulating in Etruria naturally became localized and acclimatized in Latium as well. The contrary theory, that the Aeneas story only reached Latium much later on, seems incredible when one reflects how well known he was, already before 500 B.C., in Etruria only just across the Tiber.

Indeed, the Janiculum Hill, on the right bank of that river, had originally been known as Aenea, having been called this, presumably, by the Etruscans during their period of occupation; evidently it did not belong to Etruscan Rome, for it was not believed to have passed into Roman hands until the fifth century B.C. But in any case the story of Aeneas must inevitably, during the preceding period when the Etruscans established their domination over Rome, have been conveyed to the Romans by way of Etruria. When, therefore, Hellanicus linked Aeneas with Rome in the fifth century B.C., he was reflecting, first, the prominence of the hero in Etruscan mythology, and, secondly, the weight of Etruscan influence among the Romans. It was as a hero of Etruria that they knew of Aeneas.

His traditional destiny, after the wars described in the *Aeneid* were over, was to found the Latin town of Lavinium, the present Pratica di Mare, seventeen miles south-east of Rome. It was therefore from Lavinium, according to this tradition, that his son Ascanius established Alba Longa thirty years later. And from Alba Longa, in turn, after a long line of Alban kings, Romulus and Remus were to go forth to found Rome itself (see chapter 4, sections 1 and 2).

These were elaborate refinements upon simpler ideas: the idea, for example, that Aeneas had been Rome's founder. The amended version was prompted by vested interests in a number of quarters, and by difficulties in establishing a mythical chronology. Even as late as the first century B.C., some writers preferred to stick to the doctrine that Aeneas was Rome's founder, regarding further complexities as unnecessary. One such person was the historian Sallust,[86] who disliked a lot of flummery and may have felt a distaste for the somewhat ambiguous mythological personality of Romulus (chapter 4, section 2). But by that time he was not in line with his contemporaries, for the more complex version had gradually become canonical.

Aeneas chose Lavinium for his new foundation because he had been told, in Epirus, to establish the settlement at the place where he would see a sow with thirty young. When he arrived in Italy, as we have seen, the god of the Tiber warned him in a dream that the appearance of the portent was imminent.

> Here your appointed home is, the resting place for your gods.
> Do not give up, or be frightened by threats of war. The swelling
> Anger of heaven has abated.
> Even now, lest you think all this but a baseless fiction of sleep,
> You shall find lying beneath the oaks on the river-bank
> A great white sow, with a litter of thirty new-born piglets
> White as she, clustered at the teats of their sprawling mother.
> Here is the site for your city, sure terminus of your travails.
> And this is the sign that, when thirty years roll by, Ascanius

Shall found the white town, Alba, the city of shining name.
I prophesy certainties.[87]

And on the next morning the prodigy duly appeared. The tale
is told in various ways: by Dionysius at considerable length,
with emphasis on Aeneas' perplexity because the site was a
poor one – he was told a better one would come later on – and
by Diodorus with a story (derived from Fabius Pictor) to the
effect that Aeneas was advised not to found a city at once, but
to wait for thirty years.[88] According to other versions this stipu-
lation of a thirty-year interval alluded not to the first foundation, that is to say Lavinium, but to the second, namely Alba
Longa which was to be established by Ascanius thirty years
after Aeneas' Lavinium. But it was alternatively held that the
thirty piglets stood, not for these thirty years at all, but for
Rome's thirty Latin 'colonies' of the future;[89] or did they refer
to the thirty divisions (*curiae*) of the Roman state? The sow
was white because the name of Alba Longa was the same as the
Latin word *alba*, white,[90] though as usual there are doubts
whether the derivation is genuine. (It seems distinctly perverse
of Lycophron to say that the sow was black or dark, *kelaine*, by
which he presumably means 'fateful', as a sort of inside-out play
on the name 'white'.)

The mythology of the Indo-European peoples is full of animals sent by heaven to guide migrating tribes, and sometimes
these are wild boars, which played a part in the warrior ideal.
This theme was not limited to Italy, for it was a boar which
guided the people of Ephesus to the site of their future sanctuary. But boars were very much a feature of Italy in ancient
times – and indeed still today, as many a restaurant menu bears
witness. As for sows, their representation on early coin-like
pieces and coins indicates that they were a tribal or civic badge
of the Latins and other Italian peoples; and there are traces of
a sow-cult at Rome itself.[91] The animal which provided Aeneas
with his portent, together with its young, was depicted by
statues at Lavinium, and in the first century B.C. its supposed
body, preserved in brine, was still on show at that town.[92]

However, the whole story of Aeneas' disembarkation near

this point of the Latin coast is likely to have been stimulated, or perhaps actually brought into existence, by the fact that a place in the vicinity bore the name of Troia. It was situated between Lavinium and Ardea, at or near the locality called Zingarini.[93] There were also places of the same name in other parts of Italy. The periods from which they date cannot be established for certain. One piece of evidence that has been quoted in favour of their earliness is an Etruscan vase of the late seventh century B.C. from Caere, which shows two men on horseback emerging from a labyrinth labelled TRUIA.[94] Trojan myths, of course, readily adhered to sites or settlements bearing this name of Troia or Truia. However, the etymological basis for such a connection may have been wholly erroneous, for it is by no means certain that the word has anything to do with Troy. Nor does it mean a sow, as a gloss of the eighth century A.D. hopefully suggested. It may signify 'fortified place', or it may, as analogies in other lands suggest, mean 'passing to and fro'. In historical times a Roman cavalry exercise was still called the *ludus Troianus* (chapter 6, section 1).

The whole story of Aeneas' foundation is redolent of a duality, and rivalry, between Lavinium and Alba Longa (chapter 4, section 1). In actual historical fact, Alba Longa had been a very important Latin centre in the earliest Iron Age periods, and Lavinium had been of very little significance at that period (chapter 1). But this disparity did not prevent Lavinium from competing later on, with very strong claims about the sanctity of its sites, rituals and myths.

Lavinium was a small town on the coastal route from Rome to Campania, comprising a port and a shrine. The discovery has been made, on this site, of thirteen archaic altars which were inspired by Greek influences from southern Italy. Their erection may mark Roman attempts, during the sixth century B.C., to claim religious control of the Latin League. In the fourth century, Aristotle had heard of the place – if his reference to 'Latinium', quoted by Dionysius, should be applied to Lavinium, as seems probable.[95] As for the origins of the latter name, Dionysius states that according to the Greek mythographers it was called after Lavinia, the daughter of King Anius of the

Aegean island of Delos, whereas the Romans, he adds, regarded Lavinia as the daughter of King Latinus. Virgil, possibly basing his version on his epic predecessor Naevius, makes her the second wife of Aeneas, his first wife (Creusa) having disappeared during the departure from Troy. Lavinia is a colourless figure, dimly reminiscent of Helen of Troy as the prize of war, and recalling Penelope as the wife to be claimed from a hostile suitor. Yet Lavinia's introduction serves an important purpose all the same, and gets over a difficulty. For Rome was sometimes said to be descended from Latinus (chapter 4, section 1) and sometimes from Aeneas, and the latter's marriage to Lavinia performs the feat of combining both these versions.

The glories of small Lavinium were two. For one thing, it was believed to have been the first foundation of Aeneas, a stepping-stone or resting point on the way to Rome. Secondly, there was a tradition that Aeneas had brought his household-gods (Penates) to Lavinium from Troy, again on their way to their permanent Roman abode (by way of Alba Longa). The possession by the Romans, in historic times, of this supposedly Trojan cult of the Penates helped to encourage the story of Aeneas' migration from Troy, which explained the presence of these gods. At Rome, the images were lodged in the Temple of the national protectress Vesta beside the Forum. But the word comes from *penus*, store-house, and in primitive times, no doubt long before the arrival of the Aeneas myth, the Penates had been the principal objects of the private cult maintained by every Roman household, in which they represented the forces or powers that each family honoured to make sure it had enough food every day. Later, at the Temple of Vesta, they became national gods and protectors (*Di Penates Publici*). Whether this development preceded the creation of the Lavinium cult or not, the establishment of the national worship, with its alleged Trojan connections, conferred additional, ancestral solemnity on the whole concept of the patriotic, protective Penates. And so the Romans, eager to stress the glories of their own Trojan ancestry, made a point of declaring that the Penates of Rome were the same as the Trojan gods of Lavinium – and had come from that town.

Perhaps they had. But whether they had or not, the claim was a plausible one, since the cult had certainly taken on a new and more solemn shape owing to the influence of Lavinium. And it is possible to suggest how and when this influence came about. In historical times its main surviving relic consisted of an annual ceremony in honour of the Penates and Vesta which the chief Roman officials still continued to perform at Lavinium year by year shortly after they had vacated their office in the capital. This ceremony is likely to have been instituted round about 500 B.C., when the Romans annexed Lavinium. When they did so, they probably found the Aeneas myth already installed there, just as it was also installed, through Etruscan influence, in other Latin towns; and they took the story over for their own purposes, together with the idea that the Penates were Trojan.[96] It was probably at about the same time that these deities became identified with Castor and Pollux, the Dioscuri (chapter 6, section 1).

During the fifth century B.C., however, less seems to have been heard of the attempt to make Aeneas a Roman founder, since from about 450 onwards Etruscan influence in the city declined. But, if that was so, the story came back into favour later on: and once again Lavinium was the place which inspired the development. For in about 338, when Rome had finally absorbed the Latin League and entered into new relations with its individual members (chapter 1), the Romans decided to project this association back into the mythical past by enhancing the Lavinian rites as a symbol of the antique Roman-Latin link. In early days the Penates, in visual terms, had been little primitive statuettes of the storehouse; they are found with cremation-urns on Roman burial sites. But gradually, after the successive developments of *c.* 500 and *c.* 338, they became complex and manifold deities with patriotic overtones and Trojan links.* This meant that Lavinium could no longer claim to be the Latin leader of the cult, since this function had passed to Rome. But Lavinium was allowed – for the greater glory of Rome – to

---

* It is possible that this two-stage process should be telescoped into a single Roman take-over in the fourth century.

retain a memorable, nostalgic role. And so the historians who came afterwards were eager to read back the destiny of the place into remote and venerable antiquity.

Timaeus (d. 260 B.C.) already recorded Lavinium as Aeneas' first foundation.[97] When he visited the town, he was shown the Trojan relics that were preserved in the Temple of Venus. They included the earthenware jars in which, as artistic representations confirm, Aeneas was supposed to have brought the Penates from Troy – one of the features identifying them with Castor and Pollux, whose cult involved the use of similar jars.[98] Some two or three generations later, the poet Lycophron brought Aeneas to Lavinium.[99] He and Timaeus show how strongly the place urged its own claims to Trojan origin, claims which Roman tradition set itself to recognize and at the same time to absorb.

The process was encouraged by Cato, who devoted special attention to the origins of Italian cities (chapter 1). And then in the first century B.C. Licinius Macer, influenced by contemporary antiquarian fashions, again concerned himself with the municipalities of Italy, because of their brutal suppression by his political enemy Sulla; and Macer displayed particular interest in the ancient towns near Rome.[100] Subsequently Augustus, who himself came from one of them (Velitrae, the modern Velletri) and was always enthusiastic about ancient observances of this kind, allowed his own Genius or spirit to be coupled with Jupiter and the Di Penates in official oaths.

Aeneas' burial place near Lavinium was also shown to visitors. The site was beside the river Numicus (or Numicius), which was a stream running down from the Alban hills to the coast.[101] Virgil links the Numicus with the Tiber as a sacred river of Rome, and mentions it first among the sights seen by Aeneas as his first day in Latium dawns. In historical times a mound was still to be seen, surrounded by a fine grove. Some said it was the tomb of Anchises (who had supposedly died in Sicily), but it was more generally regarded as the burial place of Aeneas. In relation to this site, he was ascribed the surname of 'Indiges'. The Indigites, it is now established, were ancestors who received worship,[102] and it is evident that the so-called grave near Lavinium was originally the shrine of a generalized divine ancestor (or perhaps a particular ancestor whose name was subsequently lost sight of). This identification with Aeneas was a later development, which had taken place at least as early as the third century B.C., when Fabius Pictor described his worship.[103]

An inscription found five miles inland, at Tor Tignosa, shows that Aeneas was also called 'Lar'. This is another term which has been variously interpreted, but, like Indiges, it seems to mean a dead and revered ancestor, and was applied to Aeneas as the ancestor of the Roman race. The inscription is apparently of the fourth century B.C. and fits in well with the assumption that the national role of Aeneas was magnified after Rome's suppression of the Latin League in 338. The ancestral Lares, like the Penates of the store cupboard, were originally little household gods, worshipped in the lararia of private homes – though perhaps they had in early times belonged rather to the farm lands and crossways, with which they always maintained a link. Thereafter, like the Penates, they became national gods, Lares Publici. Once again, Augustus skilfully made use of the institution, merging the veneration of his own Genius with the Lares of the Crossroads and thus giving a new impetus to their cult. Henceforward they were called the Lares Augusti. They appear on reliefs with the prophetic sow. They are also found in connection with the apotheosis of Julius Caesar, the divine ancestor who had launched the imperial house.

This was particularly apt, since Aeneas, like Caesar, had come to be thought of as a Roman god – just as he was a god in various other parts of the Mediterranean world. It was stated by some authorities that he was drowned in the Numicus stream and then deified; modern anthropologists refer to the practice, authenticated in various other countries, of apotheosis by strangulation, which they trace back to early ritual customs. But Livy's version is that Aeneas died in battle, apparently against the Etruscans. He goes on to note the deification that ensued, though the bewildering variety of names attributed to the deity, including the name of Jupiter himself, encourages him to display a touch of the questioning spirit which, for all his feeling for the Roman religion, were aroused in him by superhuman interventions. Or perhaps he found this scepticism in the source he was following, and did not see fit to modify it. 'Aeneas lies buried,' says Livy, 'whether it is fitting and right to term him god or man, on the banks of the river Numicus. People call him, however, Jupiter Indiges.'

The process that had taken place has already been indicated in discussing Hercules (section 1 above). According to the doctrines formulated by Euhemerus in the early third century B.C., Hercules was thought of as a man who, by merit, had become a god. Ennius popularized Euhemerism at Rome, and Aeneas was interpreted in the same way; and so was Romulus (chapter 4, section 2). Their elevation to godhead was much spoken of in the first century B.C., when Caesar, too, was raised to the gods. And the same destiny was clearly in store for Augustus – as was shown, *inter alia*, by his association with the Lares and Penates.[104]

4 DIDO

Virgil's most startling personal contribution to the Aeneas myth, although it has obsessed the civilized western world as a work of art, never secured acceptance in the Roman mythological canon. This was the deeply, to some almost intolerably, moving story which told how Aeneas, between his two visits to Sicily, had landed in Carthage; how the queen and founder of that city, Dido, had fallen in love with him; and how he had responded to her love, but had been compelled by the order of Jupiter to leave her and go on his destined way. And she took refuge from her sorrow in death.

Dido perhaps means 'the wanderer'. It was her name among the Carthaginians, whereas at Tyre, the great Phoenician city which had founded Carthage or 'New Town' (allegedly in 814 B.C.), she was known as Elissa. This name was derived from a divinity, El. That is to say, Dido-Elissa was originally a goddess.[105]

It has been conjectured that she was first converted from a goddess into a human queen in some Greek work of the later fifth century B.C. When this development had taken place, it was stated that she was a daughter of a king of Tyre, known to Virgil as Belus, the god Baal. After her husband, called Sychaeus by Virgil, died at the hands of her brother Pygmalion (now king of Tyre), Dido was said to have escaped with some followers to north Africa, where she founded Carthage. As far as our knowledge goes, her first appearance in literary history is not until the early third century B.C., when Timaeus recounts that in order to escape marriage with the king of Libya (Iarbas in Virgil) she built a pyre, as though for a sacrifice, and leapt into the flames.

And then, at some time or other, there arose the story of Aeneas' sojourn at Carthage, echoing, though with far deeper significance, the lingerings of Odysseus with Circe and Calypso. The surviving fragments of the epic poem written about the First Punic War by Naevius, who died at Utica near Carthage (201 B.C.), include a famous passage which has been interpreted by many modern authorities to signify that he wrote of Aeneas' visit to Dido, thus providing Virgil with his model. In this tantalizing excerpt, someone is asked by someone else how Aeneas left the city of Troy.[106] Perhaps Dido is the asker, and perhaps it is Aeneas himself who is asked. Controversy still rages on the identity of these two persons, and all that can be safely said is that they *could* be Dido and Aeneas. It would certainly be reasonable to suppose that the story which brought Aeneas to Carthage originated, or gained currency, at the time of the Punic Wars. And it is particularly reasonable to attribute such a story to Naevius, who is referring to Aeneas – and he refers to him in another passage also – in a poem about the war with Carthage. So we cannot exclude the possibility that Naevius already interpreted and extended the Trojan legend (or borrowed its interpretation and extension from others unknown) by setting forth the relations between Aeneas and Dido; though this still remains no more than a possibility.

In the first century B.C. Varro, who was familiar with the idea that Aeneas came to Carthage, made Dido's sister Anna, not

Dido herself, kill herself for love of Aeneas.[107] Now Varro was an older contemporary of Virgil, who only outlived him by eight years. But whether, when Varro wrote, the alternative form of the myth, attributing this tragic death to Dido rather than Anna, was already in existence or known to him his words do not enable us to say. Moreover, neither Livy nor Dionysius refers in any way whatever to the entire Carthaginian episode of Aeneas. So far, then, we have no cogent reason to deny that the inspiration behind this utterly compelling tale, which defies history, chronology and established mythology alike, is Virgil's own.[108]

Or was there some tragic play on the subject in existence at the time when he wrote? The whole story, as he tells it, is very much in the spirit of Attic tragedy, and indeed almost amounts to a characteristically quick-moving, concise, selective Greek play in itself. But the concept of womanhood which Virgil's treatment reveals is no longer that of the Athenian tragic dramas which have come down to us. The *Medea* of Euripides (431 B.C.) still belonged to a classical world in which self-willed passionate love between man and woman is not accorded the degree of emotional sympathy it receives from Virgil. However, there is reason to believe that if one of Euripides' other plays, the *Andromeda*, had survived, it would have displayed more than a touch of romantic love. Later, in the third century B.C., the figure of Medea in the *Argonautica* of Apollonius Rhodius of Alexandria had taken on a new, romantic character which, as has often been remarked, was not without influence upon Virgil.[109] He was an epic poet, but it is possible that some pre-Virgilian dramatist too, either a Greek before him or a Roman after him, may have written a play about Dido in which this same romantic note was superimposed upon the tragic features of the story; though such a conjecture may well be an unfounded reflection on Virgil's originality. At all events, his Dido is a true tragic heroine, whose catastrophe, reversing her former great prosperity, is derived from a flaw in her own noble character, and from a bitter moral conflict. The crux is her marriage to Aeneas, if marriage it was.

Now Dido and the prince Aeneas found themselves
In the same cave. Primordial Earth and presiding Juno
Gave the signal. The firmament flickered with fire, a witness
Of wedding. Somewhere above, the Nymphs cried out in
  pleasure.
That day was doom's first birthday and that first day was the
  cause of
Evils: Dido recked nothing for appearance or reputation:
The love she brooded on now was a secret love no longer;
Marriage, she called it, drawing the word to veil her sin.[110]

Mythological marriages were often consummated in caverns.
Aeneas and Dido are like Jason and Medea, or Peleus and Thetis.
The thunder and lightning declare the oneness of the God of
Heaven with the Earth Mother: it is a Sacred Wedding, a *hieros
gamos*. But in Virgil's solemn and elevated description scholars
have also detected the echoes of antique formulae of Roman
marriage – and a marriage, of a kind, the union of Dido and
Aeneas could be said to be. Innumerable readers, Saint Augustine
among them, have reproached Aeneas for abandoning Dido.
But he could not stay with her after Jupiter had ordered him to
go, for his actions were ordained by Fate. He was the destined
founder of Rome's line. And his sadness at departing, for he
would never again love like this, is part of his transformation
from the individualistic Homeric hero into the servant of a
divine and Roman mission.

But Virgil, in the lines quoted above, makes a rare personal
intervention in order to censure Dido. This is a warning that
we must not be carried away, as he almost was, by sympathy
with her misery. She had lost control of herself: and her
marriage with Aeneas was not a marriage after all, but a sin.
It was a breach of the vow she had made to her husband
Sychaeus, now dead. For she had sworn to him that she would
never marry again.[111] According to the older, austerer traditions
of Rome, which were being deliberately revived by Augustus,
her fault was a grave one. It was also a fault related to the
general, propagandist idea that the Carthaginians were corrupt
and perfidious people.[112]

She and Aeneas both had to pay for their time of weakness.

His payment was the removal of the last chance of personal life and love he would ever have. Her payment was death. True, she had not acted of her own volition – for it was the scheming of Venus and Juno that had caused Aeneas to come to her. It was a misfortune for her to get enmeshed in the divine plans for Aeneas. But this could not exonerate her for violating her oath.

A Roman of Virgil's time, learning from the *Aeneid* how the foreign, exotic Dido detained the progenitor of Rome and charmed him with rich gifts,[113] could not fail to think of the recently defeated female enemy, Cleopatra, who had been built up by Augustan propaganda into an insidious oriental temptress luring Antony into her eastern self-indulgence and threatening to sap the virility of Rome itself. Virgil's artistry could not permit anything like a direct comparison – especially as Dido wins such a measure of sympathy from the reader. Yet Cleopatra's Alexandria does, all the same, play a part in the depiction of Dido's Carthage. Later on, the incompatibility of the two sirens with the destiny of Rome is emphasized once again by the contrast between Dido's luxury and the simple early Rome of Evander.[114]

Aeneas' visit to Carthage symbolizes all Rome's conflicts with more advanced cultures. And above all, this African crisis and tragedy was seen as the direct preface and cause of the Punic Wars, and as their mythical dress-rehearsal: it was in those terrible struggles that the curse which Dido calls down on Aeneas' head was fulfilled.[115] Moreover, in the very year of Virgil's death, when he was giving the *Aeneid* the form it now possesses, the Romans were celebrating another triumph over a people of north Africa, this time the proverbial Garamantes of Libya. They had been defeated by Lucius Cornelius Balbus, a powerful backer of the Augustan regime who was the last senator ever to be awarded the honour of a Triumph.[116]

Aeneas has to leave Dido because the voice of Jupiter and duty calls. No call of duty was ever so difficult for Aeneas to obey, or so necessary. Schoolboys have often been scandalized by

reading how the hero himself declares: 'I am pious Aeneas!'
But that is what *pius* means, obedience to the will of the gods,
the religious obedience that was to make Rome great. And it
was an appropriate quality to attribute to Aeneas, because
already in the *Iliad* he had been 'beloved of the immortal
gods'.[117] His father Anchises, too, was called *pius* in early Roman
poetry.[118] The word also means loyalty to one's country – which,
indeed, when one's country was Rome, seemed to be the same
thing as obedience to the gods. Aeneas, like a few other mythical or legendary heroes such as Romulus and Camillus, was the
fatalis dux, the leader who carries out the divine ordinances of
Fate. It was a conception which went back to Herodotus and
other early Greek historians. Since then, the idea had been in
abeyance, but Virgil and Livy boldly revived it, and caught the
mood of their generation.

In addition, the *pietas* of Aeneas refers, very specifically, to his
dutifulness towards parents and kinsmen. On the whole, ethical
considerations of this kind came into being rather later than
religious and patriotic concepts. Yet Homer, of course, had
already possessed a morality of a kind, the morality of his age,
and by the time of the philosopher Heraclitus of Ephesus
(*c.* 500 B.C.) such doctrines were beginning to take abstract
shape. However, it did not need much abstraction to praise
loyalty to one's family, and this would obviously be one of the
first ethical qualities to appear. It was also the quality which
Aeneas displayed in its highest form, when he rescued his father
and son from the flames of Troy.

> And now more clearly over the town the
>   fire's roar
> Was heard, and nearer rolled the tide of its conflagration.
> 'Quick, then, dear father,' I said, 'climb onto my back, and
>   I will
> Carry you on my shoulders – that's a burden will not be
>   burdensome.
> However things turn out, at least we shall share one danger,
> One way of safety, both of us. Let little Ascanius walk
> Beside me ...'[119]

The scene reappears in many other writers, for instance Propertius:

> The flames in reverent fear
> Those filial shoulders dared not sear
> When old Anchises from the wreck
> Clung trembling to Aeneas' neck.[120]

Such was the event reduplicated on countless artistic representations, beginning, as far as we know, with those of Etruria during the later sixth century B.C. (section 3 above). These representations were surely intended, from the start, to convey the *pietas* of Aeneas, his dutifulness towards his family. Greek literature took up the message, indicating that it was because of this dutiful action that the Greek conquerors had allowed him, when he left Troy, to take his possessions with him.[121] (And, incidentally, here was an interpretation which disposed of the charge [see section 2] that the Greeks had permitted him to go because he had treacherously favoured their cause.) In particular, it was customary for migrants from one country to another to take their household gods with them. This was what Aeneas, too, had done, and the emphasis placed on this aspect invested his story with a special sanctity.

Flight from a city, in defeat, might not seem a particularly positive form of heroism; as Churchill remarked, retreats from Dunkirk do not win wars. And so Ennius emphasized Aeneas' reluctance to leave, in spite of his father's plea, and stressed that it was only the intervention of his mother Venus that persuaded him to do so. Besides, as the warlike designs on vases are at pains to stress, Aeneas' escape from Troy was a successful piece of fighting – the achievement of the great warrior whom we know from the *Iliad*. Moreover, as Virgil immediately points out, his escape was commanded by destiny: he was 'a refugee by fate', *fato profugus*, so that his escape was an act of *pietas* towards the gods. But his principal *pietas* still lay in his preservation of his father and son, recorded by so many works of art.

The Romans, in spite of, or because of, their frequent lapses of conduct, were a profoundly, intensely moral people, and their myths are laced through and through with this morality (chapter 7, section 2). Such a tendency was, of course, greatly accentuated by their adoption of Greek ethical and religious ideas; and it was at a comparatively early stage of this infiltration that they vowed a temple to the personification of Pietas in 191 B.C. and dedicated it ten years later. But it is evident that the representations of Aeneas with Anchises and Ascanius had reached them centuries earlier from Etruria, and so, therefore, had the appreciation of the hero's *pietas* which these representations conveyed. We may well ask ourselves, then, whether there were not other early ethical concepts, too, which would likewise be traceable to Etruria if only our Etruscan literary sources had not vanished (chapter 2, section 2).

Certainly, Italy and Rome were acquainted with such ideas at an early date. For example, there was a very antique Roman priestly corporation, the Fetials, one of whose most prominent duties was to ensure, or make it appear, that any war in which Rome was engaged was both *justum* and *pium*. After various modifications of their function, the Fetials lapsed in the last century of the Republic, but they remained the subject of antiquarian interest, and Octavian revived them, and became a Fetial himself, in order to make a solemn declaration of war against Cleopatra, which thus became an act of *pietas*. Moreover, after the war was over, he officially adopted the concept as one of the four Cardinal Virtues which the philosophers had made fashionable. And so the *pietas* of Aeneas was satisfying to the emperor from every point of view, religious, patriotic and ethical, with special reference to the sanctity of families, an ideal which he went to great pains to revive. The abnegation of *Pius Aeneas* provided an appropriate contrast, in every way, to the ruinously egotistical public figures of the late Roman Republic, whose anarchic goings-on the new regime set itself to stamp out and supersede.

And so the myth of Aeneas was closely associated with the family and person of Augustus, who claimed direct descent from him by right of adoption by Julius Caesar. In Augustus' funeral procession, the effigy of Aeneas was carried among the effigies of other ancestors. This was in accordance with tradition, for an important point of the Aeneas myth had been its jealous conservation by those families which were able to claim Trojan descent. For the past three hundred years, it is true, the story had often been brought out and paraded for national purposes. But except, perhaps, in the homes of the supposedly Trojan families there had never been a cult of Aeneas at Rome as there was at Lavinium (section 3 above). Nor, indeed, did even Caesar, or Augustus, go so far as to introduce one. Aeneas belonged, rather tenuously, to the Roman pantheon, but none of the numerous Roman festivals or public games was devoted to his honour.

However, the impact of the *Aeneid* gradually transformed the situation. In matters of cult, there was no conspicuous change; and even Virgil could not manage to weld on to the tradition the startling tragedy of Dido. But owing to the influence of the *Aeneid* the Trojan genealogy ceased to be the prerogative of the imperial family and became the property of the Roman people. The myth had been diffused from above; and it was as a manifestation of national solidarity that the impending 900th anniversary of the traditional foundation date of Rome (A.D. 148) inspired the emperor Antoninus Pius to issue a series of brass medallions which gave pride of place to the city's Trojan origins.

4   ROMULUS

I PREPARATIONS FOR ROMULUS

The people whom Aeneas encountered when he came to the country subsequently known as Latium were generally believed to have been called Aborigines, a name which, among various other suggestions,[1] has lately been interpreted as meaning 'mountain peoples' rather than the more obvious 'aboriginals'. Cato indicated that they only changed their name to Latins after their fusion with Aeneas' Trojans.[2] Dionysius, who wanted the origins of all the communities in the region to be Greek, was happy to quote Cato's view that the Aborigines were Greeks as well, though he had to confess that the suggestion was dubious.[3]

The king of this tribe at the time of Aeneas' arrival was stated to be Latinus, dwelling at Laurentum, a little town which disappeared from view in imperial times and became merged with Lavinium under the name of Laurolavinium. Virgil does not exert himself very much over Latinus, whom he is content to leave as a symbol. The Latinus of the *Aeneid* is an ineffective old man; other writers described him as young, but Virgil felt that something had to be done to win sympathy for him, and that grey hairs would help. Latinus lacks the power to control those of his compatriots who are hostile to Aeneas. All the same, however, he is earmarked by the poet and the gods, in the end, to symbolize the alliance that will emerge between Trojans and Latins as an aftermath and consequence of the events described in the *Aeneid*.

Latinus, as the ruler of Latium, was by no means a novelty. He had appeared very early on in the Greek tradition. The *Theogony*, attributed to Hesiod, had already known of him as the strong and faultless son of Odysseus and Circe (chapter 3, section 2) who, together with his brother Agrius, 'far off in a

nook of the sacred isles ruled over all the renowned Tyrrh-
enians'.[4] The passage has been variously ascribed to the eighth,
seventh and sixth centuries B.C. But it harmonizes particularly
well with the last of these periods, since it identifies Latium
with Etruria, a confusion between conquerors and conquered
which is suggestive of the Etruscan domination over Latium in
the years before and round about 500.

Latinus' genealogy was very vague and varied. He was said to
be son of the god Faunus,[5] but there was also a tradition that
Hercules was his father. Latinus is variously described as fighting for Aeneas and against him; in some accounts he was killed
in the war, in others he survived. There were also many divergent statements of his paternal or grand-paternal relationship
with the founder or founders of Rome, all directed towards the
thesis that Rome was a Latin foundation. And the divergences
between the accounts of the war itself (if it ever took place, as
the mythologists did not wholly agree among themselves) are
reflected in the brisk assertion by Ovid that even the partici-
pants did not know what it was about.

> Some hoped that when their navy turned to mermaids
> The Rutuli would read that sign as warning
> To stop the war – but still the war went on.
> Gods ranged on either side to help their favourites,
> And both sides took their stand, brave as the gods.
> They even lost the reason why they fought,
> Even forgot the virgin bride-to-be,
> Her father's name, and all his wealthy kingdom.
> They fought for nothing else but victory
> Against the thought of yielding to defeat.
> At last the goddess Venus saw her son
> Aeneas take the field and win the day.[6]

In other words, the mythological tradition was a bit feeble at
this point. Hence a certain lack of interest in Latinus. But the
mythical wars themselves, in general terms, were of funda-
mental importance, because they were seen as the prototypes of
all the Italian wars which the Romans were actually destined
to fight so desperately, for century after century, before they
could master their enemies and dominate the peninsula.

According to Virgil, the leader of the anti-Trojan party, along with the Etruscan Mezentius,[7] was Turnus, prince of the Rutuli of Ardea.[8] Virgil performs the same feat as he undertook for Dido. He makes this villain so close to a hero that we find it hard not to sympathize with him: though on reflection we have to conclude that he was at fault. This was because Turnus was guilty of the sin of pride, *superbia*. That is a quality which ranges all the way from splendid valour to the tyrannical arrogance of Tarquinius Superbus, traditionally believed to be the last Etruscan monarch of Rome (chapter 5, section 2): Turnus, for all his magnificence, has much in common with Tarquinius, and indeed in more than one sense he is his mythical forerunner. For his name, as certain ancient writers appreciated, seems to be Etruscan – related to Tyrrhenus, Tursnus – and so does Rutulus, the name that belongs to the Rutulian tribe. It seems probable, therefore, that the Turnus myth originated in about the sixth century B.C., when Latium was under Etruscan domination; and the story may have developed further in the fourth century, when the Marcian family, who came from this part of Latium, produced their first authentic hero, Gaius Marcius Rutilus (chapter 5, section 1). But as far as our information goes, Turnus is introduced to literature by Cato, who already makes him an ally of the Etruscan Mezentius and an enemy of Aeneas.[9]

Ardea was the sort of little Latin town that Cato was interested in. Situated twenty-five miles south of Rome, just beyond Lavinium and Laurentum, it is now seven miles from the sea, but in about 500 B.C. it had quite a flourishing port (Castrum Inui, at the mouth of the Fosso dell' Incastro).

Ardea appeared on the Roman horizon at various solemn dates, and was regarded as the source of a number of Roman customs. Greek writers stated that a heroine of that name was one of the offspring of Odysseus and Circe, and thus a sister of Latinus. But the archaeology of the Ardean site tends to deny this Greek descent, since what it instead reveals is a fairly advanced native population without a trace of Greek or oriental objects. The hostilities of Turnus and Aeneas may reflect early tensions between Ardea and its neighbour Lavinium.

But Lavinium's far more serious rival was Alba Longa – not in terms of power, for Alba Longa, while it lasted, was far the more powerful of the two, but in the impressiveness of its myths (chapter 3, section 3). Its foundation was in accordance with the promise given by Jupiter to Venus, the divine grandmother of Ascanius.

> Fear no more, Cytherea. Take comfort, for your people's
> Destiny is unaltered; you shall behold the promised
> City walls of Lavinium, and exalt great-hearted Aeneas.
> I say it now – for I know these cares constantly gnaw you –
> And show you further into the secret book of fate:
> Aeneas, mightily warring in Italy, shall crush
> Proud tribes, to establish city walls and a way of life,
> Till a third summer has seen him reigning in Latium
> And winter thrice passed over his camp in the conquered land.
> His son Ascanius, whose surname is now Iulus –
> Ilus it was, before the realm of Ilium fell –
> Ascanius for his reign shall have full thirty years
> With all their wheeling months; shall move the kingdom from
> Lavinium and make Long Alba his sure stronghold.[10]

Ascanius had not played an obtrusive part in Homer, though he had emerged in subsequent Greek writers as an inheritor reigning in the region of Troy. However, when the Trojan story became known in Rome, he came into immense prominence as the link upon which the Julian family based their descent from Aeneas and Venus. For, in pursuance of the line taken by Cato,[11] the Julii identified him with Iulus, whom they equated, as Virgil says, with Ilus ('man of Ilium', Troy), and claimed as their founder. Livy admits to a great deal of perplexity about who Ascanius really was.[12] This is because he evidently has two sources before him, one affirming and the other denying the identification with Iulus. The two sources emanate from the political quarrels of the early first century B.C. For Lucius Julius Caesar (consul 90 B.C.), who made capital out of his family's alleged sacred origins, was strongly pro-Sullan and anti-Marian, and this seems to have inspired the 'popular' pro-Marian historian Macer to put forward a version denying the Julians the coveted connection with Ascanius.

Later, however, Gaius Caesar, the dictator, possessed Marian sympathies which would surely have reconciled Macer to the idea if he had not died as early as 66 B.C.[13]

Aeneas was believed to have founded Lavinium *three* years after his arrival in Italy. A schematic thirty years later Ascanius founded Alba Longa, and took the Penates there from Lavinium. Now, unlike Lavinium, Alba Longa was, as we have seen, the most important centre of the Latins in the early days of Rome; a separate, half-suppressed Etruscan tradition reflects its political relations with Veii.[14] But, in regard to the myths, Alba

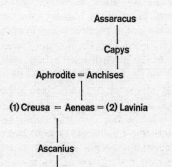

Assaracus
|
Capys
|
Aphrodite = Anchises
|
(1) Creusa = Aeneas = (2) Lavinia
|
Ascanius
|
?11 generations

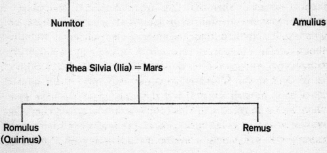

Numitor   Amulius
|
Rhea Silvia (Ilia) = Mars
|
Romulus   Remus
(Quirinus)

Longa and Lavinium were in sharp competition, and there are constant rivalries, analogies and parallels between one and the other. Timaeus was convinced of the priority of Lavinium, but Fabius Pictor related the portent of the white sow, the *alba sus*, to Alba Longa instead (chapter 3, section 3). According to Ennius, it was the daughter of the king of Alba, not the king of Lavinium, whom Aeneas married. There was even a Lavinian story that the Penates were not pleased to be moved to Alba, and like homing dogs or cats vanished and reappeared at their old homes. In fact, Alba having been so much more important in early times, the Alban versions of the various stories are probably the older, and did not seriously begin to lose ground to the Lavinian versions until the fourth century B.C. The Alban stories had probably come to Rome much earlier than that, when Alba was absorbed into the Roman state. Traditionally this had occurred in the seventh century B.C., though perhaps a date at the end of the sixth century would be nearer the mark – the time when Lavinium, too, was absorbed. When Alba Longa fell to the Romans, they took over, as privileged patricians, the principal Alban families, not only the Julii[15] but others: the Curiatii and Quinctii and Cloelii and Geganii and the ambitious, treacherous, incompetent Servilii, a family that played a long and chequered role in the history of the Republic and, at its end, provided Caesar with his principal mistress.

Greek researchers into chronology, notably Timaeus and then Eratosthenes of Cyrene (d. 194 B.C.), made the Romans aware that their myths were still much too thin upon the ground. For, once it was established that the Trojan War had taken place – that Aeneas and Ascanius had lived – at a date not far from 1100 B.C.,[16] and that Rome had not been founded until three hundred years later, there remained a subsequent yawning gap to be filled. And so the mythographers duly filled it – with a list of the kings of Alba Longa. A few traditions on this subject dated back to earlier times. But the king-list, as we have it, is made up by historians of the third, second and first centuries B.C.; or more particularly by Cato, whose interest in such towns prompted him to attempt a circumstantial account. Nevertheless, the stories which thus arose remained pretty barren and jejune conceptions, with a minimum of supporting myth, drawn mainly from the sagas of Aeneas or the later kings of Rome.

In developing this rather boring vulgate, Cato recounted that Ascanius, after founding Alba Longa, subsequently handed it over to his half-brother (in some versions his son) Silvius,[17] who thus became the first Alban king. His name, unlike those of the other Alban monarchs,[18] may be one of the fairly old elements in the tradition. But this version was evidently not regarded as satisfactory by the Julian family, since it deprived their supposed Ascanius (Iulus) of the foundership of the dynasty. So Dionysius adds that, when the arrangement was made, Ascanius was compensated with 'a certain sacred authority and honour preferable to the royal dignity'.[19] This consolation prize was offered as a compliment to the special religious interests of the Julian house, which culminated in Caesar's election to the chief priesthood (63 B.C.) and in the subsequent religious offices and reforms of Augustus, who became chief priest fifty-one years later.

The gap which required the insertion of the Alban king-list was implied by Timaeus, who fixed the date of the city's foundation at 814 B.C. This date, however, bore no relation to any historical facts or deductions. Timaeus was keen to relate the different chronological systems and traditions of different cities one to another. This was praiseworthy in itself, but was vitiated by an over-pious love of coincidences. In particular, he was determined, thus incurring the implied disapproval of Dionysius,[20] to synchronize the foundations of Rome and her arch-enemy Carthage – of which the traditional foundation date was 814. Fabius Pictor preferred 748–7 for Rome, perhaps partly because this provided exactly four centuries before the Secular Games attributed to 348 (these Games marked the progress of centuries, unless, as was sometimes the case, they stood for periods of a hundred and ten years). Cincius Alimentus favoured 729, Cato decided upon 751 – adjusting Pictor's calculations so as to permit the interpolation of certain names which Cato wished to insert into the list of consuls. Varro, adjusting again for similar reasons, established the date at 753, which subsequently became canon-ical. But it was not too canonical to prevent Dionysius, amid some doubts, from preferring Cato's figure instead. All these dates are speculative and mythical. Alleged correspondences with archaeological facts are often quoted today, but, if such correspondences occur – and it is doubtful if they do – they are wholly fortuitous (see chapter 1).

The founder of Rome was variously described as a woman and a man. The woman mentioned by Hellanicus in the fifth century B.C. was called Rhomē. Sometimes she was a Greek, but this was also said to be the name of the Trojan captive[21] who, when a group of Greeks from Troy landed storm-bound in Latium, urged on her fellow prisoners to burn the ships (Virgil transposes the scene to Sicily, chapter 3, section 2). Rhomē was also, according to a Syracusan historian Callias (c. 300), the name of Latinus' wife (or sister, as others said, or daughter). In the early years of the second century B.C. she was described as the daughter of Ares (Mars), like the Amazons.[22] But she re-mained foreign to Roman tradition, although by this time an attempt had been made to marry her to Aeneas or Ascanius. Whatever the real derivation of *Roma* – probably, like *Romulus* (see next section), it was Etruscan, the ancient Etruscan name for the Tiber being 'Rumon'[23] – it was declared by would-be etymologists that the name came from the Greek *rhomē*, strength, and that the place had at one time been called Valentia, meaning strength or power (from *valere*), the quality *par excel-lence* attributed by Naevius to Jupiter.

Sometimes, however, the founder was named not Rhomē but Rhomus. Eratosthenes, Naevius and Ennius called him the grandson of Aeneas. But he was alternatively described as Aeneas' son – though chronologically-minded writers were at pains to refute such impossible views, since they ignored the wide gulf between Aeneas and the city's foundation. Rhomus was also allotted a wide range of other fathers as well. The idea that he was sole founder of Rome is only traceable to quite a late date, perhaps in the third century B.C. or possibly a little earlier. It was a dull and normal process in foundation litera-tures[24] to conclude that a man called Rhomus must have founded

Rome, in the same way as Italus colonized Italy and Chaeron established Chaeronea.

2 ROMULUS AND REMUS

In due course Rhomus among the Greeks became Romulus at Rome. The dramatic tale of the best known of all Roman myths may be briefly summarized, in Livy's version, as follows:

After the kings of Alba Longa had ruled for nearly three hundred years, strife broke out between two brothers, Numitor and Amulius. Amulius, the younger of the two, seized the throne, driving out Numitor, and imposing upon his daughter Rhea Silvia perpetual chastity as a Vestal Virgin. But she was raped – it was said by the god Mars – and gave birth to twin sons, Romulus and Remus. King Amulius imprisoned her and ordered the boys to be drowned. But the men told to do the deed left them in a basket on the edge of the flooded Tiber, at the spot where the Ruminalis fig-tree was growing. The basket was left high and dry by the receding water. But a she-wolf, coming down from the hills to quench her thirst, heard the babies crying and suckled them herself; and the royal herdsman, Faustulus, found her licking their bodies. Faustulus took the infants to his hut and gave them to his wife Larentia to nurse.

The name Romulus is probably Etruscan like Roma which, although subjected to various etymological guesses (cf. above and note 23),[25] appears to have come from the same root. Perhaps an Etruscan family with some name of the kind had settled in Rome, or their name may have been closer to 'Aremulus', the version preferred for the city-founder by certain ancient authorities. The suffix *-ulus* is Etruscan, and denotes a founder, like Caeculus at Praeneste. Romulus is the Roman *par excellence*, Romanus, just as Siculus (Sicelus) in Sicily corresponds to 'Sicanus'.

But much of the paraphernalia of the story relating to the infancy of the twins was borrowed from similar stories told by the Greeks about the infancy of other heroes, notably Oedipus and Theseus. As far as we know, the myth of Romulus and Remus is first mentioned in the fourth century B.C., by the Sicilian historian Alcimus. It must have been at about that time – conceivably it was even a little earlier – that the Romans adopted the tale for themselves, since it is full of details of local topography and religion which are likely, in some cases, to be fairly old. Nevertheless, the Romans were quite content to retain all the Greek features of the narrative, blending them with these indigenous details.

During the fourth and early third centuries B.C. Romulus gained the upper hand over Aeneas as the supposed city-founder. Then, in the Punic Wars, new factors revived the Aeneas saga (cf. chapter 3, section 2). But interest in Romulus and Remus still continued to grow, and successive versions progressively became more elaborate. A full-dress narrative was given by Fabius Pictor, who got most of what he said, Plutarch tells us, from an unknown Greek writer called Diocles of Peparethus, who had possibly flourished in about 300. A considerable part in the development of the saga was also played by Naevius' lost plays *Romulus* and *The Wolf*, two tragedies (unless, as is possible, they are different names for the same tragedy) which he devoted to Roman themes (*fabulae praetextae*) and launched just before the Second Punic War (chapter 2, section 3).

So famous a legend naturally developed numerous variants. Many of these centred round the figure of the twins' mother, whose conspicuous role was a sign of the greater interest in feminine personality which characterized these Hellenistic times; Ennius, on whose account Virgil's version is believed to have depended, told of her prophetic dream.[26] She was called Silvia like Silvius the Alban King (chapter 4, section 1), and her other name Rhea was perhaps taken from the Greek goddess of that name.[27] But another name given to the mother of Romulus and Remus (for example by Ennius) was Ilia, probably because, like Ilus-Iulus (Ascanius), she had originally been regarded as a child of Aeneas. Rather shamelessly, the great patrician clan of the Aemilii tried to substitute an Aemilia in her place!

The rape of Rhea Silvia or Ilia by Mars, which was said to have taken place in the god's sacred grove, is a story that has parallels in many cultures, going back at least as far as the Bronze Age. It is a prestige myth, to invest the birth and deeds of a popular hero with an aura of mystery and wonder; the sort of tale which exploits the ambiguous borderline between gods and human beings.[28] Mars, later identified with the Greek Ares, was in origin a good deal more than a war god, being concerned with agriculture as well. Indeed, he was a high god of the Italians in the same sort of way as Jupiter. Direct divine interventions are rare in the myths of the Romans, who found them embarrassing: Livy for example deplored Alexander the Great's claim to divine paternity. And so he and other writers of the imperial age felt obliged to try to justify Mars' rape of Rhea Silvia on the familiar grounds that Rome's greatness warrants the assumption that supernatural circumstances attended its origins (cf. chapter 2, section 3). However, there remained a feeling of discomfort that so violent a deed should be ascribed to a god, and this is expressed by Dionysius who lengthily suggests a number of alternative, purely human explanations for what really happened.[29]

But there is also quite a different version of the conception of the twins. This originated in Etruria and survived in the pages of Plutarch, though it had failed to pass into general Roman currency. He tells the story as follows:

For to Tarchetius, they say, king of Alba, who was a most wicked and cruel man, there appeared in his own house a strange vision, a male organ that rose out of a hearth and stayed there for many days. There was an oracle of Tethys in Tuscany which Tarchetius consulted, and received an answer that a virgin should give herself to the apparition, and that a son should be born of her, highly renowned, eminent for valour, good fortune, and strength of body. Tarchetius told the prophecy to one of his own daughters, and commanded her to do this thing; which she avoided as an indignity, and sent her handmaid. Tarchetius, hearing this, in great anger imprisoned them both, purposing to put them to death, but being deterred from murder by the goddess Vesta in a dream, enjoined them for their punishment the working of a web of cloth, in their chains as they were, which when they finished they should be suffered to marry; but whatever they worked by day, Tarchetius commanded others to unravel in the night.

In the meantime, the waiting-woman was delivered of two boys, whom Tarchetius gave into the hands of one Teratius, with command to destroy them; he, however, carried and laid them by the river side, where a wolf came and continued to suckle them, while birds of various sorts brought little morsels of food, which they put into their mouths; till a cowherd, spying them, was first strangely surprised, but, venturing to draw nearer, took the children up in his arms. Thus they were saved, and when they grew up, set upon Tarchetius and overcame him.[30]

A similar story of a miraculous male organ was again told to account for the conception of one of the later Roman kings, Servius Tullius (chapter 5, section 2), and the paternity, in that case, is ascribed to the fire-god Vulcan or a household divinity. There is also a related tale of a fertilizing spark from Praeneste. Myths of such a type illustrate the widespread Italian veneration of sexual vigour, though there are also Celtic parallels in a number of different settings. It seemed understandable that women should conceive by exposure to fire or light, since this is synonymous with life: the fire, literally, put life into them. The writer to whom Plutarch attributes the story, a Greek historian of Italy named Promathion, is unknown, and has been variously attributed by modern scholars to dates as far apart as the fifth and first centuries B.C. But, whatever his own date, the tale he tells surely goes back to a date before 100 B.C., and perhaps a good deal earlier than that.

Promathion's name is Greek, but the myth is Etruscan. It is true that Tarchetius is described as king of Alba Longa, but when the Etruscans controlled Latium in the sixth century, Alba, too, became for a time an Etruscan town. Tarchetius is an unmistakably Etruscan name, akin to Tarchon and Tarquitius. The 'oracle of Tethys', deity of the waters, to which Plutarch refers, is probably the shrine of the Etruscan divinity who was worshipped at Caere's port Pyrgi and identified by Greeks with their sea-goddess Leucothea.[31] The story is evidently an attempt to Etruscanize the origins of Rome. It only just managed to survive; for in the general tradition, it was superseded by the quite different canonical Roman version which is so much more familiar.

The kings who appear in that version do not include Tarchetius at all, but are called Numitor and Amulius. These rulers are independent of the rather sterile Alban king-list, but their own mythological basis is equally jejune and insubstantial. Their rivalry, introduced to explain the exposure of the twins, was based on the mutual hatred between the Greek brothers of the Theban epic cycle, Eteocles and Polynices. It seems quite likely that the name Numitor is just an echo or duplication of Romulus' successor Numa (chapter 5, section 1). But the name of Amulius, who already appeared in Naevius, and who according to Ennius ordered the mother of the twins to be thrown into the river, cannot be explained away so easily, and might be based on an older and more tenacious tradition.

The presence of twins in the story is surely due to Greek influences, since founders of Greek cities were often twins.[32] Remus is likely to have been a survival and by-form of Rhomus (section 1 above), whose traditions thus persisted alongside Romulus (otherwise known as Aremulus) in this new form. An inscription shows that Remus was already known to the Greeks in the third century B.C.[33] The etymology of the name was and is abundantly disputed, but Rome possessed quite a number of sites beginning with 'Rem ...'[34] which could have helped to bring it into existence and favour – under the impulsion, very probably, of the families of the Remmii and Reminii which, despite their dimness in historical times, may well have possessed sufficient influence, at an earlier date, to mould the tradition.

The exposure of the twins, and the floating cradle, are age-old mythical themes, conferring upon the children an upbringing which sets them apart from our common destiny. They are motifs which have attracted the keen interest of Jung and other psychoanalysts.[35] Already in the third millennium B.C. Sargon of Mesopotamian Akkad had told of his own exposure on the waters; and the story of Moses among the reeds is in the same tradition. So, too, are myths of the Maori hero Massi, and of Vainamoinen in the Finnish *Kalevala* who 'floated above dark waves'.

But the immediate precedent was obviously one of the very

numerous stories of Greek infants who were believed to have been exposed, and then suckled by animals.[36] The best known was the tale of Tyro, who exposed her twin sons Neleus and Pelias, born to her of the god Poseidon. They, too, were suckled by animals and brought up by shepherds. There was also, allegedly, an Arcadian version with a different human cast; and Miletus, founder of the city of that name, was said to have been suckled by she-wolves. But the myth of Tyro was the most familiar, largely because it had been the subject of two Greek plays by Sophocles. Both are now lost, but one or both of them inspired a Latin poem, the *Song of Neleus*, which has likewise disappeared (except for seven lines) but seems to have been written as early as the third century B.C.

By that time, however, the myth of Romulus and Remus had already been established, either by adaptation from the Sophoclean original or from some Latin precursor of the *Song of Neleus* which cannot now be identified. Or, quite probably, the link lay in Etruria, because an Etruscan relief from Certosa di Bologna, which seems attributable to the fourth century B.C., shows an animal which may be a she-wolf suckling a human figure. Moreover, although wolves were venerated in many parts of Italy, the superb bronze she-wolf in the Capitoline Museum at Rome, though it does not seem to have had anything to do with Romulus and Remus, may well be a south Etruscan work of *c.* 500 or *c.* 400 B.C.

At all events, in 296 B.C. two Roman brothers, Quintus and Cnaeus Ogulnius Gallus, who were colleagues in a Roman magistracy, the aedileship, employed the fines they had collected from usurers to set up a statue of the wolf and twins. Or perhaps what they did was to add statuettes of the twins beneath an existing effigy of a she-wolf.[37] The scene then appears on coins of *c.* 269[38] and was reduplicated thousands of times on visual representations for century after century.

Meanwhile a host of writers had taken the story up; though Dionysius, who draws upon many of these accounts in his enormously long account of Romulus, indicates that there were a number of rationalizers who preferred to deny and explain away the whole tale.[39]

Its original, Roman feature was the extremely firm localization at venerable sites in the capital. Thus the children were exposed, we are told, at a section of the river beside the south-western corner of the Palatine hill, marked by the fig-tree called Ruminalis – and it was there that the Ogulnii set up their statue. The tree still existed, Livy claimed, in his own day. In Italy, as elsewhere, the milky juice of the fig was much valued as a fertility-charm, being regarded as symbolical of human breast-feeding. And so it was already suggested in ancient times, quite correctly in all probability, that the word Ruminalis was connected with *ruma*, breast, and Rumina, an early divinity of suckling.[40] It was because of this etymology that the fig-tree came to be associated with the story of the twins. (The further suggestion, implied by Livy, that Ruminalis and Romulus came from the same verbal root – the former, according to this theory, having been originally called Romularis – has less to recommend it, since the word Romulus, as we have seen, was apparently of Etruscan origin.)

This association of the fig-tree with the twins did embarrassing violence to topography, because an older tradition pointed to another Ruminalis fig-tree which was nowhere near the river at all, but beside the Comitium (place of Assembly) next to the Forum. However, the problem was solved, perhaps in about the fourth century B.C., by planting another fig-tree beside the river and the Palatine. Henceforward, then, there were two different trees of the same name. A fiction had to be invented to reverse their chronological order; and the proximity of the tree in the Comitium to the statue of a legendary wonder-worker, Attus Navius, seemed to provide the answer.[41] For it was soon asserted that Navius had magically moved the tree from the site by the Tiber, which was now alleged to have been its original location, to the Comitium; and that another one had grown beside the river in its place.

The introduction of the she-wolf into the story, as we saw, echoed the Greek tale of the infant hero Miletus, who was said to have been suckled by such animals. And probably it recalled unknown Etruscan myths, or variants of myths, as well. But the choice of this particular beast (among all the others supplied for such occasions by Greek mythology) was again due to a topographical consideration. For the fig-tree by the river (mythologically the first, historically the second) grew beside the Lupercal, the grotto which has been described in connection with Evander, and its name was believed, perhaps rightly, perhaps wrongly, to have been derived from *lupus, lupa*, a wolf, a derivation which readily brought it into relation with the twins and their she-wolf. Livy follows a tradition which does not mention the Lupercal at this point – though in the very next chapter (note 53 below) he refers to the twins taking part in the Lupercalian ceremonies. So does Dionysius, to whom we owe our description of the grotto (chapter 3, section 1). But he also indicates that the she-wolf, when she was first discovered with the twins, hid herself in this cave.[42] The emphasis on the Lupercal in such a connection may well go back to the Fabii, who traditionally played a leading part in its rites – and the link was no doubt made much of by their loyal historian, Fabius Pictor.

The king's shepherd (says Livy), who found the animal suckling the twins, was traditionally believed to have borne the name of Faustulus. His figure already appears on coins of *c.* 125 B.C., issued by a moneyer bearing a contracted form of the same name, Fostlus,[43] who displays his mythical ancestor beside the Ruminalis fig-tree. Near the historically earlier of the two trees, in the Comitium, there was an antique holy place, now known to us as the Black Stone – from the black pavement later built over the ancient structures – and famous for the discovery of an inscription of *c.* 500 B.C. This Black Stone, among other interpretations, was believed to cover Faustulus' tomb.[44]

He was regarded as having brought up the twins without anyone's knowledge. Or more probably, some authorities maintained, he was assisted secretly by the deposed king Numitor. Another version indicated that Faustulus was not the man who found the children but the recipient of Amulius' instructions that they should be cast adrift. Faustulus was said to have been of Arcadian extraction, descended from one of the companions of Evander. But this idea may have come from the supposition that his name was a by-form of the god Faunus, with whom Evander was identified (chapter 3, section 1). The name of

Faunus was believed to have come from *favere*, to favour, and *faustus*, lucky; and whether this was the case or not that is evidently the correct derivation of 'Faustulus'.

As Livy rightly says, the appearance in the story of Larentia, who is stated to be the wife of Faustulus, has something to do with the fact that she was known as *lupa*, which meant both she-wolf and whore. This gave the opportunity for a process that the Romans so greatly favoured, the explanation of an ancient, no longer understandable institution. For Larentia, or Acca Larentia as she was also called, was a minor Roman divinity, honoured by an annual festival. She had some connection with the Underworld, and when mythical genealogies of the Greek style came into fashion, she was regarded as the mother of the Lares who were the ghosts of the dead (chapter 3, section 3).[45] This etymological association brought her readily into relation with Romulus and Remus, who were the most famous of national ancestors. Since, moreover, they had been suckled by a she-wolf, Acca Larentia too became *lupa*, the prostitute-saint who is familiar to anthropologists.[46] She is already described as a prostitute by Cato,[47] and by the next century her identification with the she-wolf was complete. Licinius Macer[48] (perhaps also Valerius Antias)[49] made her into the wife of Faustulus, a step that was facilitated by the fact that she had become known by the similar-sounding name Faula (Fabula), a common designation of whores. And yet, in spite of this moral reputation, the Roman family of the Accoleii were still glad to honour Acca Larentia as their ancestress,[50] to judge by a coin of theirs of *c.* 37 B.C. which apparently depicts her head.

Meanwhile, however, there was a totally different story in circulation which indicated that, being called Fabula, she was the same as a Fabula who, during Hercules' visit to Rome (chapter 3, section 1) became the god's mistress. She owed this privilege to the keeper of Hercules' temple who, defeated by the god at dice, had lost a bet which compelled him to give the winner a free supper and a girl. He duly provided Fabula, and she, at a later date, married a certain Tarutius, and subsequently bequeathed to the Roman people the extensive property which he had left her or which she had earned by prostitution.[51] This curious tale, current in the first century B.C., was preserved by Plutarch, who had also, as we have seen, offered a deviant version of Romulus' birth (chapter 4, section 2). That story we have identified as Etruscan, owing to the appearance of the name Tarchetius, and it also involved a Teratius whose name resembles Tarutius in the present story: this too then was evidently yet another fable from Etruria which narrowly survived after having been officially shelved in favour of the canonical Roman tale. It may well owe its preservation, in part, to Lucius Tarutius Firmanus, a religious antiquarian of the first century B.C. (chapter 2, section 2). So great was the divergence between the two versions that Plutarch believed there were two distinct Acca Larentias.[52]

And so the twins grew up; and as they became strong enough, Livy records, they began to attack robbers and divide the stolen goods with their friends the shepherds.

The Palatine Hill was already the scene of the annual Lupercal festival, at which young men ran about naked and engaged in various horse-play. As Romulus and Remus were attending the festival, brigands, infuriated by the loss of their plunder to the brothers, laid a trap for them. Romulus escaped, but Remus was captured and delivered to King Amulius. The brigands complained that the youths had been leading raids upon the lands of the king's brother, Numitor; and to Numitor Remus was handed over.

But now the truth about the boys' birth gradually came out, and the young men murdered Amulius and saluted Numitor as king. They also planned to establish a new settlement, for the surplus population of Alba Longa, upon the place where they had been left to drown as babies and had been subsequently brought up. But unhappily the brothers' plans for the future were marred by the same curse which had divided their grandfather and Amulius – jealousy and ambition. A disgraceful quarrel arose from a matter in itself trivial. As the brothers were twins and all question of seniority was thereby precluded, they determined to ask the tutelary gods of the appropriate sites to declare by augury which of them should govern the new town once it was founded, and give his name to it. For this purpose Romulus took the Palatine Hill and Remus the Aventine as their respective stations from which to observe the auspices. Remus, the story goes, was the first to receive a sign – six vultures; and no sooner was this made known to the people than double the number of birds appeared to Romulus. The followers of each promptly saluted their master as king, one side basing its claim upon priority, the other upon number. Angry words ensued, followed all too soon by blows, and in the course of the affray Remus was killed.

There is another story, a commoner one, according to which Remus, by way of jeering at his brother, jumped over the half-built walls of the new settlement, whereupon Romulus killed him in a fit of rage, adding the threat 'So perish whoever else shall overleap my battlements!'

This, then, was how Romulus obtained the sole power. The newly built city was called by its founder's name.[53]

The individual features of this story require more detailed analysis. In the first place, according to Livy, the twins, as they grew to manhood, had led a sort of Robin Hood existence, attacking only undesirable enemies such as brigands and wild beasts. Dionysius of Halicarnassus offers the less romantic statement that when they were about eighteen they had a dispute about pasture-land with the shepherds of Numitor, whose herds used to graze on the Aventine. It was for this reason that the young men were kidnapped at the Lupercalia, a version dating back to Tubero, who attributes the initiative not (like Livy) to the brigands but to Numitor's henchmen.[54]

The arrest of Remus, followed by Numitor's approach to Romulus, led to the discovery who the twins were. Their recognition is played down by Livy, who attributes it somewhat off-handedly to Numitor but adds that Faustulus had always entertained suspicions about their origin. Perhaps, as a part-time rationalist, he found the story too corny. Dionysius, who has no such qualms, makes a big event of the Recognition, in which the identity of the twins dawns successively on Numitor and Amulius. This situation, in which the survival of the cradle played its part, was in the most familiar traditions of Greek drama. And here again the writers who first launched the story of the Recognition, and particularly Fabius Pictor who gave it literary currency, are very likely to have been influenced by Sophocles' *Tyro*, either directly or through some intermediary.

Then followed the murder of Amulius. This was a rather awkward subject since not everyone, in historical times, welcomed the idea that the founder of Rome had been a murderer. Livy may have declared outright that both the twins killed Amulius in collaboration. Yet the text is disputed, and it is possible that what he really said was that Romulus alone was the killer.[55] But Dionysius hedges uncomfortably, not liking to eliminate the youths from the murder altogether but shifting the initiative onto Numitor. Naevius, however, had been acquainted with an altogether different tradition, emanating from Etruria and (once again) tenuously preserved but excluded from the canon. For according to a fragment of his poem *Amulius*, in this version a wise old man who rejoiced at the preservation of the twins, was at some unidentifiable point of the story greeted the king of Veii.[56] This monarch, whose name Viba (?) recalls the famous Etruscan heroes called Vibenna (chapter 5, section 2), may possibly, in a subsequent passage that is now lost, have helped Romulus to kill Amulius. In any case this Etruscan rendering of the story evidently assumed quite a different form.

According to the version that has come down to us, Romulus and Remus planned jointly to found a new city. Or, according to Dionysius, it was Numitor's idea. Dionysius adds that Romulus chose the Palatine for a number of reasons and particularly because, as a child, he had been exposed and reared there, while Remus preferred the Aventine (where a site was said to have been named after him).[57] Livy, eager to give the Palatine absolute priority, does not refer to any difference of opinion about the site, merely stating that they took the Palatine and Aventine respectively as the augural stations at which they would perform their acts of divination. The dispute, according to him, centred upon which of them should give the new city its name. This version goes back to Ennius, whose account has survived almost complete:

> Their contest would decide the city's name
> As Rome or Remora. The multitude
> Expectant looked to learn who would be king.
> As, when the consul is about to give
> The sign to start the race, the people sit
> With eyes intent on barrier doors from whose

Embellished jaws the chariots soon would come;
So now the people, fearful, looked for signs
To know whose prize the mighty realm would be.
Meantime the fading sun into the shades
Of night withdrew and then the shining dawn
Shot forth its rays. 'Twas then an augury,
The best of all, appeared on high – a bird
That on the left did fly. And, as the sun
Its golden orb upraised, twelve sacred birds
Flew down from heaven and betook themselves
To stations set apart for goodly signs.
Then Romulus perceived that he had gained
A throne whose source and prop was augury.[58]

Nothing is said here about the six vultures which Remus, in
Livy's version, was first believed to have seen. But the twelve
birds of Romulus had become an important talking point by
the middle of the first century B.C., when an Etruscan sooth-
sayer Vettius declared that they meant Rome would last for
twelve *saecula*[59] (periods of a hundred or a hundred and ten
years). And then in 43 B.C., the young Octavian, seizing the consulship, asserted that he, too – the heir of the divine Caesar and
therefore of the divine Romulus as well – had seen an omen of
twelve vultures in the sky.[60]

The fighting and killing of a brother is an extremely common
theme in the mythologies of the world. Cain and Abel, and the
Egyptian gods Osiris and Seth, have their Greek counterparts
in Theban tales of the strife of Eteocles and Polynices (who had
also been the models, as we have seen, for the struggle between
Numitor and Amulius). Succession-tensions within the family
lay at the very core of early thought, and modern anthropo-
logical interpretations of the numerous stories of this type have
abounded.[61] However, just as many Romans shied at the idea
that the founder of their city had murdered their great-uncle
Amulius, the idea that he had slain his own brother inspired
them with even greater distaste. This seemed a painfully ominous
anticipation of the civil wars of the later Republic – and indeed Horace and others specifically and directly derived those
upheavals from the fatal primary deed.[62] Livy, in dealing with

this delicate matter, hints to us that he has two divergent sources in front of him. The first indicated that Remus saw six vultures and that Romulus outbid him with twelve. This was an ambiguous situation which did not give the latter an indisputable victory, to say the least,[63] and so Ennius, as we have seen, had preferred to ignore the claim of Remus. Livy's second version, on the other hand, distracts attention from the guilt of Romulus by specifically putting the blame on Remus, since he had tried to jump over the half-built walls. It was very wrong and sacrilegious of him to do this, since, as every reader of Greek mythology was well aware, contempt for the sanctity of walls attracted severe and merited retribution.[64] Besides, by acting in such a way, he was flouting the principle of collegiality, upon which, exemplified in the annual pairs of consuls, Rome's whole Republican opposition to tyranny depended (chapter 6, section 1).

But, even so, some people still felt uneasy about the part Romulus had played. One of these worriers, whether his anxiety was copied from others or was his own, seems to have been Dionysius, who not only emphasizes the extreme distress felt by Romulus at his brother's death, but refrains from explicitly ascribing responsibility to Romulus, and goes on to quote a view that the overseer of the building work was the man who did the deed.[65] Some writers went even further and declared that Remus was not killed at all in the famous quarrel, but survived.[66]

For generations, the whole business was red-hot politics. When the Etruscans and Latins were being put down by Rome in the fourth century B.C., and the Samnites in the next century, they were probably quoting this story of Romulus and Remus, in the *first* of the two forms recounted by Livy, to show the sort of fratricidal way in which the Romans were accustomed to treat their enemies. If so, that was also, in all likelihood, the time when the Romans propounded the second version which spared Romulus much of the discredit. The unfavourable version was no doubt revived by the historians of the second century B.C. who were hostile to Rome, on the occasion of Pyrrhus' invasion of Italy and Sicily (chapter 3, section 2). This point is suggested by Dionysius, when he attacks writers who curry favour with barbarian kings by giving sordid accounts of Rome's origins.[67] For he seems to be thinking of the authors who curried favour with Pyrrhus. Owing to writers who took this sort of attitude, there was a time when the Romulus myth was under a cloud at Rome – or at least when it was felt to need a good deal of apologetic interpretation.

And then, starting with Scipio Africanus the elder (d. 184 B.C.), there came a long list of Romans who, amid the cut-throat quarrels of the day, were accused by their political enemies of seeking autocracy for themselves; and to all of these the first hostile version of Romulus' action could be meaning-fully and maliciously applied. Some of the alleged villains were right-wing and some left-wing, some *optimates* and some *popu-lares*, but if they were accused of autocratic ambitions the mythological analogy could be put forward with equal viru-lence for and against either side. Shocked by the Gracchi, the conservatives on the Senate were always talking about contem-porary would-be tyrants; and conversely, the conservative Sulla, who had actually made himself absolute ruler after a blood-bath, seemed an all too obvious reincarnation of the murderous Romulus. We may assume, therefore, that the historian Licinius Macer, who loathed Sulla, was largely responsible for the first of Livy's two versions. At some stage, too, some historian or other propounded the idea that the Aventine had been Remus' hill. Ennius does not seem to say anything about this. But once again Macer comes to mind. For this reference to the Aventine was a clear echo of the conflict between the Orders in the half-legendary fifth century B.C., when the Aventine was supposed to have been the place to which his plebeians seceded (chapter 6, note 48). But, as so often, people of the second and first cen-turies B.C., who wrote about the ancient conflict of the Orders, were really thinking of the strife between *optimates* and *popu-lares* in their own day.

Yet at the same time, from well before 100 B.C., there was growing up quite a different tradition that Romulus, so far from being a murderer and fratricide, had been a virtuous figure, an ideal monarch. This alternative interpretation was already current among historians of the second century B.C., such as the

Greek Polybius and the Roman Lucius Piso Frugi. After the year
100 it was perhaps stimulated by an anonymous *Constitution of
Romulus*, which may have been written by supporters of Sulla
in praise of Romulus' supposed system of government. Cicero
echoed the tone of these publications,[68] and Dionysius took
much the same line. But he is also careful to add that Romulus'
authority was not arbitrary and absolute like that of the kings
who could still be seen in other parts of the Mediterranean area
in his own day.[69]

But at the very time when Dionysius was at work, the mythology of Romulus had entered a highly significant new phase.
For the first emperor of Rome, before adopting the title
'Augustus', had toyed with the idea of calling himself Romulus.
This idea he gave up, because he did not want to offer hostile
propagandists an obvious opportunity to label him either as a
king or as a fratricide. Nevertheless, without crudely identifying himself with Romulus, he gave his memory great prominence, engraving the story of the Foundation on the Altar of
Augustan Peace and placing in his new Forum an inscription
which read : 'Romulus, son of Mars, founded Rome.' The whole
imperial theology emphasized that whereas Romulus had been
the first founder, Augustus was the second. This is the theme
emphasized in the descriptions of the Romulean system offered
by Livy and Dionysius, and a long series of allusions and implications by Virgil conveys the same message.[70]

   The deification of Romulus was obviously very relevant here.
For there was a tradition that, when he died, he was taken up to
heaven as a god. The same had been the destiny of Hercules
and Aeneas, and Julius Caesar, after his death, was made a god
of the Roman state, so that his heir Augustus called himself
divi filius, son of a God; and he, too, was obviously moving in
the same direction (cf. chapter 3, section 3). As for the apotheosis
of Romulus, the oldest and most straightforward tradition stated
that his father Mars came down from heaven to seek his son,
who thereupon vanished into thin air, and became a god himself – an orthodox end for Greek heroes. This was probably the
version of Ennius, who bestowed upon Romulus the apotheosis

that Hercules had received of old – in pursuance of a prophecy of Jupiter.[71] The story of how this came about was told in later days by Ovid.

> From this Mars knew Jove's promise was secure,
> And vaulting with his spear he leaped aboard
> His blood-stained chariot and cracked his whip.
> Descending through the air he glided near
> The green-hilled Palatine where Romulus
> Was handing out (with splendid moderation)
> New laws to waiting lines of citizens.
> Mars took his arm and swept him off the earth.
> Then, as a ball of lead shot from a sling
> Becomes a nothingness in distant air,
> The mortal features of brave Romulus
> Vanished before he reached the heights of Heaven.
> Quirinus was the heavenly name they gave him,
> And beauty fit to rest in godlike ease
> And wear the clothes that the immortals wear.[72]

However, other writers, before and after Ovid, felt greater doubts about the deification of Romulus. Plutarch, for example, gathers together a varied assemblage of contradictory traditions. First he says that Romulus, as his reign advanced, seemed to neglect and even affront the patricians who were his senators. For this reason, continues the biographer,

On the king's sudden and strange disappearance a short while after, the senate fell under suspicion and calumny. He disappeared on the Nones of July, as they now call the month which was then Quintilis, leaving nothing of certainty to be related of his death; only the time, as just mentioned, for on that day many ceremonies are still performed in representation of what happened. Neither is this uncertainty to be thought strange, seeing the manner of the death of Scipio Africanus the younger, who died at his own home after supper, has been found capable neither of proof or disproof; for some say he died a natural death, being of a sickly habit; others, that he poisoned himself; others again, that his enemies, breaking in upon him in the night, stifled him. Yet Scipio's dead body lay open to be seen of all, and any one, from his own observation, might form his suspicions and conjectures, whereas Romulus, when he vanished, left neither the least part of his body, nor any remnant of his clothes to be seen. So that some fancied the senators, having fallen upon him in the temple of Vulcan, cut his body into pieces, and took each a part away in his bosom; others think his disappearance was neither in the temple of Vulcan, nor with the senators only by, but that it came to pass that, as he was haranguing the people without the city, near a place called the Goat's Marsh, on a sudden strange and unaccountable disorders and alterations took place in the air; the face of the sun was darkened, and the day turned into night, and that, too, no quiet, peaceable night, but with terrible thunderings, and boisterous winds from all quarters; during which the common people dispersed and fled, but the senators kept close together. The tempest being over and the light breaking out, when the people gathered again, they missed and inquired for their king; the senators suffered them not to search, or busy themselves about the matter, but commanded them to honour and worship Romulus as one taken up by the gods, and about to be to them, in the place of a good prince, now a propitious god. The multitude, hearing this, went away believing and rejoicing in hopes of good things from him; but there were some who, canvassing the matter in a hostile temper, accused and aspersed the patricians, as men that persuaded the people to believe ridiculous tales, when they themselves were the murderers of the king.[73]

And Plutarch goes on to describe three mythical Greek precedents or parallels for such disappearances and assumptions.[74]

The writers of the first century B.C., when the story was keen topical politics, had made the same effort to weigh up the conflicting versions of the apotheosis of Romulus. Cicero gave the matter his attention at a time when Caesar had not yet been murdered and deified, but when the tradition about Romulus, in the light of contemporary political preoccupations, was evidently the subject of keen discussion. In spite of the orator's dislike of autocracy, he felt able to take a favourable view of Romulus, on the grounds that the latter had always paid deference to the senate – the opposite view to the tradition preserved by Plutarch. Nevertheless, Cicero will not allow that Romulus was translated to heaven on grounds of merit, insisting that he died a natural death. And he draws critical attention to the credulity of people who accepted the fable that he had been carried off to the sky during an eclipse.[75]

1. A local inhabitant kisses Hercules' hand after he has slain the monster Cacus on the Palatine hill (the Aventine according to Virgil). One of a series of brass medallions issued by Antoninus Pius to celebrate the mythical past of Rome, A.D. 140–43. Bibliothèque Nationale, Paris.

2. Aeneas rescuing his father Anchises and his son Ascanius (Iulus) from burning Troy. Relief from Intercisa (Dunapentele) in Budapest Museum.

3. Aeneas and Dido embracing. Mosaic at Low Ham, Somerset.

4. The temple of Venus on the summit of Mount Eryx in Sicily. Venus, the mother of Aeneas, was claimed by the Julian family as their ancestress. Silver coin of Gaius Considius Nonianus. British Museum.

5. The sow and piglets which Father Tiber told Aeneas, in a dream, that he would see. At the place where he saw them he was to found the city of Lavinium. From Obulco (Porcuna) in southern Spain. Vatican Museum.

6. Over a pig, held by a kneeling youth, Aeneas and Latinus swear an oath of union between Trojans and Latins. The double head is of Janus, the god of beginnings. Silver coin of the late third century B.C. British Museum.

7 *top*. The walls of Lavinium; with a statue of its founder Aeneas carrying his father. The sow and young are also to be seen. Medallion of Antoninus Pius, A.D. 138–9. Bibliothèque Nationale, Paris.

8. The building of the walls of Alba Longa, the city established by Aeneas' son Ascanius (Iulus), the supposed founder of the Julian house. Drawing of a tomb-painting in the Museo Nazionale delle Terme, Rome.

9. The god Mars appears to Rhea Silvia, to rape her and beget
Romulus and Remus. Found at Aquincum (Budapest). Budapest
Museum.

10. The she-wolf suckling Romulus and Remus: a theme popular
throughout the empire for many centuries. This relief was found
at Aventicum (Avenches in Switzerland) and is in the local museum.

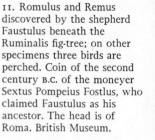

11. Romulus and Remus discovered by the shepherd Faustulus beneath the Ruminalis fig-tree; on other specimens three birds are perched. Coin of the second century B.C. of the moneyer Sextus Pompeius Fostlus, who claimed Faustulus as his ancestor. The head is of Roma. British Museum.

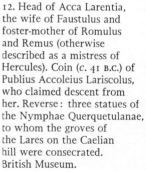

12. Head of Acca Larentia, the wife of Faustulus and foster-mother of Romulus and Remus (otherwise described as a mistress of Hercules). Coin (c. 41 B.C.) of Publius Accoleius Lariscolus, who claimed descent from her. Reverse: three statues of the Nymphae Querquetulanae, to whom the groves of the Lares on the Caelian hill were consecrated. British Museum.

13. The rape of the Sabine women by the Romans. Relief from the Basilica Aemilia in the Forum Museum, Rome.

14. The rape of the Sabine women and the head of their king Titus Tatius, who allegedly became joint king of Rome with Romulus, on a coin of Lucius Titurius Sabinus. British Museum.

15. Relief of Marcus Curtius, who, according to one version of the myth, leapt on horseback into the chasm of the Lacus Curtius, sacrificing himself for Rome in obedience to an oracle. Palazzo dei Conservatori, Rome.

16. King Numa Pompilius, mythical founder of religious institutions, sacrificing before a lighted altar. Coin of Lucius Pomponius Molo, who claimed to be his descendant. British Museum.

17. Statue of Numa Pompilius (of the second century A.D. but based on an earlier model) from the House of the Vestal Virgins beside the Forum. Forum Museum, Rome.

18. Numa Pompilius and his grandson Ancus Marcius, the legendary Sabine kings of Rome, on a coin of Gaius Marcius Censorinus, whose family claimed descent from them. Reverse: prow and stern of ships.

19. Part of fresco from the François Tomb, Vulci, depicting an Etruscan saga. Here Macstrna (Mastarna) of Vulci is cutting the bonds of Caile Vipinas (Caeles Vibenna), after whom the Caelian hill was believed to take its name. The emperor Claudius identified Mastarna with the Roman king Servius Tullius. Palazzo Corsini, Rome.

20. Also from the François Tomb: an Etruscan hero of Vulci, M. Camitlnas, surprises and slays a man whose name shows him to be a Roman and a Tarquin (Cneve Tarchunies Rumach=Cnaeus Tarquinius Romanus).

21 *left*. Another duel from the François Tomb. The slayer is Avle Vipinas (Aulus Vibenna, the brother of Caeles), who also appears in myths as Olus. The victim may be a man of Falerii.

22 *below left*. Two heroes, partly or wholly mythical, of the early Republic: Lucius Junius Brutus, 'first consul', and Gaius Servilius Ahala, slayer of the usurper Spurius Maelius (attributed to 439 B.C.). The coin was apparently issued in the fifties B.C. by Marcus Brutus, Caesar's future assassin, who claimed descent from both these adversaries of tyrants.

23 *below*. Gaius Mucius Scaevola, who, having tried and failed to kill Rome's Etruscan enemy Lars Porsenna of Clusium, showed his indifference to pain by holding his right hand in the fire. Relief from Intercisa (Dunapentele) in Budapest Museum.

24. Horatius Cocles, watched by three Roman and two Etruscan warriors, swimming to safety after his defence of the Sublician Bridge against Lars Porsenna and his Etruscans. Medallion of Antoninus Pius (A.D. 140–43), Bibliothèque Nationale, Paris.

25. The Dioscuri, Castor and Pollux, who miraculously appeared at the battle of Lake Regillus (499 or 496 B.C.) to help the Romans against the Latins. Coin of the later third century B.C.

26. The sacred geese which by their cackling alerted Marcus
Manlius Capitolinus to the night attack on the Capitol by the Gauls
(390 or 387 B.C.). Ostia Museum.

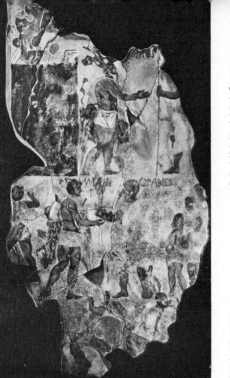

27. A painting of *c.* 200 B.C. illustrating an unknown exploit of one of the families that were most prominent in Roman myth and history, the Fabii. Quintus Fabius, in a long white mantle, is seen parleying with Marcus Fannius, in Samnite helmet and goatskin. Palazzo dei Conservatori, Rome.

28. New myths continued to be created in historical times: when the cult of Aesculapius was brought from Epidaurus in Greece to Rome in 293 B.C., his sacred snake leapt ashore from the ship to the Tiber island. Medallion of Antoninus Pius. Bibliothèque Nationale, Paris.

Livy, who says there was a thunderstorm not an eclipse, uses his talents to produce a brief and brilliant evocation of the mysterious aura which surrounded the event. He leaves it to his readers to decide whether a miracle really happened, or whether the truth may not rather have been that the senators tore Romulus to pieces. As so often, Livy has two sources before him, presumably Valerius Antias who favoured Sulla and was therefore prepared to see autocrats deified, and Licinius Macer, who preferred to see Romulus (Sulla!) torn in pieces by his enraged subjects. Livy's own comment either shows that he has not digested his sources or is a masterpiece of indecision.[76] Dionysius, too, in his long-winded way, deals with equally ambivalent material. For he suggests that the event gave authority to the Euhemerist view that great men become gods after their death – although, immediately beforehand, he had decided for the view that it was a case of murder, perpetrated for various reasons but mainly because of Romulus' tyrannical rule.[77] Caesar, too, had been first murdered and then deified. But when even historians who were so very loyal to the Augustan regime tied themselves in such knots about Romulus' deification, one begins to appreciate why Augustus did not care to be regarded as the second Romulus. The king was suitable as a venerable forebear and founder, in a general sense, but it would certainly have been a mistake for the emperor to seek complete identification with so equivocal a personage

Nevertheless, the Julian family, not content with their adoption of Aeneas, had also attempted to link their destiny to that of Romulus, as Augustus well knew. This manoeuvre took the form of a description of his epiphany, Greek and un-Roman in character, but suitably adapted to the Roman context. The version of the story which reached Plutarch was as follows:

Things being in this disorder, one, they say, of the patricians, of noble family and approved good character, and a faithful and familiar friend of Romulus himself, having come with him from Alba, Julius Proculus by name, presented himself in the Forum; and, taking a most sacred oath, protested before them all that, as he was travelling on the road, he had seen Romulus coming to meet him, looking taller and comelier than ever, dressed in shining and flaming armour; and he, being affrighted at the apparition, said, 'Why, O king, or for what purpose have you abandoned us to unjust and wicked surmises, and the whole city to bereavement and endless sorrow?' And that he made answer, 'It pleased the gods, O Proculus, that we, who came from them, should remain so long a time amongst men as we did; and, having built a city to be the greatest in the world for empire and glory, should again return to heaven. But farewell; and tell the Romans that, by the exercise of temperance and fortitude, they shall attain the height of human power; we will be to you the propitious god Quirinus.' This seemed credible to the Romans, upon the honesty and oath of the relater, and indeed, too, there mingled with it a certain divine passion, some preternatural influence similar to possession by a divinity; nobody contradicted it, but, laying aside all jealousies and detractions, they prayed to Quirinus and saluted him as a god.[78]

Yet this story of the miraculous appearance of the dead Romulus to Julius Proculus had not been given an undisturbed passage. Ennius had introduced someone, whose name does not survive in the existing fragment, to tell of this manifestation,[79] and the family of the Julii, reviving in the later Republic, had managed to get him accepted as a Julius, a man from Alba Longa descended from Ascanius. This enabled them to combine their Alban origin with a solemn part in the foundation of Rome: a little confusedly, since tradition did not import the Julii until two reigns later.[80] Cicero knew the story, but called Julius Proculus an untutored peasant who published (or invented?) the story at the request of the senators because they did not want people to think they had murdered the king.[81] Dionysius says the man was blameless and truthful. But Livy, at this point, evidently had an anti-Julian source in front of him.[82] For although he describes Julius Proculus as a man who carried political weight, he then concludes sharply by expressing surprise that the people and army believed his story as they did. Tales of deification presented no problems to Greek hero-cult, as we have seen before, but they created difficulties for the educated Roman mind.[83]

And then there was another equally problematical question. Even if it was really true that Romulus had turned into a god, was it his body or his soul that went to heaven, or neither or both? Plutarch, after narrating the various versions, concludes in philosophical vein that we ought not to believe that the bodies of good men go to heaven, but only their souls. A spokesman in Cicero's *Nature of the Gods* firmly contradicts even the latter assumption, with reference to Romulus and others 'admitted to celestial citizenship in recent times, by a sort of extension of the franchise'.[84]

Virgil, on the other hand, concludes that Romulus is a god, and indeed that he stands at the head of the gods of the Roman state. When the poet prays that Augustus shall be allowed to rescue shipwrecked Rome, it is to Romulus and Vesta that he addresses his prayer.[85] Romulus was a god because he had been identified with the god Quirinus, a process that may well not have taken place before the time of Ennius[86] but was celebrated on the coins of Numerius Fabius Pictor (*c.* 110 B.C.) – a relative of the historian; and then subsequent developments under Caesar and Augustus provided a further great stimulus. Quirinus had been granted a temple in 293 B.C. But his cult was much earlier, because in antique times he had been a high god of the Italians, like Jupiter and Mars with whom he was traditionally linked or sometimes identified. He was worshipped on the Quirinal hill, and when Sabine writers claimed that hill as the original Roman settlement of their tribe, they asserted that he was their god.[87]

And now the time has come to discuss this alleged Sabine contribution to Rome in greater detail.

3 ROMULUS AND THE SABINES

With an eye on the future, recounts Livy, Romulus, after becoming king, sought to increase the population of the city by establishing a sanctuary for fugitives on the Capitoline Hill, an assertion which probably corresponds to the racial mixture that characterized the early community, though it did not, in fact, include the Capitol at so early a date (chapter 1). But a serious shortage of women, adds the historian, meant that Rome's new strength was not likely to last for more than one generation. He sent envoys to many states to propose marriage alliances, but the fear and contempt in which the new community was held earned these proposals a uniformly bad reception. However, the king now planned a new move, to coincide with an annual festival.

For on this occasion [said Livy] large crowds flocked to Rome. Not only were the neighbouring Latin townships represented, but the Sabines came too, with their wives and children; and they were lavishly entertained and shown round the city. But when the festival began, all the able-bodied male inhabitants of Rome rushed through the crowd and seized the young women who were among the visitors. Most of the girls were taken by whoever first got hold of them, but some especially beautiful ones were reserved for themselves by leading senators, who sent gangs to fetch them. The festival broke up in panic, and the girls' parents, shouting curses and prayers, had to depart.

The abducted women, too, were furious and fearful for the future, but Romulus went from one to another with reassurances. Promising that they would enjoy all the privileges of married Romans, and suggesting that children, when they came, would form a bond with their new husbands, he urged them to forget their wrath and give their hearts to those to whom chance had given their bodies. Often, he said, a sense of injury yields in the end to affection; and their husbands would treat them all the more kindly in that they would try, each one of them, not only to fulfil their own part of the bargain, but also to make up to their wives for the homes and parents they had lost. The men, too, played their part: they spoke honeyed words and vowed that it was passionate love which had prompted their offence. No plea can better touch a woman's heart. The women in course of time lost their resentment.[88]

The festival with which this Rape of the Sabine Women was traditionally associated was in honour of the god Consus, a harvest-deity for whom a temple on the Aventine was vowed or dedicated in 272 B.C. by Lucius Papirius Cursor, who belonged to a family well placed for the manipulation of records and myths (cf. chapter 6, section 2). The name of the god is nowadays generally believed to be derived from *condere*, to store, but there was an ancient belief that it came from *consilium*, a plan, because of Romulus' clever plan to seize the Sabine women. The festival was one to which, as Livy says, it would be natural to invite the neighbours of Rome; and it is not impossible that on one or more occasions the guests at the festival (or hosts) really did seize one another's wives. The exchange of women, forcible or otherwise, is known to anthropologists as one of the recognized bases of human relationship.[89] There are obviously occasions when a community suffers from a dearth of women. The villagers of Frattoli in the Abruzzi, for example, were in this predicament in 1961, and appealed to the authorities for a supply.[90]

Livy, as has been seen, ascribes the exploit of Romulus to the same type of situation, as a result of which the population of Rome was likely before long to dwindle away into nothing. Dionysius, on the other hand, who devotes some analysis to the causes of the deed, rejects the theory that the motive was a scarcity of women. He also rejects another interpretation, no doubt favoured by enemies of Roman imperialism, according to which the motive for the deed was a desire to create a pretext for war with the Sabines. He himself, instead, supports the alternative view, favourable to Romulus, that his action was prompted by a statesmanlike desire to contract an alliance based on affinity with the neighbouring cities.

Moreover, in order to lend dignity to the proceedings, and at the same time indulge his passion for Greek origins, he makes Romulus point out that the seizure of wives was an ancient Greek custom, and, indeed, that this was the most distinguished way of acquiring a spouse. Dionysius, or his source, probably inferred this point from symbolic survivals of violence in Spartan wedding customs.[91] But the reason why the story became established among the Romans was surely by way of explanation for similar features of their own wedding ceremonies, in which the bride was traditionally pulled away from her mother by force, and her hair was parted by a spear.[92]

The story of the Rape, a familiar theme in Roman works of art, was already well known by the time of Ennius, who devoted a tragic play to the subject. The version given by Livy retains a dramatic structure, built up from a rapid sequence of inspiring scenes, with the captured women playing the part of a Greek tragic chorus. Dionysius, on the other hand, tries to be pseudo-historical, taking an immense amount of trouble to assign the whole business to a definite date, and thus illustrating the characteristic and slightly ludicrous desire of his contemporaries to create a firm mythical chronology. For he comments adversely on an attribution of the event to the first year of Romulus' reign. It is not likely, he says, that a newly-built city would undertake such an enterprise before establishing its government. Therefore Cnaeus Gellius, he adds – the historian of the second century B.C. (chapter 2, section 3) – is much more likely to be right in ascribing the Rape to the *fourth* year of Romulus' reign.

Further efforts to achieve a plausible, bogus exactitude are apparent in differing estimates of the total number of the Sabine women who were captured. They were variously stated to number five hundred and twenty-seven (Valerius Antias) and six hundred and eighty-three (King Juba of Mauretania). But there was yet another version stating that only thirty women were concerned. Cicero says that the thirty wards or *curiae* of Rome were named after them[93]; whereas another theory linked the number with the sow and thirty piglets of Lavinium.

Although the coerced brides gradually became reconciled to their lot, their parents and relations were far from resigned, and the Sabine communities thus despoiled of their women sent an army to launch an attack on Rome. Their monarch, Titus Tatius, pitched his camp beneath the Capitoline Hill, but saw no means of storming the heights. Dionysius' version of what followed, with its meticulous assessment of divergent sources, throws light on the processes by which the Roman mythological tradition gradually came into being.

While Romulus was thus at his wit's end, he met with an unexpected piece of good fortune, this strongest of fortresses being delivered up to him in the following circumstances. It seems that, while the Sabines were passing by the foot of the Capitoline to view the place and see whether any part of the hill could be taken either by surprise or by force, they were observed from above by a maiden whose name was Tarpeia, the daughter of a distinguished man who had been entrusted with the guarding of the place. This maiden, as both Fabius Pictor and Cincius Alimentus (chapter 2, note 39) relate, conceived a desire for the bracelets which the men wore on their left arms and for their rings; for at that time the Sabines wore ornaments of gold and were no less luxurious in their habits than the Etruscans. But according to the account given by Lucius Calpurnius Piso Frugi, the ex-censor, she was inspired by the desire of performing a noble deed, namely, to deprive the enemy of their defensive arms and thus deliver them up to her fellow citizens.

Which of these accounts is the truer may be conjectured by what happened afterwards. For this girl, sending out one of her maids by a little gate which was not known to be open, desired the king of the Sabines to come and confer with her in private, as if she had an affair of necessity and importance to communicate to him. Tatius, in the hope of having the place betrayed to him, accepted the proposal and came to the place appointed; and the maiden, approaching within speaking distance, informed him that her father had gone out of the fortress during the night on some business, but that she had the keys of the gates, and if they came in the night, she would deliver up the place to them upon condition that they gave her as a reward for her treachery the things which all the Sabines wore on their left arms. And when Tatius consented to this, she received his sworn pledge for the faithful performance of the agreement and gave him hers. Then having appointed, as the place to which the Sabines were to repair, the strongest part of the fortress, and the most unguarded hour of the night as the time for the enterprise, she returned without being observed by those inside.

So far all the Roman historians agree, but not in what follows. For Piso, whom I mentioned before, says that a messenger was sent out of the place by Tarpeia in the night to inform Romulus of the agreement she had made with the Sabines, in consequence of which she proposed, by taking advantage of the ambiguity of the expression in that agreement, to demand their defensive arms, and asking him at the same time to send a reinforcement to the fortress that night, so that the enemy, together with their commander, being deprived of their arms, might be taken prisoners; but the messenger, he says, deserted to the Sabine commander and acquainted him with the designs of Tarpeia. Nevertheless, Fabius and Cincius say that no such thing occurred, but they insist that the girl kept her treacherous compact. In what follows, however, all are once more in agreement. For they say that upon the arrival of the king of the

Sabines with the flower of his army, Tarpeia, keeping her promise, opened to the enemy the gate agreed upon, and rousing the garrison, urged them to save themselves speedily by other exits unknown to the enemy, as if the Sabines were already masters of the place; that after the flight of the garrison the Sabines, finding the gates open, possessed themselves of the stronghold, now stripped of its guards; and that Tarpeia, alleging that she had kept her part of the agreement, insisted upon receiving the reward of her treachery according to the oaths.

Here again Piso says that, when the Sabines were ready to give the girl the gold they wore on their left arms, Tarpeia demanded of them their shields and not their ornaments. But Tatius resented the imposition and at the same time thought of an expedient by which he might not violate the agreement. Accordingly, he decided to give her the arms as the girl demanded, but to contrive that she should make no use of them: and immediately poising his shield, he hurled it at her with all his might, and ordered the rest to do the same; and thus Tarpeia, being pelted from all sides, fell under the number and force of the blows and died, overwhelmed by the shields. But Fabius attributes this fraud in the performance of the agreement to the Sabines; for they, being obliged by the agreement to give her the gold as she demanded, were angered at the magnitude of the reward and hurled their shields at her as if they had engaged themselves by their oaths to give her these. But what followed gives the greater appearance of truth to the statement of Piso. For she was honoured with a monument in the place where she fell and lies buried on the most sacred hill of the city, and the Romans every year perform libations to her (I relate what Piso writes); whereas, if she had died in betraying her country to the enemy, it is not to be supposed that she would have received any of these honours, either from those whom she had betrayed or from those who had slain her, but, if there had been any remains of her body, they would in the course of time have been dug up and cast out of the city, in order to warn and deter others from committing the like crimes. But let everyone judge these matters as he pleases.[94]

Livy is much less informative about variant versions of the myth, because as usual he tells a more economical tale. But he, too, leaves it open whether Tarpeia was overwhelmed by shields or by bracelets and rings, and whether, as the second-century historian Lucius Piso had suggested, she may not have been a traitress at all but a heroine actuated by the noble motive of depriving the enemy of their defensive protection.[95]

Plutarch goes on to quote sources recording that, after Tarpeia had suffered for her crime, her father (variously described as Spurius Tarpeius and Titus Tarpeius) was prosecuted and found guilty of treason.[96] However, the biographer sharply rejects quite a different version put forward by the Greek biographer Antigonus of Carystus (*c.* 240 B.C.) and others, who indicated that she was the daughter of the Sabine king and 'being forcibly detained by Romulus, acted and suffered thus by her father's contrivance'. Nevertheless, either Antigonus' view that she was a helpless tool martyred by her father, or Piso's idea of her as a heroic figure, must have obtained some currency, since families which claimed royal Sabine descent placed the image of Tarpeia on their coins, including the Petronii who were proud to trace their cognomen Turpilianus back to her.[97]

Plutarch is very contemptuous about a rival suggestion that Tarpeia herself, not her father, was the commander of the Capitoline garrison. This idea that Romulus had put a young girl in command, he says, must have been invented by someone who wanted to make the founder of Rome look a fool. And the biographer will likewise have nothing to do with another remarkable fluctuation of the story. This was its attribution to an occasion over three hundred years after the mythical date of Romulus, namely the capture of Rome by the Gauls at the beginning of the fourth century B.C. According to this version, which is ascribed to an unknown Greek poet Simylus, she betrayed the Capitol to the Gauls because she had fallen in love with their king. However, in spite of Plutarch's strictures, this may very well have been the original form and context of the story. The 'bracelets' sound like typical fourth-century Gallic gold ornaments;[98] and the story, although it conceded the fall of the Capitol to the Gauls, which the Romans never admitted (chapter 6, section 2), otherwise fitted in very suitably with the disaster suffered at their hands because it provided a satisfactory explanation why the Romans were defeated, an explanation which did not reflect upon their bravery.

Furthermore, the application of the tale to the earliest period of Roman mythical history, the time of Romulus, was in any case seriously anachronistic, because the Capitoline hill, as was recalled at the beginning of this section, did not come within the boundaries of Rome at all until about the sixth century B.C. The transfer of this event to a hypothetical earlier date was evidently due, as so often, to a desire to explain an antique place-name. This was the Tarpeian rock, at the south-western end of the hill (above the present Piazza della Consolazione). Here, as Dionysius records on the authority of Lucius Piso Frugi, there was an alleged Tomb of Tarpeia which was the object of an annual libation ceremony. At first, we are told, the whole hill had been called the Tarpeian mount, until the Etruscan kings of Rome – who were, in historical fact, the first Roman occupants of the hill during the six century B.C. – changed its name to *Capitolium*.

There is something of a mystery here, since Tarpeia proves to be an Etruscan word, akin to Tarquinius.[99] What has happened, apparently, is that the Sabine families who settled at Rome, of whom more will be said shortly, claimed the hill, which at that time was called 'Tarquinius', as their own peculiar property. Consequently they changed its name to the Sabine form 'Tarpeius' (since the Sabines used the letter 'p' where the Etruscans and Romans said 'q', e.g. 'Pompilius' for 'Quinquilius'). The name of the Tarpeian rock was not as Sabine as it looked, for it had first been Etruscan. And so, therefore, had the name of the maiden Tarpeia, though its Sabinization had evidently taken place before the myths about her fate were concocted.

The Augustan poet Propertius declares that the hill was named after the story:

> The gateway sold, her city crushed by foes,
> She claimed her fee: to wed the day she chose.
> Tatius, who though a foeman loathed her crime,
> Said: 'Come, my bed and throne are yours to climb'.
> Battered beneath his followers' shields she fell:
> A bridegroom's gift that paid her service well.
> The traitorous guide has given the hill its name:
> False guardian, thus unjustly crowned with fame.[100]

But it was really, of course, the other way round. The myth did not give the hill its name, but it was the name of the Tarpeian rock, together with its so-called tomb, which prompted the myth. And another important contribution to the story was the reputation of the rock as the place where traitors were cast down to their deaths. One might have expected Tarpeia's punishment to have taken the same form, thus mythically initiating the custom. But instead, it was concluded that the rock had taken its name from the first person to have been guilty of the crime of treachery.

The proximity of this rock was what – despite the protests of Lucius Piso – made this mythical female lose her good name. For, in origin, she had been a figure of religious significance. There are hints of this in our tradition. Livy's account suggested that Tarpeia encountered the Sabine king because she had gone outside the walls to fetch water for a sacrifice. But Propertius, more explicitly, states that her errand was in connection with the rites of Vesta, since she was a Vestal Virgin. This version does damage to mythical chronology, since the Virgins were not supposed to have existed until the time of Romulus' successor Numa (chapter 5, section 1). But the attribution of Vestal rank to Tarpeia was probably intended to explain a statue which was still to be seen in historical times. This was identified as a Vestal Virgin named Tarquinia, who was supposed to have presented the Romans with lands in the Tiber plain beneath the Capitol – beneath the Tarpeian rock.[101] More generally, too, this sacred Vestal status (while making Tarpeia's alleged infamy all the worse) casts a religious aura over her memory. Indeed, this was as it should be, since the original Tarpeia or Tarquinia, after whom the rock and so-called tomb were named, had been a goddess. She presided over the hill and rock, or over one of its springs. And she was originally beneficent, for her image stood in the Capitoline Temple of Jupiter, Juno and Minerva.[102]

Yet owing to the sinister character of the rock which bore the same name, it became customary to regard her as an evil figure, indeed as a text-book example of one particular kind of evil. For she was corrupted to betray her country. Sometimes it was said that she was corrupted by gold, and sometimes by love. Perhaps the former version, which was adopted by Fabius Pictor, is the earlier one, but there are abundant parallels for both ideas, not only in far-distant cultures such as those of Scandinavia, but, above all, in the mythology of Greece, where half-a-dozen possible precedents can be identified.[103]

They were greatly elaborated – and in some cases invented – in Hellenistic times, when this sort of moralizing element was so very fashionable. But there were no moralists so determined as the Romans (chapter 7, section 2), and Livy was the most determined of them all. He spells out this particular moral succinctly: the Sabines acted as they did *to show by example that there must be no trusting a traitor.*[104] Moreover, there was another ethical lesson, too, which, although secondary, could be hung on a convenient Augustan peg. This was the message, conveyed forcibly by Tatius and his Sabines, that treachery may be welcome, but traitors are distasteful, even to their beneficiaries. The Macedonian King Antigonus I the One-Eyed (d. 301 B.C.) had once said as much. And so did Octavian, just before the battle of Actium, when a Thracian prince Rhoemetalces deserted to his side from Antony and Cleopatra.

After gaining possession of the Capitol in this way,[105] the Sabines moved down again to meet the advancing Romans. In the battle that followed, the Sabine champion was recorded to have been a certain Mettius Curtius. 'Comrades!' Livy makes him cry, 'We have beaten our treacherous hosts, our feeble foes. They know now that catching girls is a different matter from fighting against men!' But this brought Romulus upon him, and

the yells of the pursuers so scared Mettius' horse that he took the bit between his teeth and plunged with his rider into the swamps. The Sabines were aghast, the imminent threat to their champion for the moment diverted them from the work in hand, and they tried to help him by shouting advice and signalling, until at last by a supreme effort he struggled out to safety.[106]

Dionysius has little to add, and he and Livy no doubt felt that a satisfactory explanation had now been provided for the pool in the middle of the Roman Forum which was known as the Lacus Curtius. A survival of the primeval Forum swamp, this pond became, in historic times, a well-known and revered site, adorned by altars and other monuments. The triangular bases of these structures, going back to about the beginning of the first century B.C., can still be seen today.[107]

Later in the same century, the antiquarian Varro was writing about the place. In doing so, however, he showed that the connection of its name with Mettius Curtius was only one of a number of possible interpretations.

In the Forum is the *Lacus Curtius* or 'Pool of Curtius'; it is quite certain that it is named from some Curtius, but the story about it has three versions: for Procilius does not tell the same story as Piso, nor did Cornelius follow the story given by Procilius. Procilius states that in this place the earth yawned open, and the matter was by decree of the senate referred to the haruspices (diviners); they gave the answer that the God of the Dead demanded the fulfilment of a forgotten vow, namely that the bravest citizen be sent down to him. Then a certain Marcus Curtius, a brave man, put on his war-gear, mounted his horse, and turning away from the Temple of Concord, plunged into the gap, horse and all; upon which the place closed up and gave his body a burial divinely approved, and left to his clan a lasting memorial.

Piso in his Annals writes that in the Sabine War between Romulus and Tatius, a Sabine hero named Mettius Curtius, when Romulus with his men had charged down from higher ground and driven off the Sabines, got away into a swampy spot which at that time was in the Forum, before the sewers had been made, and escaped from there to his own men on the Capitoline; and from this the pool found its name.

Cornelius and Lutatius write that this place was struck by lightning, and by decree of the senate was fenced in: because this was done by the consul Gaius Curtius Chilo (who had Marcus Genucius as his colleague), it was called the *Lacus Curtius*.[108]

Lucius Calpurnius Piso Frugi – the historian of the second century B.C. who put in a word for Tarpeia – is the authority for the version naming Mettius Curtius, which was followed by Livy and Dionysius. But Varro also quotes a certain Procilius, possibly a man of that name who was tribune in 56 B.C., for the alternative version identifying the warrior with the brave young Marcus Curtius who was said to have immolated himself in 362 B.C. to save his country. He is shown doing so on a relief in the Capitoline Museum which dates from about 100 B.C., but may go back to an earlier original. And finally, Varro quotes a writer called Cornelius, who is unidentifiable, and Lutatius, the learned consul Quintus Catulus of 102 B.C. (who took an unfavourable view of Aeneas, chapter 3, section 2) for a third interpretation, according to which the pool was named after Gaius Curtius Chilo, consul in 445 B.C., who consecrated the spot after it had been struck by lightning. No fully canonical version emerged from this three-fold choice, partly no doubt because Livy and Dionysius, out of eagerness to place the event as far back as possible in the venerable past, preferred the attribution to Mettius Curtius, whereas the more romantic exploit of Marcus was more likely to commend itself to the public.

We cannot tell which of the three explanations for the name of the pool was correct: probably none of them, since the etymologies of these old place-names were buried in the mists of antiquity. But holes in the ground, whatever had caused them, were commonly regarded as ports of communication with the Underworld, and the explanation of such cavities and caverns by telling of heroes swallowed up in the ground was a very ancient mythological proceeding, to be found in many parts of the world. In Greece, the tale of Amphiaraus is a story of this type,[109] and the versions of the Curtius tale which have come down to us are Greek importations, duly adjusted to the requirements of Roman typography and mythical history.

As for the Curtian family itself, it was to the fore once again in the first century B.C., when an influential knight named Gaius Curtius was a backer of Caesar, and though he cannot very convincingly have claimed descent from the ancient Curtii, he would have welcomed a compliment to their name. Later, Augustus, as was his custom, exploited the site in his own interests, allowing one of his officials to carry out repairs. He also sanctioned the continuation of a custom by which men of every walk of life threw a small offering into the water every year.[110] But from now onwards, very characteristically, this practice was to be accompanied by good wishes for the emperor's own welfare.

The battle between Romans and Sabines was still under way, with victory (according to one version) tending towards the Roman side, when the captured Sabine brides decided to intervene. With hair streaming and clothes torn in an access of grief, they thrust their bodies between the combatants, and appealed to them to stop fighting. The effect of their appeal was instantaneous, and a moment later the rival commanders stepped forward to make peace, Romulus the Roman king on one side, Titus Tatius king of the Sabines on the other.

And they did more than just make peace; for the story goes on to tell how they now reached a momentous decision. The two states were henceforward to be united under one single government. Rome was to be its single capital city,[111] but Romulus and Tatius were to reign as joint rulers.

> They thought it best to have a brace of kings
> And Tatius joined his reign with Romulus.

But Tatius is a dim and colourless figure.[112] Before his arrival at Rome, he is supposed to have been king of the Sabine town of Cures (on the left bank of the Tiber close to the Via Salaria). But the tradition maintained that he died before Romulus – leaving the latter sole monarch of Rome once again, so that, in effect, Tatius sank almost without trace. He was never considered solid enough, as a part of history or even as myth, to take his place in the Roman list of the Seven Kings. He merely served, with the aid of his supposed first name Titus, to provide an etymological explanation for one of the original 'tribes' or 'centuries' of Rome (Tities, Titienses, chapter 5, note 63), and a priesthood called the *sodales Titii* – though in fact his name, whatever its real origins may be, surely has nothing to do with any of these institutions. He also came in useful, as coins of *c.* 74 and *c.* 70 B.C. show, as an alleged ancestor of the families of the Titurii and Vettii, who used the surname Sabinus.[113]

Yet Tatius did serve other important purposes as well. One was to provide, by his association with Romulus, a regal precedent for the dual consulship of the Republic – emphasizing the continuity of the constitution. And then, in the hands of determinedly pro-Sabine historians, such as Cato in all probability, and certainly Varro,[114] he was retrospectively assigned the Capitoline and the Quirinal as his sphere. In fact, however, as we have seen, the Capitoline was not inhabited at nearly so early a date as this notional eighth century, and there is no firm archaeological reason to regard the Quirinal as originally Sabine, or to postulate a primitive duality between a Latin Palatine and a Sabine Capitoline, Quirinal or Esquiline (chapter 1).

But this was the way chosen by these pro-Sabine historians to get themselves out of a real difficulty. The difficulty was this. Out of the six greatest patrician families in Rome, the *gentes maiores*, three, the Valerii and Claudii and (probably) Fabii were of Sabine origin. It was therefore embarrassing that there were so few definite relics of Rome's great past that could be identified as distinctively Sabine. The reason for this deficiency is clear enough: it is because in the early days, when the Sabine element was incorporated in Rome, Sabine culture had been relatively feeble, and had left little specific mark. In other words, the situation regarding the Sabines was exactly the opposite to the situation regarding the Etruscans. Etruscan civilization had been powerful and Etruscan influence on Rome substantial, but the Etruscan tradition, for political reasons, had been largely suppressed, so that the background behind this power and influence can only be reconstructed from time to time, when chance happens to permit. Sabine culture, on the other hand, had been backward. The great Sabine families, when they arrived in Rome, were still too barbarous to exercise any cultural influence. Yet in later days, vociferous representatives of the Sabine tradition in high Roman society, and then in Roman literature, had insisted on carving out the whole myth of the dual Rome to accommodate their ancestral pretensions.[115]

The Valerii were particularly insistent, even inserting one of their number retrospectively, along with Mettius Curtius, among the Sabines who stayed on at Rome with Tatius after their treaty with the Romans.[116] And this was a family which had a historian, Valerius Antias, to make sure their claims were not forgotten. The Fabii were somewhat in eclipse in his time (they provided no consul between 116 and 45 B.C.), but, long before that, they had possessed their own influential historian, Fabius Pictor; and Cato the elder, too, displayed Fabian loyalties. It seems that the claims of the Fabii to have been pre-eminent from the earliest days of the Republic were authentic enough. But they went one better, or rather two better. For one thing, they were able to assert a Romulean date for themselves, since their family priesthood associated with the Lupercalia (section 2 above) was supposed to go back to that time. And what is more, they even claimed descent from a nymph Tiberina, who was said to have been one of Hercules' mistresses. They were very ready to keep alive the apparently unfounded story that the Quirinal Hill had always been the Sabine sphere, since this was where they themselves traditionally lived.[117] So did the arrogant, unscrupulous, bogus-progressive Claudii; and their family tomb was at the foot of the Capitoline. And so they, too, were happy to cherish stories about early Sabine dominance over the Capitoline, Quirinal and Esquiline hills.

However, the Sabine image at Rome was heavily clouded by the unfortunate fact that their three great families often did not get on at all well with one another. For example, relations between the Valerii and Claudii in the early first century B.C. were very strained, so that when Valerius Antias writes even about events alleged to have taken place three or four hundred years previously, the Claudii get a bad time. And there was a great mutual distaste between the Fabii and the Claudii ever since the latter rose to prominence towards the end of the fourth century B.C.[118] This enmity, too, was exploited by historians, and above all by Fabius Pictor.

As a genuine reflection of the fact that the Claudii were relatively late starters, there was a circumstantial report that they had first come to Rome not earlier than *c.* 504 B.C., when

Attus Clausus (Appius Claudius) brought in from the Sabine country a large band of dependents, who were welcomed with him and given Roman citizenship.[119] However, this tradition was not good enough for every later Claudius, because we have seen that their fellow-Sabines the Valerii and Fabii could, at a pinch, claim to date back as far as Romulus. And so the Claudii, too, developed a version of their own Romulean ancestors, in order to compete with them.[120] But until then, if their enemies like Fabius Pictor chose to post-date them by two centuries, some of them may have felt happy or philosophical enough about the alleged later date because they could point out that it linked them with the glorious first years of the Republic (which was believed to have started only a few years before 504, cf. chapter 5, section 1) instead of the more equivocal older times of the kings. What was not so satisfactory was a rival, and presumably hostile, theory which gave them neither the one advantage nor the other, placing them in the last days of the monarchy, the period of the wicked Tarquinius Superbus (chapter 5, section 2). In fact, whether the date 504 is authentic or fictitious, and whether certain other Sabine families had arrived earlier than that time or not – they may well have – the truth probably is that the Sabines infiltrated into Rome gradually, over a considerable period. In the process, having little of their own to offer, they were completely absorbed, so that, later on, the various Sabine myths that interested writers were so eager to compile had to start from scratch.

At all events, the internal enemies of the Claudii did not attempt to reject the date 504. But what they did instead was to attack the leader of the supposed immigration, Attus Clausus, classing him with Appii Claudii of allegedly evil character,[121] and treating him and his later followers as degraded fugitives from Roman conquest rather than as the high-minded, voluntary settlers of Claudian tradition. But in the time of Augustus, this hostile propaganda had an extremely powerful opposing current to contend with, since the emperor's own favoured sons-in-law Marcellus and Tiberius were Claudii. Later on, Tiberius, who was also his stepson, succeeded him on the imperial throne. But even before that time, and even before his succession was certain, it would have taken a bold man to go on blackguarding the Claudii of history and myth too enthusiastically. Even the fact that, for a time, Tiberius seemed to fall out of favour with the emperor was not enough to encourage confident denigration. That tricky combination of circumstances could conceivably have provided one of the reasons why Livy, who, following his sources, had done his share of criticizing the family, decided to call a halt to his history altogether (chapter 2, section 3). It may, incidentally, have been the emperor Tiberius (A.D. 14–37), or one of his successors Claudius (A.D. 41–54), a keen antiquarian of the same house (chapter 5, section 2), who finally decided that it was right and proper to say that the Claudii had come to Rome in the early, venerable times of Romulus.

One of the unconvincing features of the carefully compiled mythical chronology of Rome is the way in which the foreign foes of the Romans were gloriously conquered again and again, yet always seem to return to the scene afresh, very soon afterwards, as dangerous foes. It is the same with the Sabines, except that, by the efforts of the strong pro-Sabine lobby at Rome, their first clashes with the Romans allegedly resulted in the voluntary, bipartite alliance made by Romulus and Tatius; and then followed the honorific reception of Attus Clausus in the capital. Yet in spite of these supposed happenings we are told that the Romans still had to repel actual occupation of the city by a Sabine force in 460, still had to defeat them in 449, and what is more (after a hundred and fifty years of silence on the subject) still had to conquer them in 290, and only granted them full citizenship in 268.

It was at some period within these later years that the Sabine myth at Rome got fully under way. The theme became fashionable again, not merely because of the pervasive personalities of Cato and Varro, but because in the eighties B.C., before and during the great Italian rebellion (the Social or Marsian War), the burning question of the day was the possibility or otherwise of a true fusion between Romans and other Italians: and was it to be by conquest or agreement? Here the ancient saga of Romulus and the Sabines was available for adjustment to suit whichever viewpoint was required.

Long before that, the Sabine stories had been bound up with the assertion, in pro-Sabine circles, that this people had always been splendidly austere, providing a moral example to others. It is amusing, however, to read in Dionysius' account of the Tarpeia myth that the Sabines were in those days, on the contrary, extremely luxurious – just as luxurious, he reports, as the Etruscans![122] This version was obviously derived from circles that resented the Sabine tradition. However, it failed to make headway against the opposite view. For this had been well instilled by Cato the elder, who had been brought up in Sabine country.[123] And their simple virility became a commonplace of Roman poetry and moralizing.

However, just as fashion required that Roman beginnings should be linked up with the Greeks, so, too, it was necessary to find Greek origins for the Sabines. This was done simply enough by tracing them back to the Spartans – ancestors of appropriate austerity. Cato cherished the connection since, however much he might dislike contemporary Greeks, he was keen to connect Rome with what he regarded as the best of Greece. And then the same theory, duly encouraged by Varro, enjoyed a great vogue at the end of the Republic and beginning of the Empire. The first known Valerius was attributed Spartan origin, and so was Attus Clausus. And the Fabii too, since they claimed descent from Hercules, were Heraclidae like the Spartans.

This Spartan descent of the Sabines, however, ante-dated Cato and Varro. It had already been fashionable, indeed it had probably originated, in the years around 300 B.C. when the Greek town of Taras (Tarentum) was the most important power in south Italy and loomed large on the horizon of Rome (chapter 1). For Tarentum was well known to be a Spartan foundation. The fact that the city had close links with the Oscan-speaking Italian tribes, including the Samnites and no doubt the Sabines as well, may have played a part in developing the view that the latter, like the Tarentum, were of Spartan origin. But the main point was an ethical one, relating to the rough simplicity that the Sabines were proud to claim. For in this respect – granted that it was the correct thing to have Greek origins – the Spartans, known to Rome by way of Tarentum, were pre-eminently suitable. Cato is quoted as saying that the ancestor of the Sabines was Sabinus, son of an indigenous deity, and that they were also, or alternatively, descended from a certain Sabus from Sparta. But from then onwards it is the latter version which prevails. A variant opinion declared Sabus to have come from Persia, another country famous for its severe morals.

THE MYTHOLOGY OF
THE ROMAN KINGS

1 NUMA AND HIS SUCCESSORS

After Romulus, according to tradition, came six more kings:
Numa Pompilius, Tullus Hostilius, Ancus Marcius, Tarquinius
Priscus, Servius Tullius and Tarquinius Superbus. They may, in
certain cases, have been real people – particularly when their
names differ from the names one might have expected to find in
early times. But even if they did really exist, this would not
necessarily mean that they were kings of Rome, or, if they were,
that they were the only ones. There may have been others who
have disappeared from view.

Including Romulus (and excluding Tatius, who did not find
his way into the list) they were seven, which was a sacred
number greatly in demand by mythologists. In spite of the
historical unreality of the list, the Romans drew up an elaborate
and detailed table of dates for their kings; just as, millennia
earlier, the Sumerian king-lists had stated that Gilgamesh was
the fifth king of the second dynasty of the city-state of Erech
after the flood.

However, from time to time a good deal of doctoring of the
dates took place. A conspicuous figure in this process was
evidently the historian Fabius Pictor, who provided the earliest
known account of the Roman monarchy, though little of it has
survived. One problem that these adjusters had to face was to
make their date for the foundation of the city agree with the
figure required by the durations of the seven reigns, reckoned
back from the canonical date for the foundation of the Republic. It is because of this sort of manipulation, for example, that
estimates of the length of Numa's reign vary between thirty-
nine years and forty-three. Cicero who supplies, briefly, our

earliest surviving story of the regal period, takes the trouble to defend the former of these two figures by citing the Greek historian Polybius. Plutarch, on the other hand, is prepared to admit that the dates of Numa's reign were uncertain.[1]

But this degree of restraint is rare among writers on such subjects. For one thing, it was easier to invent regal than Republican 'facts', since, in dealing with the kings, there were no annual Fasti to inhibit people's imaginative powers. By the time of Cato a canon was more or less established, and it was possible to set up statues of the kings on the Capitol, with the years of their reigns inscribed on the bases. But these chronologies cannot be taken at all seriously. For one thing, the durations ascribed to the reigns are quite improbably long: in so undeveloped a community more than seven kings would be needed to fill two hundred and forty years. This would especially be the case if, as was supposed, the monarchy for most of the time had been elective. For under that system reigns are short; by the time such kings come to the throne their ages are already fairly well advanced, since they have to be old enough to have had distinguished careers.

The mythical reign of Numa, as described by Livy and others, is briefly summed up by a writer of the second century A.D., Florus (chapter 2, note 66), in the following terms:

The successor of Romulus was Numa Pompilius, whom, while he was living at Cures in the territory of the Sabines, the Romans of their own accord invited to become king owing to the fame of his piety. He instructed them in sacred rites and ceremonies and all the worship of the immortal gods. He established pontiffs, augurs, the Salii, and the other priesthoods. He divided the year into twelve months and appointed the days upon which the courts could and could not meet. He gave the Romans the sacred shields and the Palladium (chapter 3, section 3, note 71), the mystic tokens of empire, and the double-faced Janus the symbol of peace and war. Above all he handed over the care of the hearth of Vesta to the Vestal Virgins, that the flame, imitating the heavenly stars, might keep guardian watch over the empire.

All these arrangements he attributed to the advice of the goddess Egeria, so that his barbarous subjects might accept them with greater willingness.

In a word, he induced a fierce people to rule with piety and justice an empire which they had acquired by violence and injustice.[2]

This account is largely based on Livy, who in turn probably derives most of his material from Valerius Antias. Plutarch, in his *Life of Numa*, adds a number of anecdotes and other material which he probably drew, to some extent at least, from the same source, but his work is less a biography than a philosophical and theological study. The oldest known literary authority for Numa was Ennius.

The powerful Sabine lobby succeeded in claiming this second of the kings as Sabine, stating that he had been born at Cures, the place of origin of Tatius, whose daughter Tatia he married. Numa was also allotted, in retrospect, a house on the allegedly Sabine Quirinal hill, a primitive structure which was still shown to visitors in Plutarch's time. But 'Nuna' is an Etruscan first name[3], and there is good reason to suppose that 'Pompilius' was likewise Etruscan, though it had been converted into a Latinized form.[4] So King Numa Pompilius is likely to have started his mythical career as an Etruscan. Or possibly, once all the accretions are sloughed off him, it was not a mythical career but a real one; though if so, we know nothing whatever about it.

He is supposed to have been elected king after an interregnum. This was a device by which historians of democratic inclinations such as Licinius Macer were conveniently able to illustrate Utopian good relations between liberal senate and sovereign assembly.[5] And the election of Numa served to demonstrate a further point also, the superiority of the personal qualities of a 'new man' over the hereditary system, an aspect which Cicero, himself a new man (the first member of his family to hold the consulship), was glad to emphasize[6]. And Augustus, also, by no means objected to the suggestion that in new situations it was proper for new constitutional expedients to emerge.

The symmetrical arrangement of the canon made it possible to suggest that all the essentials in Roman history had already been anticipated by the first four Roman kings.[7] And it was even possible to claim that the essentials were covered by the first two, the warlike Romulus and the peaceful Numa. They were descended from the same Indo-European origins as the Sanskrit divine pair Varuna and Mitra, the frightening magician and the pacific lawgiver. And one of the oldest Etruscan myths, too, spoke of the duality between king and priest, between Lucumo and Arruns.

For Numa, the inventor or originator of customs and religious practices, is one of the most familiar figures of folklore. Indeed it was sometimes suggested that the very name of this king, who sought to replace the fear of external enemies by the fear of the gods, was derived from *nomos*, the Greek word for law. Instead it was, as we have seen, Etruscan, and so, likewise are many of the institutions which the writers fathered upon him. But when the Romans, in historic times, became self-conscious about the origins of their national religion, they gathered together a list of many practices which Rome had adopted from the Etruscans – and 'nationalized' them by con-cocting this even more antique Roman, Sabine father-figure as their author. Typical of this process is the so-called 'Calendar of Numa', which cannot, in fact, be traced back to the eighth century B.C., the notional epoch of Numa, but belongs to the sixth century, when Rome was under Etruscan control (chapter 2, section 3).

Numa's association with religion caused him to be regarded as a disciple of the Greek philosopher Pythagoras, who was well known in Italy because he had established a religious community at Croton in the south of the peninsula. Greek analogies and alleged precedents were always welcome,[8] and the Pythagorean connection with Rome – which was extended, or had originated, by allowing him two Etruscan disciples – seemed to account for certain similarities between early Roman religion and the Greek cults of southern Italy. But the link may, originally, have been introduced owing to the purely fortuitous circumstance that another Pythagoras won an Olympic prize in the Olympiad (four-year period) during which Numa was believed to have become king. This Pythagoras, like the more famous one, was believed to have visited Italy, and Plutarch reported that in some people's view it was the athlete not the philosopher who advised Numa. For, as Plutarch went on to point out, to suppose that the philosopher was Numa's teacher would have played havoc with the traditional chronology, since, according to this, Numa reigned nearly two whole centuries before the lifetime of Pythagoras.

Cicero was annoyed by this stupid mistake, as he considered it to be.[9] But he was not the first to recognize the error, since Cato, for one, had already done this. The link between Numa and Pythagoras was already being claimed in Cato's time. Indeed, the connection probably dates from an earlier epoch still. The place which acted as intermediary in bringing the knowledge of Pythagoras from south Italy to Rome was surely Tarentum, which had succeeded Croton, from the fifth century onwards, as the chief seat of the Pythagorean order. When the Romans first formed close relations with Tarentum in the second half of the fourth century B.C., they took a keen interest, like other Italic peoples, in the religious beliefs of Tarentum, the principal Greek town of south Italy, which seemed to provide analogies with their own practices. It cannot, therefore, have been at all long before they learnt a great deal about Pythagoras.

For he rapidly became the favourite religious prototype of the Romans. It was he, rather than Socrates or Plato, who seemed to them to represent the height of Greek wisdom. Consequently, in the latter half of the fourth century B.C., they actually erected a statue of Pythagoras in the Comitium beside the Roman Forum.[10] And at about the same time a Sicilian poet declared that the philosopher, in his lifetime, had been made a Roman citizen.[11] Under the influence of the Tarentine Aristoxenus (born between 375 and 360), a number of Greek cities of Sicily and south Italy had claimed Pythagorean origin for their laws and constitutions; and it seemed natural for the Romans to do the same. This encouraged them to assume a connection between Pythagoras and Numa, especially as the concept of Philosopher-Kings was now widely current. A further stimulus in the same direction was the fashionable doctrine of divine sanction as the basis for social patterns. This idea greatly appealed to the Romans and may well have gone back to Pythagoras, or at least was regarded as doing so.

A particular step in this direction was taken by Appius Claudius the Blind (censor, 312 B.C.), who was eager to introduce Pythagorean and Tarentine thought to Rome (cf. chapter 2, section 3). Closer acquaintance was gained with these ways of thinking after Tarentum signed a treaty with the Romans at this time (chapter 1), and subsequently, during the First Punic War, passed into their power. The writings of Ennius (d. 169), who himself came from south Italy, show traces of Pythagoreanism, notably in the preface of the *Annals*. But a curious incident occurred in 181 B.C. In that year a certain man from Tarentum claimed to have discovered two stone chests on Rome's Janiculum hill, one being the coffin that had contained the body of Numa but was now empty (the hill had been associated with his name) and the other still containing twelve books allegedly written by Numa, including writings on Pythagorean philosophy.[12] The books were brought before a Roman praetor, who ordered them to be burnt.[13] He had a good pretext for his action, if he possessed a historical sense, seeing that Numa, if he ever existed, died so long before Pythagoras was born. But the real reason why the books were destroyed was because Pythagorean works were held to be subversive, partly on the general grounds that many people took a low view of all Hellenic intrusions but chiefly because the schemes of initiation and mystic purification in which the Pythagoreans were interested seemed (as Christian doctrines seemed in later epochs) too other-worldly to be patriotic. The fraudulent discovery may well have been a try-on by Pythagorean-minded persons eager to supply a dramatic demonstration of the historical authenticity of their beliefs.

It seems strange that after this débâcle, and after the proof by Cato and others that Numa could not have known about Pythagoras, Cicero and other writers still felt it necessary to point out, with some urgency, that the connection between the two figures was fictitious. This was presumably because the considerable revival of Pythagoreanism which took place in the first century B.C., a revival that aroused keen interest in Varro, had brought the link with Numa into fashion once again.

At all events, Numa remained in people's minds. He was kept there by the families which claimed descent from him; though how early they got to work we cannot say – except that this cannot have been later than the fourth century B.C.

First and foremost among them was one of the six greatest Roman houses, the Aemilii, who asserted that Numa's son Mamercus was their ancestor (though according to other accounts he was the son of Pythagoras himself). Mamercus' brother Pompo was said to be the forebear of the family of the Pomponii,[14] who were connections of the elder Scipio Africanus and were later kept well in the forefront by Cicero's friend the knight Titus Pomponius Atticus (though he can scarcely have regarded himself as their descendant). As for Numa's third son Calpus, the family of the Calpurnii, which achieved fame and possessed its own historian (Lucius Piso Frugi) in the second century B.C., alleged that he was the man from whom they were descended.[15] And the Pinarii detected an ancestor in yet another son, Pinus, a claim which ill accorded with their even more ambitious assertion that they had served the worship of Hercules ever since the god's visit to the site of Rome (chapter 3, section 1). Finally, it was supposed that Numa had a daughter, and that she became the mother of the next king but one, Ancus Marcius whom the Marcian family declared to be their ancestor (cf. below, this section). A historian of the second century B.C., Cnaeus Gellius, must have pleased the Marcii, but must equally have annoyed a great many Aemilii and Pomponii and Calpurnii and Pinarii, when he expressed the opinion that this girl was Numa's only child, and that, far from having four sons, the king had not possessed any sons at all! And Cassius Hemina, in about the middle of the century, chose to take the same sort of sceptical attitude.

By this time, however, the Numa myth had gradually assumed its full dimensions. Hemina himself mentions one of Numa's laws,[16] and there may be an earlier reference to another in a fragmentary calendar of 187 B.C.[17] For this was the time when Cato, with his Sabine interests, was giving the figure of Numa a strong boost, laying stress on those aspects of the king's career which harmonized with the belief that the Sabines were the religious people *par excellence* (chapter 4, section 3). In the next century that patriotic Sabine Varro emphasized the same view, and Varro's contemporary, Valerius Antias, probably revived and stressed the idea that the Roman religion was established by Numa to defend the social order. For Antias was writing with an admiring eye on the contemporary dictator Sulla, since Sulla claimed to be defending the traditional society by his measures.

By this time a marked ethical component had entered into the Numa story. Its strongest expression was the tradition that Rome's Temple of Fides (Good Faith) went all the way back to a cult established by Numa. Although, in fact, the temple was not founded until 254 B.C., there seemed to be a grain of plausibility in this version, seeing that the Romans had, indeed, worshipped a similarly designated god of Good Faith (Dius Fidius)[18] from an antique date; his temple was attributed to 466 B.C. This early emphasis on the idea was in keeping with their insistence that wars and other dealings should be, or should at least look, pious and just (chapter 7, section 2). But the concept of good faith really came into its own when Rome became involved with Greek states during the third century B.C. Pictor and Cato stressed the importance of this 'virtue', and emphasized Rome's adhesion to it, and a lot was again said about the matter during the strained relations with fellow-Italians which culminated in the Social (Marsian) War of 91–87.[19] Throughout those troubled years the Roman side were no doubt emphasizing the venerable link with Numa. And Rome's successive enemies, on the other hand, were surely at pains to belittle the Numa tradition, as part of their denial that the Romans possessed any venerable tradition of good faith at all.

During the same first century B.C. Numa Pompilius aroused keen interest for quite another reason also. This was because Julius Caesar was insistent on his own descent, through the Marcii, from King Ancus Marcius, said to be the grandson of Numa. Nor is it at all surprising, thereafter, to see the Augustan writers emphasizing Numa's role. For the king played a vital part in the publicity of Augustus, who had passed, as it were, through a warlike, Romulus phase to the peaceful, reconstructive tasks of a second Numa. He also laid particular stress on Fides, with whom the name of Numa had come to be linked. And so Virgil, in the sixth book of the *Aeneid*, envisages the emperor standing flanked by Romulus on one side and Numa on the other.[20]

To publicize these points, Augustus made use of one of his moneyers. For the time being, in order to show his concern for traditional institutions, he had retained the old custom by which the national currency was signed by the young men of good prospects who, at the beginning of their careers, served on an annually elected board of three moneyers. And one of these youths, under Augustus, was a certain Cnaeus Calpurnius Piso, a member of the great Calpurnian family which he had managed to attach to his regime. This Cnaeus Piso signed not only normal coinage, but a number of commemorative brass or copper medallions; and on them he placed the head of King Numa. At first sight this might seem like a simple repetition of the old Republican practice by which moneyers adorned their issues with designs illustrating their family history. But the pieces signed by the young Cnaeus Piso clearly had a much wider significance than that. For one thing, the existence of such a medallic issue at all was quite exceptional. Furthermore, on one side of the pieces was Numa, on the other Augustus: the juxtaposition was no accident. When moneyers of Augustus displayed their family history they preferred to select incidents that combined the family reference with a topical, imperial significance: and there was no doubt about Numa's Augustan role. Indeed, the issue may well have been timed to coincide with the sweeping moral and social reforms with which the emperor prefaced his new Golden Age, officially inaugurated in 17 B.C.[21]

And then, more than a century later, Plutarch envisaged Numa Pompilius as a sort of crowned philosopher on the throne, a reflection of the pattern of the Good Ruler which was very much in people's minds at that time.

*

Numa was not only associated with the legendary Pythagoras, but was believed to receive love and advice from Egeria, described as a goddess or nymph with divine insight into the future. True to the distaste of the Romans for overtly superhuman interventions (chapter 4, section 2), Livy suggests that the report to this effect was a pure invention by Numa himself. Dionysius of Halicarnassus, likewise, regards it as fictitious, but says it was invented by someone else. Whereas Plutarch, who repeats the tale and discusses it at length (carefully asserting that the king only associated with Egeria after the death of his wife Tatia!), sees clearly that it is on a par with various Greek stories which told of other divine men. However, the story may not have been Greek, for the Etruscan nature of Numa's names and supposed religious innovations suggest that this, like other elements in his career, may have been introduced from Etruria. The diviners *par excellence* were the Etruscans. And, in particular, the Etruscan nymph Vegoia or Begoe gave counsel about law and order to King Arruns Veltumnus of Clusium, just as Egeria was the consort and adviser of Numa.[22]

Moreover, another of the relatively few surviving Etruscan myths tells of Tages, whose grey head and child-like face emerged from a furrow at Tarquinii and revealed the art of divination to all Etruria (cf. chapter 2, section 2). It is true that Tages' revelations concerned the specially Etruscan skills relating to divination by birds and the intestines of animals, whereas the form of the art ascribed to Numa was divination by water or hydromancy – which was also attributed to Pythagoras. But this hydromantic element was necessary in order to bring the myth into connection with Egeria, since she was probably, in origin, a goddess of water. In this capacity she came to be identified with a further set of water-deities, the Camenae. They had a grove and spring outside the Porta Capena at the southern extremity of the Caelian Hill – and this was the place where 'King Numa had nightly meetings with his mistress'.[23] The Camenae were equated with the Greek Muses, who likewise had their spring, Hippocrene;[24] so that Egeria, too, was sometimes called a Muse, and her concern for the intellectual pursuits of Numa seemed to fit in with this picture. Hence, too, her relevance to divination, since the ancients sometimes, erroneously, derived the name of the Camenae from *carmen*, a song or prophecy. Besides, the priestesses who served the goddess Vesta, the Vestal Virgins, were accustomed to draw water from the spring of the Camenae, and the Vestals, in spite of anachronistic views to the contrary (chapter 4, section 3), were generally supposed to be the creation of Numa.

The site of this spring was named after its divine visitor and called the Egeria Valley. But this cannot have been a very early development since the spring-goddess Egeria originally came not from Rome but from Aricia south of the Alban Lake.[25] Her name was that of a prominent early Latin family, one of whose members was said to be the founder of the great Arician cult of Diana traditionally brought to Rome by Servius Tullius (section 2 below).[26] Egeria's link with the place was recognized by Ovid, who, on the death of Numa, makes her proceed to the Arician grove to bewail her loss.[27] Aricia played a very prominent part in the life of Rome during the little known times that marked the transition from monarchy to Republic, for those were the years when the place gradually succeeded Alba Longa as the most important town in Latium (chapter 1). But not long afterwards Aricia, in its turn, was absorbed by the Romans, who took its cults and transplanted them to Rome.

Livy describes Egeria's relationship with the king in hard-boiled terms. Fearing his peace policy might make the Romans idle and luxurious, Numa Pompilius

decided upon a step which he felt would prove more effective than anything else with a mob as rough and ignorant as the Romans were in those days. This was to inspire them with the fear of the gods. Such a sentiment was unlikely to touch them unless he first prepared them by inventing some sort of marvellous tale. He pretended, therefore, that he was in the habit of meeting the goddess Egeria by night, and that it was her authority which guided him in the establishment of such rites as were most acceptable to the gods, and in the appointment of priests to serve each particular duty.[28]

The translator whose version has been used here suggests that this passage contains 'a shrewder comment than Livy was aware of on the practicalness of Roman official religion, and perhaps upon the practical aspect of religion in general'.[29] Now, it is true that Livy, who had such a lot of writing to get through, sometimes copied his sources without thinking the matter out for himself. But almost every educated Roman, more or less strongly, held precisely this view of his national religion and mythology, that it was something to keep the people quiet, and Numa, if he ever existed, was by no means the last to adapt mythology to this purpose (chapter 7, section 2).

So, in various ways, Numa's reign was made to mirror the pre-occupations of later ages. And, in the cause of this process, events and institutions belonging to periods considerably subsequent to his mythical eighth century were pressed into service.

But this is not true of all the tales associated with his name. Some of them are very ancient indeed.

For instance, it was said that a shield fell from heaven as a gift from Jupiter to Numa (or was discovered in the house of Numa), who in order to prevent it from being stolen ordered the manufacture of eleven duplicates. The name of the shield, *ancile*, means 'indented on both sides',[30] and artistic representations show that it was of a figure-of-eight shape which is familiar from Cretan and Mycenaean shields of the second millennium B.C. and was depicted on Athenian 'Geometric' vases in the early centuries of the first millennium. But votive plaques or dancers' shields of the same shape appear in several parts of Italy in and after 700 B.C.,[31] and the patron goddess of Lanuvium, Juno Sospita, is similarly equipped. These shields considerably antedate the heavy infantry methods of fighting which were apparently introduced to Rome during the sixth century B.C. (see below, section 2), so that this item of myth relating to Numa seems to belong to a stratum a good deal earlier than most of his other innovations.[32]

So does Mars' priestly order of the Salii, men who at the god's festival each year leapt round the town carrying these shields, in a magical dance to ward off evil – a ceremony which was originally a fertility-rite, and subsequently became a war-dance. Statuettes of such dancers appear on a bronze urn from Visentium (Bisenzio) on Lake Bolsena. This urn dates from the eighth century B.C., when Etruscan civilization was shortly about to assume its distinctive forms (chapter 1). Moreover, similar rites still seem to have been practised by the people of the same area after they became fully recognizable as Etruscans. For the institution of the Salii was attributed, according to one interpretation, to a king of Etruscan Veii, known as Morrius or Mamurrius.[33] However, even if these dances came to the Romans from Etruria, the shape ascribed to the *ancilia* at Rome suggests that they preceded the period when the Etruscans were in control of the city (see section 2 below).

The Salii were makers of magic, and the mythical Numa also accumulated round his personality a few other quaint tales which bring in further magical themes, such as are found in the folklore of a thousand different countries.

One of them starts in a familiar enough Greek way. It tells of two gods or demi-gods. They are called by the non-Greek names of Faunus and Picus. Faunus we have encountered before (chapter 3, section 1), and Picus was the subject of many marvellous stories of Greek Alexandrian type about his changes of shape and amorous activities. Numa Pompilius, according to the story, surprised and trapped the two divine figures by mixing wine and honey with their drinking water; and thereupon they transformed themselves into a number of weird shapes.[34] Yet the king persisted in his attempts to catch them, and when they saw that he had finally succeeded, they revealed to him many prophecies and secrets. One of them was a charm against thunder and lightning (*procuratio fulminis*) – performed, strangely enough, with onions and hair and pilchards. This recipe was still remembered in historical times. However, according to another version of this story they did not tell Numa about the charm after all, but employed their magic to bring Jupiter down from heaven.

This is an attempt to explain why, on certain solemn occasions, the god was called 'Elicius'. It seems probable that he really owes the name to his alleged capacity to procure or elicit rain. But the present tale, associated with thunder and lightning, is intended to suggest the alternative explanation that the epithet meant 'called down' or 'elicited' from heaven.[35]

Numa was introduced because there was a tradition preserved by Livy that the altar of Jupiter Elicius on the Aventine had been founded by him (though the inclusion of the Aventine in the city did not belong to anything like so early a period as the eighth century which was the mythical epoch of his reign).

The story of Faunus and Picus was told by Valerius Antias,[36] and Ovid is amused by its atmosphere of folk-tale and comic drama.

> 'Cut off a head,' says Jove. 'It shall be done,'
> Said Numa, 'we will pluck an onion.'
> 'A man's,' said Jove. 'Yea, thou shalt have his hair.'
> 'A life I'll have.' 'A fish's life, I swear.'
> Jove laughed: 'Then those my bolts shall expiate,
> Man not to be repelled from god's debate.'[37]

Ovid is clearly right to suggest that the onions, hair and fish are substitutes for human sacrifice. But, although he weaves a jocular unifying thread, he makes no serious attempt to explain why these particular items were selected. This was because he did not know; and nor do we. Though the anecdote is thrown into a sophisticated shape, the magic formula may be of remote antiquity.

Tullus Hostilius, traditionally the third king of Rome, was believed to have built the Roman senate house (Curia Hostilia), and the capture and destruction of Alba Longa were also attributed to him. He was seen as a man of war: a reversion from Numa to Romulus, whose achievements and character, in some measure, he duplicates:

> The successor of Numa, destined
> To shake our land out of its indolence, stirring men up to fight
> Who have grown unadventurous and lost the habit of victory.[38]

Tullus Hostilius owes this reputation, in part, to the resemblance of his second name to *hostis*, an enemy.[39]

His story had probably taken shape by the later third century B.C. It was told in detailed fashion by Ennius, but Livy follows other versions, perhaps derived from Valerius Antias. Tullus' home was said to be the Alban township of Medullia (Monte

Rotondo). But the pro-Sabine tradition endowed him with a Sabine grandmother,[40] and the desire to give him a paternal pedigree prompted the invention of a father who had been a companion of Romulus – though Cicero, who speaks well of Tullus,[41] no doubt does so partly because the king was reputedly a self-made man. According to other accounts he deteriorated into impiety, and, in particular, he was guilty of faulty religious observance, which was a vital matter to the Romans. His failure related to the ritual relating to Jupiter Elicius, which has just been mentioned in connection with Numa.

In the figure of Tullus Hostilius, as of Numa, we have a personage who, in spite of the mythical features of his career, may well have actually existed under some such name. For the Hostilii were a plebeian family of so little power during the fourth and third centuries B.C., when the Roman mythology was coming into being, that he is hardly likely to have been invented. The Hostilian house became eminent, it is true, in the second century B.C., but before that it is hard to see how they could have exercised sufficient influence to inject a wholly fictitious monarch, bearing their own name, at so prominent and antique a point in the mythical chronology.[42] For similar reasons the name given to the Roman senate-house at a very early date, *Curia Hostilia*, seems to suggest that there really was, at some antique time, an important individual called Hostilius. Whether he was a king of Rome or not, genealogically speaking he was a flash in the pan, since the family of that name only became prominent so very much later. And although these subsequent Hostilii no doubt claimed descent from the king, their claim – even on the assumption that he had really existed – must have been unfounded.

But the attribution of the downfall of Alba Longa to so ancient a date (672–640 B.C.) is implausible, since there are such strong reasons for supposing that the town remained the most important centre in Latium until it was superseded by Aricia in c. 500. The highlight of Tullus' war with Alba Longa, in the mythical tradition – the first emergence of the place out of the shadows for a very long time past – was the duel between two sets of brothers, three on either side, to determine the fate of the war. On the Roman side these champions were the Horatii, and the Albans were the Curiatii. The only victor, indeed the only survivor, was a single one of the Horatian brethren. However, this Horatius, returning home with his triple spoils, was met by his sister, who had been promised in marriage to one of the Curiatii. Horatius saw that she was weeping; whereupon he killed her, crying: 'So perish every Roman woman who mourns a foe!'[43] He was found guilty of treason, for taking the law into his own hands and usurping a function of the state. But he appealed to the Assembly and was acquitted.

The main features of the story had appeared in Ennius.[44] Then Livy, and in his more long-winded fashion Dionysius, made it into a lively psychological drama, lacking, for once, too strong an infusion of morality. Indeed, as Livy says, Horatius was acquitted 'more in admiration of his valour than from the justice of his cause'. Dionysius stresses this 'remarkable and unexpected reversal of fortune',[45] a theme suitably reminiscent of the fifth-century Athenian historian Thucydides, on whose work he wrote a treatise.

The Horatii, traditionally a leading family in the early years of the Republic (chapter 6, section 1), were one of the ancient houses, like the Hostilii, which had faded from view before history began – although, unlike the Hostilii, they did not enjoy a revival in the second century B.C., or indeed ever again.[46] Strangely enough, the Curiatii, although defeated according to this version of the tradition, were happy to play a part in keeping the tradition alive, for in later days the family still used the surname Trigeminus (triplet). They claimed a consul in the fifth century B.C., and later in the second century a Gaius Curiatius Trigeminus served as a moneyer.[47] But historians, Livy tells us, were divided as to whether the Curiatii were the Albans and the Horatii Romans, or vice versa – so it was evidently possible, if you were a later Curiatius, to say that yours was the side that had won. However, the majority view, Livy says, allocated the Curiatii to the Alban side, and Dionysius follows the same opinion. The latter adds, however, that the two sets of heroes were cousins, whose mothers were the twin daughters of an

Alban called Lucius Sicinius. This betrays the hand of the historian Gaius Licinius Macer, whose patronage demonstrably extended not only to past Licinii but to Sicinii as well, presumably on the erroneous grounds of an etymological connection between the two. And so not content with finding a brave, democratic Sicinius Dentatus in the fifth century B.C., Macer contrived to trace the family back into the even more mythical times of the grandparents of the Horatii and Curiatii.

Duels between champions are frequent enough in the mythology of Greece: and Robert the Bruce, in Scotland, and Cuchulain in Ulster, were comparable heroes who, like Horatius, fought against three opponents at the same time. Moreover, Horatius' killing of his sister had a parallel in the anti-feminist activities of Cuchulain, who disdained the provocations of a naked woman. Parsifal, too, made his escape from feminine wiles, and Siegfried rebuffed Brunhilde. Male tyrannizing over women is a common theme of European initiation myths, which require the heroic fury to burn itself out in this way.[48] But Horatius is brought down by his sister all the same, for the hero victorious over men but ruined by a woman is another very common mythological theme.

When this had happened to Horatius, it was necessary for him, like Cuchulain, to be reintegrated into society by a special ceremony, recalled by the expiatory rites and sacrifices which subsequently remained a tradition in the Horatian family.[49] Cuchulain was plunged into three successive vats to cool him down, and Horatius had to pass beneath a special yoke. This was identified as a beam, still surviving in Augustan times, which formed a cross bar over a street on a spur of the Esquiline hill, near the site of the future Colosseum. It was known as the *tigillum sororium*, and the story of Horatius is invoked to explain it on the assumption that the latter word comes from *soror*, sister – an assumption shared by Dionysius, who declares that after Horatius had murdered his sister an altar was erected to Juno 'to whom the care of sisters was allotted'.[50] As usual, however, this etymological zeal is misapplied, since the term had nothing to do with *soror*, sister, but was connected with Juno Sororia, the goddess who presided over the passage of girls into puberty (from *sororiare*, the first swelling of the breasts). When the altar was erected to Juno, another, it was added, was set up in honour of Janus Curiatius, Janus being the god of beginnings, linked with *ianua*, a gate. This was, in fact, a cult parallel to that of Juno Sororia, and was concerned with the initiation of boys into puberty as warriors. The bringing in of the boys from each ward (*curia*) may have provided the epithet of Janus, and subsequently the name of the Curiatian family which no doubt served him.[51] The Horatii, on the other hand, had at some stage given their names to a pillar ('Horatian Spears', *pila Horatia*) and a tomb with which it was associated. These monuments were, in due course, interpreted respectively as the pillar Horatius had adorned with his triple spoils, and the grave where his sister was buried. And there were five other ancient tombs on the way to Alba Longa, which could conveniently be identified as the burial places of his slain brothers and enemies. Indeed, they may have helped to establish the tradition that six warriors were involved.

The myth of their combat seemed useful to the Romans because it stressed the legal justification of Rome's succession to Alba Longa; although, curiously enough, the duel is followed in Livy's account by a battle (in which the Romans were victorious) between the two armies, a story which evidently represented the survival of a rival tradition. But this was not the only way in which the Roman mythologists, as very often happened, allowed their remarkable legal-mindedness to run riot over this saga. In particular, they used it as a text for the right of Appeal to the sovereign Assembly (*provocatio*). We are told that Horatius put forward such an appeal, although in historical fact the regulations governing this process did not exist even in embryo until *c*. 450 B.C., and did not become law until 300. Elsewhere, we find the Romans, in the passion to give venerable antiquity to their institutions, assigning the right of appeal to the first year of the Republic.[52] But here it is set back much further still, to the third of the kings – though what sort of an Assembly really existed in the seventh century B.C. we cannot tell. Emphasis upon this right of appeal to the Assembly, and upon the ancient date of such a right, was a tradition which would find special favour among the democratically minded, anti-Sullan historians of the first century B.C. such as Licinius Macer, who were keen to stress the antiquity of the Assembly's sovereign powers.

After Tullus Hostilius, in the accepted list of kings, came Ancus Marcius, a man of peace following a man of war just as, previously, the peaceful Numa had followed the warlike Romulus.[53]

The events attributed to the reign of Ancus Marcius include the building of the first wooden bridge across the Tiber and the first colonization of Rome's port of Ostia. There are, however, doubts whether either happening can, in reality, be dated as early as the period to which Ancus' reign was assigned (642–617 B.C.). The bridge seems rather more likely to belong to Rome's Etruscan period in the sixth century. And Ancus' alleged settlement at Ostia, although recorded by Ennius,[54] has so far lacked any archaeological corroboration. This in itself might not be very significant, since the colony could have been located in one of the unexplored sectors that lie to the east of the modern or ancient town of Ostia. But it does seem an ominous coincidence that the first demonstrable settlement in the place, during the fourth century B.C. – the period which reveals the first archaeological traces of the town –was the work of a man with Ancus' family name, Gaius Marcius Rutilus. His colonization of Ostia, evidently authentic, followed a victory over the Etruscans.

He was the first Marcius to appear in the Fasti,[55] and it was probably in the time of his great career that the Marcii became a family important enough to influence the national mythology. They were, moreover, a plebeian family, and therefore needed a mythical origin more urgently than the great patrician houses, which could afford (though one does not always notice it) to make less exaggerated claims. The suspicion that Ancus Marcius owes his place in the king-list to the prompting of later Marcii seems to be confirmed by the fact that the surname of one branch of the family was Rex. This cognomen was, in fact, originally adopted to indicate descent from the first plebeian *rex sacrorum*, the holder of a priesthood which, in the earliest days of the Republic, took over some of the functions earlier possessed by the monarchy (chapter 1). But the surname could also easily be reinterpreted to give the impression that it went all the way back to a king of Rome instead.

The Marcii were probably a family from southern Latium – hence the mysterious Cnaeus Marcius Coriolanus (connected with Corioli in that area) who bore their name (chapter 6, section 1). But they also managed, with the help of Varro, to cash in on the tendency to exalt Sabine origins. For Ancus Marcius was declared to be a grandson, on his mother's side, of the Sabine Numa Pompilius,[56] a tradition which resembles Greek, Celtic and German myths in its reflection of customs involving succession through the female line – the myths imported from unidentifiable earlier matrilinear societies by peoples that had later come to live by patriarchal customs. It was in pursuance of this supposed link of kinship between the two monarchs that a Marcius of 90 B.C., serving as moneyer at a time when his family was standing high once again, depicted Numa and Ancus together on his coins.[57] He was Gaius Marcius Censorinus, a prominent Marian and anti-Sullan; and Julius Caesar, on the death of his father's sister Julia, the widow of the great general Marius, delivered a funeral address tracing her descent and his own back through her mother, who was the daughter of a Marcius Rex, to Ancus Marcius. Moreover, in the following decade Julius Caesar's niece Atia, marrying for the second time, became the wife of a member of the Marcian house (Lucius Marcius Philippus, consul, 56 B.C.), who thus became the stepfather of Octavian; and a second Atia, perhaps the younger sister of the other one, married Philippus' son of the same name (consul 38). So in view of these connections with Octavian, who became Augustus, a favourable eye was likely to be turned upon the family's ancestral claims and upon the mythical king Ancus Marcius on whom they depended.

Yet in spite of this dynastic emphasis two quite different contradictory traditions about Ancus persisted and survived. Livy and Dionysius both offer a very favourable verdict on his reign, and Cicero had already done the same. For here was another 'new man' – even the very name of Ancus' own father, the orator is glad to point out, was unknown.[58] In marked contrast, however, Virgil outspokenly criticizes the monarch as a noisy demagogue – 'too boastful Ancus, already overfond of the breath of popular favour'.[59] This version, wherever it originated, was clearly favoured by people who did not look kindly upon eulogies of his royal Marcian ancestry uttered by Julius Caesar (about whom Virgil is ambivalent). And indeed, in order to denigrate Ancus Marcius further, it was suggested that Tullus Hostilius did not die from a divine judgement after all, as had been suggested, but was actually murdered by his successor Ancus, 'with many of the Roman's aiding him'. Dionysius, who quotes the story,[60] goes on to declare that he does not believe it. But it rang satisfactorily in the ears of conservatives of the first century B.C., who feared over-ambitious *populares* and demagogues like Caesar. The tale itself, however, may well be earlier than Caesar's time, because it fitted in with a theory, fashionable in the second century B.C., which held that the main forms of government and constitution habitually succeed one another and each deteriorate one after another. People who held these views liked to detect a consistent process of decline in the Roman monarchy after Numa, and were therefore predisposed to find fault with Ancus.[61]

2 THE ETRUSCAN MONARCHY AT ROME

A Greek named Demaratus, Livy tells us, came from Corinth in Greece and settled at Tarquinii in Etruria. Then, during the reign of Ancus Marcius, his son Lucumo and Lucumo's wife, an Etruscan woman called Tanaquil, moved from Tarquinii to Rome, where they were received into the friendship of the king. Lucumo assumed the name of Lucius Tarquinius Priscus, and after the death of Ancus was unanimously elected to the throne in his place. He fought wars, enlarged the senate, constructed Rome's principal drain (the *Cloaca Maxima*), began work on the Temple of Jupiter, Juno and Minerva on the Capitol, and brought Etruscan customs and craftsmen to Rome.

As a single individual, Tarquinius Priscus may well never

have existed, any more than we can necessarily believe in the existence of his grandson, Lucius Tarquinius Superbus. Indeed, there is, in many respects, a confusion and duplication between the activities of the two Tarquins.[62] True, similar confusions cloud the distinction between Elijah and Elisha, but it would not be legitimate to conclude that the distinction between them has to be abolished. On the other hand it is easy to believe that the duality of the Tarquins was invented because it was necessary for the last Tarquin to be a tyrant, defeated and replaced by the glorious Republic (chapter 6, section 1), and it seemed uncomfortable that the increase of prosperity which undoubtedly came to Rome with the Tarquins should have to be attributed to one and the same man. Perhaps the distinction between the two kings was first made as early as the fourth century B.C. But there is reason to suppose that a large part in the creation of the tradition was played by the historian Fabius Pictor, writing during or after the Second Punic War.

On the other hand the events associated with the figure of Tarquinius Priscus do symbolize our arrival at least on the borderlands between mythology and history. For the traditional dates of his reign (616–579 B.C.), and the belief that he imported Etruscan institutions (though this belief was blurred by the usual attempts to antedate a number of them),[63] harmonize dramatically, for the first time, with the findings of archaeology. For it was precisely in the last quarter of the seventh century B.C. that excavations display the transformation of Rome into an Etruscan city (chapter 1). It remained Etruscan for a century or more, and indeed still remained more or less Etruscanized (though not necessarily under an Etruscan king) during the earlier part of the fifth century (chapter 6, section 1).

The figures of Tarquinius Priscus and Tarquinius Superbus are too few to represent the whole of that period, or even that part of it during which Rome was still unmistakably a monarchic state. There must have been more 'Tarquins' than that; though they did not necessarily all bear the same name. But those that did, or some of them, presumably belonged to the recorded Tarchna family. It cannot, however, be considered at all certain that the Etruscan city from which they came to Rome was necessarily Tarquinii. This may only have been chosen because the presence of a Tarquin at Rome so obviously recalled the name of the place. More probably, the Tarchna came from Caere, where (Latinizing their names as Tarquitius) they possessed a family mausoleum, containing tombs from the fifth to the third century B.C. (chapter 2, section 2). Besides, unlike Tarquinii, which was forty miles away, Caere was only just across the Tiber from Rome, and always enjoyed far closer relationships with the Romans.

However, theories that Etruscan Rome was subject to Caere, or to any other city of Etruria, are implausible. It was another independent Etruscan city-state. A tradition noted by Dionysius recording that five other Etruscan cities, in the northern part of the country, formed a coalition against Tarquinius Priscus,[64] preserves a dim memory of the vigorous inter-city politics of the time, in which, despite the existence of a federation of the city-states of Etruria (largely religious in character), these states, grouped in variously shifting alliances, were often at war with one another. As for Priscus' supposed original name 'Lucumo', it is merely the Etruscan word for king or chieftain. Both Tarquins, however, on becoming adoptive Romans, were retrospectively invested with the Roman first name (*praenomen*) of Lucius. This gave them the full three names customary at Rome. In historical fact, however, this form of nomenclature did not come into existence for at least two centuries after the downfall of the Etruscan monarchy. 'Lucius' seems to have been inferred, by a Romanizing process based on sound rather than etymology, from 'Lucumo' which had been the title of these Etruscan kings.[65]

Tarquinius Priscus is symbolic of another genuine historical development as well. For, at least as early as Fabius Pictor, he was stated to be the son of the wealthy and noble Greek Demaratus, who had fled from his native Corinth to escape Cypselus, the latter being an authenticated 'tyrant' who overthrew the aristocratic Corinthian families in *c.* 657 B.C. Pliny the elder adds a detailed account of the craftsmen whom Demaratus brought with him from Corinth to Etruria, and he even gives their names.[66] This tradition, coupled with the belief, voiced by Cicero, that Priscus was the man largely responsible for the influx of Greek culture into Rome,[67] fits in remarkably well with the discovery by modern archaeologists that Corinthian pottery was being imported in very large quantities into Etruria and Rome, and imitated by Etruscan and Roman copyists, at precisely the epoch in which Tarquinius Priscus was supposed to have reigned. If we like to use the word 'myth' for purely fictitious stories, and the term 'legend' for stories which although largely fictitious have a core or basis of historical fact (chapter 7, note 24), the tales about Tarquinius Priscus come under the heading of legend. Even if the career ascribed to Tarquinius Priscus may be partly or largely fictitious, or distributable among a number of other figures whom we cannot identify, these stories purporting to relate to him represent developments that really took place.

Demaratus was remembered by fourth-century Greek historians drawing on Corinthian records and traditions. But Roman writers of later days felt uncomfortable about Tarquinius Priscus; and according to their own political and racial standpoints, they formed two divergent opinions about him. The fact was that the mythology of the Tarquins, reflecting as it did an embarrassing but at least partially historical course of events, was rather indigestible. 'Roman pride', as R. M. Ogilvie observes,

was always aware that the Tarquins were interlopers and that Rome had fallen into the hands of a foreign power, but it was equally reluctant to explain this humiliation by an Etruscan conquest of Rome. In this dilemma the historians, while accepting the appearance of the Tarquins in the king-list of tradition, were anxious to dispute their legitimacy.[68]

Thus Livy, for example, is somewhat hostile to the first Tarquins,[69] emphasizing the restless pride of Priscus' wife Tanaquil, and her husband's intrigues. These were displayed by a tricky exclusion of his nephew from an inheritance, and by unfair treatment of Ancus' sons at Rome: insertions which go back to the second century B.C., when this type of legalistic material tended to be introduced into distant epochs of the past. Dionysius, on the other hand, avoids any implied censure of

Tanaquil, relying, apparently, on the favourable version of Ennius,[70] and refraining from any suggestion of impropriety regarding the accession.

Quite apart from the high feelings which the question of Etruscan influence perennially aroused at Rome (chapter 2, section 2), there were two issues here which could invite conflicting interpretations in the first century B.C. One, already encountered twice before, was the desirability or otherwise of 'new men' obtaining great office; and Tanaquil is made to invoke this principle explicitly, in truly Ciceronian fashion (though, for the benefit of the people who liked pedigrees, there was the usual alternative version of a Lucumo who had been a contemporary of Romulus).[71] She and her husband also insist on the precedents and justifications for allowing people from other parts of Italy, Etruscans like themselves or Sabines like supposed earlier kings, to occupy high places in the city. Here one can detect the influence of the controversies about Rome's attitude to the Italians which broke out in 91 B.C. into the Social or Marsian war. And, as we shall see a little later on, the same theme subsequently became dear to the emperor Claudius.

Livy utilizes the figure of Priscus' wife – whose name Tanaquil is Etruscan – in order to introduce a highly theatrical element. Cicero and Dionysius had played this down and at an earlier stage Polybius seemed to approve of Tanaquil. Fabius Pictor even tried to make her into a Roman matron. Moreover, instead of her Etruscan name, she is sometimes given a Roman one, Gaia Caecilia,[72] the name of a family which enjoyed long periods of predominance in the Roman state during the third and particularly the second century B.C., and again in the time of Sulla of whose supporters they formed the nucleus (chapter 3, section 1). This is yet another example of divergent and rival Etruscan and Roman traditions (cf. chapter 4, section 2). In the present case, rather unusually, it is the Etruscan name which has prevailed – thanks to Livy – because of the greater dramatic possibilities of the story it represents. Nevertheless, the idea that Priscus' wife was not an Etruscan at all, but an honest Roman housewife who occupied herself in the blameless weaving of woollen clothes, did not die out, for her alleged spindle and distaff were still shown in historic times within a Roman temple, and a toga she had woven was displayed in another shrine.[73] But Livy, possibly following some Latin play that has not come down to us, has painted a vivid picture of a formidable woman who secures the throne first for her husband and then for her protégé who succeeds him. We are back in the world of forceful females which Greek historians had so greatly enjoyed, following the supreme example of Herodotus. And now Augustan historians, having the ogress Cleopatra in mind, were not sorry to tackle the theme again.

Livy's treatment of the subject reminds us that we are in the presence of a Roman tradition which disapproved of the licence accorded to Etruscan women. Votive statuettes from Caere suggest that the ordinary Etruscan was more interested in goddesses than in gods; and on the human plane, the women of Etruria, or at least the greatest of them, enjoyed a liberty and power to which wool-weaving, stay-at-home Roman matrons could never aspire. The grave-ornaments of the princess Larthia, from Caere,[74] show how resplendent such ladies must have been. And the vividness of Livy's Tanaquil, typical of the whole Tarquin family whom he galvanizes into a life which his Romulus or Tatius wholly lacked, is surely indebted to a vigorous Etruscan tradition, now lost but seen dimly through the mirror of Augustan Romans and Greeks.

One of the most potent and durable elements in this Etruscan tradition was the belief that the Tarquins, between them, had begun (Priscus) and completed (Superbus) the construction of the Capitoline temple of Jupiter, Juno and Minerva. It must have been tempting for the Romans to ascribe this sacred national shrine to the ostensibly Roman regime of the Republic which so nobly overthrew the kings. And, indeed, the tradition did its best by withholding the final dedication of the temple from the kings, so that it could be located in the first year of the Republic (chapter 6, section 1). But the historians did not go further than that and attribute the entire enterprise to the Republic, for the detailed tradition of the Etruscan origin of the temple made this an impossible task.

Varro knew of a report that the temple's statue of Jupiter,

made of clay and painted with cinnabar, was commissioned by Tarquinius Priscus from an Etruscan sculptor, Vulca of Veii.[75] This was the sort of major work of art which, together with the small statuettes of Aeneas and others produced by Veii and other centres (chapter 4, section 3), stimulated the Romans to picture the gods and goddesses more clearly in human shape and to clothe them in a mythology.[76] It is true that Rome succeeded, in many ways, in suppressing its Etruscan tradition, or in concealing it by partial absorption. But religion and myth were vital portions of the inheritance which could not by any means be entirely suppressed. Or, if attempts were indeed made to do so, Roman and Etruscan antiquarians of the first century B.C. and later made it their business to try, still in the face of anti-Etruscan opposition, to disinter them.

The alleged successor of Tarquinius Priscus was Servius Tullius (578–535). After supernatural signs and portents had accompanied his conception and childhood, he was brought up in the king's house as a slave. It was believed that the sons of Ancus Marcius murdered Priscus, because they were indignant at Servius Tullius' rise to favour; and then Tanaquil arranged for Servius, who was in her confidence, to ascend to the throne. And so he became king, and the tradition maintained that he undertook important constitutional reforms, built the first wall round Rome, and instituted the cult of Diana on the Aventine Hill.

   This account, reproduced by the Augustans, was probably based, in most respects, on Fabius Pictor. But during the intervening years his version had been modified by conflicting views that arose about Servius Tullius. Some authorities praised him as a Latin who temporarily interrupted the domination of the Etruscans over Rome; the point was emphasized by recounting the wars he fought against the cities of Etruria.[77] Others, however, found it impossible to forget that the monarchy, after the first two kings, was supposed, according to a constitutional theory we have already encountered under Ancus, to be in a state of continuous decline, so that Servius Tullius had to be made to show at least a hint of tyrannical character. But

Valerius Antias, who introduced into his narrative some of the doom-laden, apprehensive air of Rome in the 80s, looked back upon Servius Tullius as an anticipation of his saviour Sulla (chapter 2, section 3). For both men, the historian maintained, made praiseworthy attempts to strengthen the conservative establishment. And at one point Antias even made Servius consider abdication, in order to provide a prototype for the abdication of Sulla.[78]

The nature of Servius' constitutional reforms is profoundly disputed. At least, however, it may be hazarded that certain reforms did take place at the time when he is supposed to have reigned, since changes of the kind were only to be expected amid the rapid expansion of sixth-century Rome (chapter 1).[79] But, in the absence of incontrovertible evidence on the subject, it was very easy for historians writing centuries later to invest these reforms with diametrically opposed interpretations. Thus Dionysius, presumably using two different and incompatible sources, first says that the innovations favoured the rich, but then goes on to declare that the king courted the support of the poor.[80] This shows the same equivocal spirit as Cicero's remark that Servius was the first monarch to be selected by the senate and not the people – a statement followed by the implicitly contradictory assertion that he ruled with popular goodwill and consent (Cicero adds that he tactfully called the rich 'money-givers' and the poor 'child-givers').[81]

These were burning issues in the first century B.C., and on the whole the second view of Servius Tullius prevailed – reflecting, it now seems, a correct view of Rome's later monarchs, who may well have laid a heavy hand on the local aristocracy. The predominance of this democratic interpretation of Servius Tullius is confirmed by Cicero's allusion to a performance of Accius' tragic drama *Brutus*, containing a reference to 'Tullius who for the citizens had made freedom firm' – words which, to Cicero's great gratification, were loudly encored with reference to himself, since he had suppressed the conspiracy of Catiline.[82] And in the previous century, too, the story of Servius Tullius had no doubt already been slanted in accordance with whether one was in favour of the 'popular' Gracchi or their pro-senatorial 'optimate' opponents. In the service of the one side or the other, the tale gained a lot of new details, and stimulated many pious frauds, in which the Struggle of the Orders in the fifth and fourth centuries B.C. was also brought into play (chapter 6, section 1).

Livy noted this dual tradition about King Servius in his sources. Indeed, if the time available to so prolific a writer permitted such an indulgence, he may even have puzzled over it. As a result, he decided to compromise, seeking to present a basically good king whose fault was opportunism, and whose merely human efforts could not prevail against the majesty of the divine plan. But this careful, indeed acrobatic, balance tended to be set awry by the irresistible claims of high drama. These theatrical possibilities, as before, centred upon the figure of Tanaquil. Greek tragic echoes abound, notably in the account of the death of Tarquinius Priscus. Aeschylus and the House of Atreus are never far from Livy's mind. For example, the figure of Servius Tullius displays more than a hint of Aegisthus, who insinuated himself into the palace of the murdered Agamemnon with the backing of the latter's wife Clytaemnestra. It is not altogether surprising, therefore, to find Virgil deciding that this was too equivocal a tradition to handle. In his panorama of Rome's future, which is vouchsafed to Aeneas, all the other kings are mentioned. But Servius Tullius is just left out. It was too difficult to know what to say about him.

There was a famous mystery about his birth. He was said to have been a slave – probably because his name Servius was believed to come from *servus*, although in fact it does not, but like his other name Tullius is probably a Latinization of an Etruscan root. But even if this servile origin was accepted, there were two possible ways of looking at it. People like Cicero, who were for their own political reasons happy enough to see men of undistinguished antecedents in power, had no reason to regard Servius Tullius as anything other than a slave by birth. But others, whose political interests required that good families should get their due or more than their due, indicated that his mother Ocresia, alleged to be a prisoner of war of the Romans, had formerly been the wife of the prince of a captured town,

Corniculum (Montecello, on the way to Tivoli);[83] and this was the version which Livy accepted. The same concern for legitimacy led to the further supposition that Servius married his predecessor's daughter.

As to his paternity, the mythical tradition assumed more sensational forms. The idea that his father was a mortal Latin or Etruscan – perhaps Tarquinius Priscus, or one of his dependents – seemed too dull. Livy, in recounting Servius' career, omits all reference to the point, but at a later stage he quotes the view that 'Servius had no father'.[84] Dionysius, on the other hand, preserves an Etruscan report that he was born to Ocresia of a male organ, belonging to Vulcan or a household god, which rose up out of the fire – exactly the story which was told in Etruria about Romulus and Remus as well (chapter 4, section 2). Knowing that the Romans were chary about endowing people with supernatural origins (chapter 2, cf. note 7), Dionysius is somewhat apologetic about this version, which he only wants to put forward 'if it be pleasing to the gods and daemons that it be related'. Nevertheless, both he and Livy also ascribe to Servius the very familiar mythological tale recounting that in his infancy a flame was seen playing round his head as he slept. And, like Numa, he was credited with a divine consort, Fortuna or the Etruscan Nortia. For Servius Tullius deserved the same sort of supernatural portent as Romulus and Numa, since he was regarded, like them, as a new Founder of Rome. He had founded the social order as Numa had founded religion, and as Romulus had founded the city itself. Consequently, a most unusual quota of solemn divine interventions was only to be expected.

To get down to earth, the tradition that Servius constructed a wall round Rome is not confirmed by the so-called 'Wall of Servius Tullius', since that must be dated to the fourth century B.C. on archaeological grounds. But remnants of earthworks designed to block the heads of the valleys leading in to the city from the east can, rather precariously, be attributed to a date approaching the notional period of Servius' reign, on the basis of fragmentary finds of Attic red-figure vases. However, a statement that Servius Tullius was the first to stamp a design on bronze coinage is totally anachronistic, since nothing of the kind, however rudimentary, existed for centuries after his alleged lifetime.[85] He was also said to have installed the worship of Diana on the Aventine. Its previous centre had been Aricia, the town which, as we have seen, took over the leadership of the Latins from Alba Longa. But Aricia was still flourishing and presumably independent in *c.* 500, so that it does seem possible that the transfer of the headquarters of the cult of Diana to Rome should be attributed to the fifth century instead, that is to say quite a bit later than the dates attributed to Servius Tullius.

In the foregoing account of Servius Tullius, whether the favourable or unfavourable versions are considered, we have been looking at what must be regarded, in the main, as a Roman tradition. But there was also an entirely different tradition emanating from Etruria. In connection with other myths, notably those of Romulus and Tanaquil, it has been suggested that dim traces can be seen, beneath the Roman version, of a largely suppressed, deviant, Etruscan rendering. In the present case both traditions happen to have come down to us, and they can therefore be compared.

We owe the continued existence of the Etruscan version to two pieces of chance: the survival of a speech by the emperor Claudius (A.D. 48), and the survival of wall-paintings from a tomb at Vulci (? 4th cent.). The speech of Claudius is preserved, to a substantial extent, upon a bronze tablet that was found at Lugdunum (Lyon). It was designed to persuade the Roman senate of the desirability of admitting a number of Gallic nobles to its ranks.

I myself deprecate that first thought of everyone, which I foresee will be my chief and first obstacle – you should not be alarmed, as if a novelty is being introduced, but rather think of all the many novelties which this city has undergone, and of the many shapes and forms which our commonwealth assumed right from the origin of our city.

At one time kings ruled the city, and yet they did not hand the kingship on to successors of their own house. Outsiders, and even foreigners, came in; Numa, who succeeded Romulus, came from the Sabines, a neighbour it is true, but in those days a foreigner, and

Ancus Marcius was followed by Priscus Tarquinius. He, owing to his impure blood – his father was Demaratus of Corinth and his mother a noble lady of Tarquinii, but poor, seeing that she had to descend to such a husband – since he was excluded from holding office at home, migrated to Rome and obtained the kingship. He, too, and his son or grandson – the authorities differ on this point – was succeeded by Servius Tullius, who was, if we follow our historians, son of the captive Ocresia, if we follow the Etruscans a former faithful companion of Caelius Vivenna and the companion of all his fortunes, who, when after various turns of fortune he had been expelled with all the survivors of Caelius' army and left Etruria, occupied the Caelian hill, so called from his leader Caelius, and changing his name (for he had been called Mastarna in Tuscan) took the name by which I have spoken of him and obtained the kingship to the great advantage of the commonwealth.[86]

The most surprising feature of this statesmanlike, if somewhat diffuse and oppressively learned, discourse is Claudius' declaration that Servius Tullius, before that was what he was called, had borne the Etruscan name of Mastarna. Claudius adds that he had been a comrade of Caelius Vivenna (elsewhere written as Caeles Vibenna), after whom Rome's Caelian Hill was named.

The same two names, Mastarna and Vibenna, recur on a remarkable series of wall-paintings from the François Tomb at Vulci in southern Etruria. They are now in the Torlonia Museum at Rome. Five pairs of figures are represented, with their names indicated in Etruscan letters. One of the five scenes depicts Macstrna, a name that is evidently to be identified with Mastarna. He is shown freeing Caile Vipinas (Caeles Vibenna) from captivity by cutting his wrist-cords with a sword; and he has brought another sword with him, for the use of his liberated friend. The other four pairs of figures are warriors pitted against one another in single combat. The cities of the defeated champions are named, but not those of the victors since they all presumably came from Vulci, where the tomb they adorned was located. Larth Ulthese, whose family name resembles that of a first-century Roman moneyer called Volteius[87], is seen killing Laris Papathnas Velznach (Lars Papatius of Etruscan Volsinii).

Rasce (Rascius) is slaying Pesna Arcmsnas Sveamach (Pesius
Arcumnius of Etruscan Suana). Avle Vipinas (Aulus Vibenna) is
cutting down Venthical ... plsachs (from Falerii?). Marce Camitlnas (M. Camitilius) is killing Cneve Tarchunies Rumach
(Cnaeus Tarquinius of Rome).

What is shown here, apparently, is a struggle which Vulci
was waging against other Etruscan city-states, such as Volsinii
and Suana which lay to its west, and against hybrid, Etruscan-
controlled cities including Rome and perhaps Falerii. Or was it
only the warrior-champions of the cities who were fighting,
since that is what 'Laris' and 'Larth' seem to mean? At all events,
they are engaged in single combat, like the Horatii and Curiatii
(chapter 5, section 1), in the spirit of the Theban cycle with its
duel between Eteocles and Polynices (chapter 4, section 2) which
these paintings from Vulci seem to echo. But whatever is happening, here is a slice of history or myth that has dropped right
out of our military tradition. Which is it, history or myth?
The paintings were made at some time between the fourth
and second centuries inclusive – perhaps in *c.* 340–310. But the
heroic deed they record must have been ascribed to some date
not later, or not much later, than the sixth century B.C., when
Rome was still an Etruscan city-state – that is to say, the pic-
tures relate to a time when it was still possible for a Roman
champion to be called Tarquinius. In other words, there is a
considerable time-gap between the alleged events and the
painter who depicted them. He is earlier, it is true, than the
surviving sources that record events of the same period, but not
so much earlier as all that. If the literary record deserves to
be called myth, then these paintings merit the same description. This is epic rather than history. But it is an epic cycle of
Etruscan Vulci, not of Greece or Rome. It is by no means unlikely that there were Etruscan epic poems, or tragic dramas,
dealing with the same range of subjects (chapter 2, section 2).

Since Mastarna was evidently a famous hero, this must be the
Mastarna whom the emperor Claudius equated with Servius
Tullius. Similar names, such as Masterna, are known from
Etruscans in the Roman army (a suggested link with *magister*
is dubious). Our literary tradition, dating from the time of

Fabius Pictor, has presented a basically Roman version of Servius. Here, on the other hand, preserved by two accidents, is an Etruscan version, identifying him with Mastarna. We are faced with a difficult choice. To ask if the king was really Roman (Latin) or Etruscan is perhaps to ask the wrong question, because the obvious myths encrusting his career make it doubtful whether a man of either name really existed, or, if he did, whether he performed any of the actions attributed to Servius. But the important point is whether the Etruscan domination of Rome, represented by Tarquinius Priscus and Tarquinius Superbus, was really, as the canonical Roman king-list indicates, interrupted by a non-Etruscan – a native Latin. The alternative possibility is that this theory is merely a patriotic distortion: and that the supposed Servius Tullius, as Claudius believed, came from Etruria. In that case we must conclude that the Roman monarchy, once Etruscan, remained Etruscan without a break until it was superseded by the Republic.

A number of arguments can be mustered in support of either of these diametrically opposed conclusions. The first thesis is favoured by the sheer weight and persistence of the Roman tradition that this new Founder was a Latin. On the other hand it is also true that the Roman writers were all too likely to take that line, whether it corresponded with the facts or not, in order to prevent some of the benefits which clearly accrued to Rome during this sixth century from being attributed to an Etruscan.[88] The emperor Claudius, however, would not be likely to suffer from any such prejudice, because he was an enthusiastic expert on the Etruscans who studied their sources and wrote about their history at great length (chapter 2, section 2) – and did so at a date when passions had cooled. He was also, perhaps, writing to flatter the Etruscan pride of one of his wives.

Claudius indicated that Mastarna was the same person as Servius Tullius, exchanging the former name for the latter. But the emperor may have been wrong. Perhaps Mastarna, if he ever existed, was not Servius Tullius at all, but some different condottiere or adventurer who raided Rome but never quite ranked as a king. However, Claudius based his identification on certain authorities, whom he does not specify (one of them is likely to have been Dionysius of Halicarnassus), and what he says perhaps possesses a kind of symbolical correctness at least. Even if the personages were mythical, he may have been right in denying that the figure of Servius Tullius indicated that there was a Latin intrusion in Rome's Etruscan kinglist. Perhaps there was no such interruption, and it was only inserted as a nationalistic Roman fiction. For we have no idea how many Etruscan kings of Rome there were. For example Cnaeus Tarquinius the Roman, whose surprise and downfall at the hands of an unknown warrior of Vulci is shown on one of the François Tomb paintings, may possibly have been a transient king[89] whose name will need to be added to those of the Tarquins of tradition, Priscus and Superbus.

Claudius suggests that Mastarna of Vulci was the hero of many romantic exploits. *Varia fortuna* is the phrase he uses for them; and these adventures, the imperial historian adds, included expulsion from Etruria 'with the survivors of Caelius Vivenna's army', followed by their occupation of Rome's Caelian hill. A literary tradition, preserved by the Augustan antiquarian Verrius Flaccus who knew and wrote a lot about Etruria, likewise records the arrival at Rome, in the company of the brothers Vibenna, of a certain Max - - - who is probably Mastarna.[90] Claudius remarks that, in consequence of the exploits of Caeles Vibenna, the hill which Mastarna occupied at Rome was named the Caelian, a view that can be traced to Varro – though he dates the saga earlier, locating it right back in the times of Romulus.[91] Tacitus too, who records that Caeles Vibenna was given the Caelian hill by a Roman king as a reward for his help,[92] is equally doubtful who the king was, or when the events happened.

These are all variants of a once extensive and prominent Etruscan tradition, which, apart from the fragmentary notices just quoted, has wholly disappeared from the Roman canon. On the paintings of the François tomb Caeles Vibenna is being freed from captivity by his hero-friend Mastarna, while Caeles' brother Aulus Vibenna is killing a warrior who may come from Falerii. Elsewhere the two Vibennas are again depicted together attacking the seer Cacus (chapter 3, section 1 and note 13). The name of Aulus Vibenna, in the form of Avile Vipiiennas, also appears on a mid-sixth-century black vase dedicated at Veii (though possibly made at Vulci), and a century later the names are found again on another vase.[93]

The same hero may also play a central part, posthumously, in a further myth. When the foundations of the Capitoline Temple were being laid, the head of a certain Olus, described as a man of Vulci, was discovered intact in the excavations; the scene is represented on Etruscan gems. Olus is probably the same as Aulus Vibenna. One source, belonging to the mid fourth century A.D. but no doubt drawing on an earlier authority, describes Olus as a king.[94] This does not necessarily mean a king of Rome, though he could have been one of the men to whom Etruscan mythology assigned such a rank during those troubled times. But whether, and at what points, these Etruscan myths – or for that matter the canonical Roman versions which have won so very much more attention – incorporate a certain measure of historical fact is extraordinarily difficult, in the present state of our knowledge, to decide: because of the very long gap between the alleged date of the events and their first written record.

According to Roman tradition, the successor of Servius Tullius, and the last king of Rome, was Tarquinius Priscus' grandson Lucius Tarquinius Superbus (the Proud).[95] Instigated by his sister-in-law Tullia (the daughter of Servius Tullius), Tarquinius Superbus murdered her husband Arruns Tarquinius in order to marry her himself. And then he murdered the old king and seized the throne, without the authorization, it was added, of Senate or Assembly.

Thereafter Tarquinius Superbus was believed to have maintained his internal power by strong-arm methods. He also waged foreign wars; and their spoils enabled him to continue work on the Temple of Jupiter, Juno and Minerva on the Capitol. He was able to seize Gabii (Torre di Castiglione, twelve miles from Rome) after his son Sextus Tarquinius, who was in the confidence of its people, had executed their leaders, having been encouraged to do so because his father, when asked what to do, had remained silent but had switched off the heads of the tallest poppies in his garden. Soon afterwards, however,

When the sons of Tarquinius Superbus had gone to Delphi and were consulting the oracle as to which of them should be king in Rome, answer was made that the first man to kiss his mother would reign. This response the princes themselves explained otherwise, but Lucius Junius Brutus, who had accompanied them, pretended to fall upon his face, and kissed the earth.

And the outcome sanctioned his act. For when Tarquinius Superbus had brought all men to hate him by the violence of his behaviour, and finally a certain Lucretia, whose chastity had been violated at night by the king's son Sextus, summoned her father Spurius Lucretius Tricipitinus and her husband Lucius Tarquinius Collatinus and, adjuring them not to leave her death unavenged, killed herself with a knife, Tarquinius was expelled, chiefly through the efforts of Brutus, after a reign of twenty-five years.[96]

Tarquinius Superbus provides a suitably bad end to the gradually deteriorating monarchy, and supplies a text for the thesis that kingship is no longer good when it has lost its original character. He displays violence and arrogance, *superbia*, and writers of the later Republic were extremely ready to see other hated figures of the past as reincarnated Tarquins. Thus Cicero compared him to Tiberius Gracchus, the democratic reformer of the second century B.C. whom the orator believed to have initiated the rule of violence;[97] and he also saw Tarquinius Superbus as the prototype of Catiline whose plot against the state he himself had put down. For it was above all attractive to identify the king – and, hopefully, his fate – with one's own contemporary political opponents. In particular, Cicero and many others were able to see this evil monarch as a prototype of the dominant autocrats of their own day, culminating in Caesar. 'Liberty' was again the livest of live issues, and Tarquinius Superbus provided the most obvious of warnings. It was his literary role to point the contrast between the flaws of the monarchy – and of rule by one man in general – and the perfection of the Republic.

He is the stock tyrant of the moralists – that is to say, a tyrant of a type highly familiar from Greek literature. Detached artificially from the more meritorious Priscus to serve this very purpose, he attracts around him a group of stories that are entirely Greek in character; indeed his career is an amalgamation of quite a number of different autocrats of Greek tradition. A clear example of the Greekness of these tales is provided by Tarquinius Superbus' silent decapitation of the highest poppies in order to show his son Sextus how to treat the leaders of Gabii. For Herodotus had told that Thrasybulus, tyrant of Miletus, advised Periander, tyrant of Corinth, how to rule by taking Periander's messenger for a walk and breaking off the loftiest ears of grain as he went along.[98] Dionysius noted the resemblance between the two stories. But he drew the conclusion that both were true, and that Tarquinius Superbus was deliberately imitating Thrasybulus; instead of deducing, as he should have, that mythologically minded historians had invented the Roman tale in imitation of the Greek one.

Gabii was a small Latin town, traditionally founded by Alba Longa, and later significant to the Romans because it was supposed to be the source of certain of their religious practices. The ancient historians do not quite appreciate that the attribution of such a miniature, parochial war to sixth-century Rome somewhat destroys their picture of a nation which was already prefiguring the imperialistic grandeur of the future.[99] In fact, though Rome was beginning to be quite an important little city-state, it was still, during the sixth century B.C., so restricted in size that a war against even so close a neighbour as this does not appear improbable. But the story was largely introduced because of an archaeological relic: a treaty with Gabii, on the oxhide-covering of a shield, was still preserved in Augustan times at the Temple of Semo Sancus Dius Fidius on the Quirinal. The treaty is commemorated by two of Augustus' moneyers belonging to the family of the Antistii, who came from Gabii.[100] There is no need to deny the authenticity of the document; at times such as this we seem to be leaving myth behind.

But the other alleged events of the reign of Tarquinius Superbus soon restore the impression that mythology is still in the ascendant. For not only is the key incident of the Gabii siege, as we have seen, of Greek origin, but the personality of Tullia is inflated by Livy and Dionysius into a fully-fledged villainess of Greek drama, who impelled Tarquin to kill her husband and her father Servius Tullius, to make her his wife, and to seize the throne. Livy, heightening the horrors with all the resources of his colourful technique, hints more or less explicitly at the analogy of Greek tragedy in general and Aeschylus' House of Atreus in particular,[101] relying, it would seem, upon a source unknown to Dionysius, which may have been one of the Latin plays of Accius relating to Roman mythological history.[102] And so Livy presents, as Dacre Balsdon puts it, his Lady Macbeth and Goneril rolled into one. Tullia plays the same dominant role as Tanaquil had played at the two previous changes of monarch; but she plays it in far more sinister fashion. Nevertheless, the historian does not forget, in the characteristically Roman manner, to plot his course of events meticulously upon an entire topographical map, including the Street of Crime (Vicus Sceleratus) which is explained – the true explanation having been lost – by the horrors perpetrated by Tullia.[103]

Young and vigorous as Tarquin was, he seized the aged Servius, carried him bodily from the Senate-house, and flung him down the steps into the street. Then he returned to quell the senators. The king's servants and retinue fled. While he himself was making his way, half-stunned and unattended, to the palace, he was caught and killed by Tarquin's assassins. It is thought that the deed was done at Tullia's suggestion: and such a crime was not, at least, inconsistent with her character. All agree that she drove into the Forum in an open carriage in a most brazen manner, and, calling her husband from the Senate-house, was the first to hail him as king.

Tarquin told her to go home, as the crowd might be dangerous. So she started off, and at the top of Cyprus street, where the shrine of Diana stood until recently, her driver was turning to the right to climb the Urbian slope on the way to the Esquiline, when he pulled up short in sudden terror and pointed to Servius' body lying mutilated in the road. There followed an act of bestial inhumanity – history preserves memory of it in the name of the street, the Street of Crime. The story goes that the crazed woman, driven to frenzy by the avenging ghosts of her sister and husband, drove the carriage over her father's body. Blood from the corpse stained her clothes and spattered the carriage, so that a grim relic of the murdered man was brought by those gory wheels to the house where she and her husband lived. The guardian gods of that house did not forget; they were to see to it, in their anger at the bad beginning of the reign, that as bad an end should follow.[104]

In this bad end of Tarquinius Superbus' reign, as in the bad beginning, another woman, too, was ascribed this same sort of leading role that women fulfilled in so many Greek mythical narratives. But instead of being a monster of evil, like Tullia, she is a paragon of virtue, the model of a thousand dramatizing moralists. This is Lucretia, whose rape by Sextus Tarquinius precipitated the downfall of the monarchy. One of those who tells the story is the Augustan historian from Greek Sicily, Diodorus.

Sextus, the son of Lucius Tarquinius Superbus, the king of the Romans, left and came to the city of Collatia, as it was called, and stopped at the home of Lucius Tarquinius Collatinus, a cousin of the king, whose wife was Lucretia, a woman of great beauty and virtuous in character. And Lucretia's husband being with the army in camp, the guest, awakening, left his bed-room during the night and set out to the wife who was sleeping in a certain chamber. And suddenly taking his stand at the door and drawing his sword, he announced that he had a slave all ready for slaughter, and that he would slay her together with the slave, as having been taken in adultery and having received at the hand of her husband's nearest of kin the punishment she deserved. Therefore, he continued, it would be the wiser thing for her to submit to his desires without calling out, and as a reward for her favour she would receive great gifts and be his wife and become queen, exchanging the hearth of a private citizen for the first place in the state.

Lucretia, panic-stricken at so unexpected a thing, and fearing that men would in truth believe that she had been slain because of adultery, made no outcry at the time. But when the day came and Sextus departed, she summoned her kinsmen and asked them not to allow the man to go unpunished who had sinned against the laws both of hospitality and of kinship. As for herself, she said, it was not proper for the victim of a deed of such wanton insolence to look upon the sun, and plunging a dagger into her breast she slew herself.

In connection with the violation of Lucretia by Sextus and her suicide because of the wrong done her, we do not believe it would be right to leave no record of the nobility of her choice. For the woman who renounced life of her own will in order that later generations might emulate her deed we should judge to be fittingly worthy of immortal praise, in order that women who choose to maintain the purity of their persons altogether free from censure may compare themselves with an authentic example.

Other women, indeed, even when such an act as this on their part is known, conceal what has been done, as a means of avoiding the punishment which is meted out for guilty acts. But she made known to the world what had been done in secret and then slew herself, leaving in the end of her life her fairest defence. And whereas other women advance a claim for pardon in matters done against their will, she fixed the penalty of death for the outrage done to her by force, in order that, even if one should wish to defame her, he should not have it in his power to condemn her choice as having been made of her own free will. For since men by nature prefer slander to praise, she cut the ground from under the accusation men who love to find fault might raise; since she considered it to be shameful that anyone could say that while her husband, to whom she was wedded in accordance with the laws, was still living, she had had relations with another man, contrary to the laws, and shameful also that she who had been involved in an act for which the laws decree the penalty of death upon the guilty should cling to life any longer. And so she chose, by a brief anticipation of death, a debt that in any case she owed to nature, to exchange disgrace for the highest approval. Consequently, not only did she win immortal glory in exchange for mortal life through her own act of virtue, but she also impelled her kinsmen and all the people to exact implacable punishment from those who had committed this lawless act against her.[105]

Here Diodorus has carried the ancient desire to point a moral to extraordinary lengths (chapter 7, section 2). Ovid prefers to dwell, with a hint of gloating, upon the horrid deed of Sextus.

> As friend this foe to Collatinus' hall
> Was welcomed: kinship made it natural.
> Ah, human blindness. All unwitting she
> Prepared a banquet for her enemy.
> The feast was done, and sleep its hour claimed.
> Night fell, and through the house no taper flamed.

He rose, and drew his gilded sword, and hied
Straight to the chamber of that innocent bride,
And kneeling on the bed, 'Lucretia,' breathed,
'Tis I, Prince Tarquin, with my sword unsheathed.'
She nothing spake: she had no power to speak,
Nor any thought in all her heart to seek,
But trembled, as a lamb from sheepfold strayed,
Caught by a wolf, lies under him dismayed.
What could she do? Struggle? She could not win.
Cry out? His naked sword would intervene.
Escape? She felt his hands upon her breast,
Never before by hand unlawful pressed.
With prayers and bribes and threats he sought to assail:
No prayer or bribe or threat could aught avail.
'What use? I'll mingle death and calumny,
Rape, and accuse you of adultery;
A slave I'll kill, say you were caught in sin.'
Fear for her name prevailed, and she gave in.[106]

Livy and Dionysius had also told of the dreadful act, with two sets of divergent details. Livy, like Diodorus, saw the tragedy as a supreme exaltation of chastity, *pudicitia*, in contrast to the evil of lust, *libido*. He wrote at a time when Augustus was planning the moral laws which would endeavour to enforce precisely this lesson. And for centuries the imperial coins issued in honour of Roman empresses depicted the personification of their *pudicitia*. Dionysius, writing as usual at greater length, added a different kind of patriotic note, asserting that Lucretia's suicide affected the Romans with such great horror and compassion that they would rather die a thousand deaths in defence of their liberty than suffer such outrages to be committed by the tyrants.[107]

The story of Lucretia had already been told by the most esteemed Roman tragedian, Accius (chapter 2, section 3), who in one of his plays, perhaps the *Brutus*, makes her reveal how 'at dead of dismal night he (Sextus) came into our home'.[108] Before that, Ennius had recounted how the outraged heroine 'looked up at the sky dotted with shining stars'.[109] And, earlier still, Fabius Pictor had recorded that Lucretia's husband, Lucius Tarquinius Collatinus, was the grand-nephew (great-grand-nephew according to Dionysius) of Tarquinius Priscus, who had appointed him governor of the Alban town of Collatia (Longh-ezza), commanding the crossing of the River Anio and the Veii–Gabii road – the place which gave Collatinus his name.

The saga bears the mark of the well-worn tradition according to which the downfall of tyrants were habitually ascribed to an insulted sister or wife who had to be avenged. Occasionally, it is true, this may have been what really happened, but it is also a favourite myth. The epoch in which the story of Lucretia first saw the light of day cannot, as usual, be determined. Per-haps it was the subject of popular Roman poems and romances of which we know nothing. If so, they were surely of Greek inspiration, for there was no lack of stories about Greek maidens who had likewise saved or recovered their honour by death.[110] But the Lucretia tale must have gained currency at Rome be-cause of efforts by the family of the Lucretii. The patrician house of that name had become extinct as early as the early fourth century B.C., but a plebeian branch which achieved praetorships in 205 and 172 no doubt clothed its forgotten past in glories such as these.[111]

6 THE MYTHOLOGY OF THE ROMAN REPUBLIC

I THE MARVELLOUS BEGINNINGS OF THE REPUBLIC

Before she committed suicide, Lucretia summoned her father and her husband, and told them she had been raped by Sextus Tarquinius; and with her father and her husband came Lucius Junius Brutus and Publius Valerius Poplicola. After she had stabbed herself and died, Brutus swore he would pursue Sextus Tarquinius and his father Tarquinius Superbus and all their house, and would never allow them to be kings at Rome, or any other man either. And his companions joined him in the oath.

Lucretia's funeral roused the people of her husband's town Collatia, and with Brutus in the lead they marched on Rome. In the Forum, he spoke eloquently against the Tarquins and their crimes, and the people demanded that the king must abdicate and be banished.

Tarquinius Superbus was at Ardea, besieging the town, when he heard of these happenings at Rome. He started back immediately to crush the rebellion, but found the city gates closed against him. And so he fled into exile at Caere, with his two elder sons. The youngest son, Sextus Tarquinius, withdrew to Gabii, where he later met his end at the hand of an assassin.

Meanwhile, at Rome, this was the end of the kings who had lasted, according to tradition, for just under two hundred and fifty years. The stock details of the story, well-worn features of the downfall of tyrants, are clearly mythical, and the date, variously ascribed between 510 and 507, has no firm basis:[1] since it cannot be fortuitous that 510 is also the date of the fall of the tyrants of Athens. As to Rome, all that can be said with any certainty is that there was once a monarchy, that it became

Etruscan in character, and that there was subsequently a Republic: so that there must have been some moment, or some series of transitional adjustments, when the one turned into the other (cf. chapter 1). The archaeological evidence shows that there was still strong Etruscan influence in Rome well on into the fifth century B.C.; though whether that also means that the kings continued until then cannot at present be determined.

In any case, the Liberation from tyranny gave mythologically minded authors an immense opportunity. Livy, and even more strongly Dionysius, placed a great deal of emphasis upon this development, extracting from it a large number of didactic morals. It is generally agreed among these and other Roman writers that the immediate result of the expulsion or withdrawal of the kings was the introduction of a dual annual consulship, such as existed in later historical times. But this is, in fact, more than doubtful, since the term 'consul' was not perhaps officially used until 366 B.C. Before that the chief officials were apparently called praetors (the title that subsequently belonged to the magistracy that came second to the consulate). Nor is it certain, either, that in the earliest Republican times they were already elected in equal couples.

When Romans of subsequent ages looked back on the changeover from monarchy to Republic, many of them interpreted it as an exciting revolutionary event. But nervous conservatives of later Republican days were not very keen about this way of looking at the transformation, because it might seem too encouraging to potential revolutionaries of their own time: if a revolution had succeeded in the past, and had been granted the halo of respectability, what was to prevent subversive characters from trying the same sort of thing again? So they did their utmost to emphasize the non-revolutionary smoothness of the transition by indicating that the penultimate king, Servius Tullius – not, be it noted, the wicked Etruscan final king, but his 'Latin' predecessor, the Second Founder – had already provided for the institution of the two consuls in 'commentaries' that had been found after his death. Livy repeats this assertion,[2] though he spoils the smooth effect by being unable, all the same, to resist the temptation of stressing the theatrical, emotional, ethical implications of the break.

With the alleged arrival of the Republic, however, the nature
of his sources has changed. For the Greek writers of Sicily and
south Italy, however brief their accounts, had found the
dramatic kings of Rome, for whom Greek analogies existed, a
good deal more interesting than they found the struggles of the
incipient Republic.³ It is true that from now on began the Fasti,
purporting to give the names of the men who were consuls in
each successive year; an annalistic tradition has succeeded a
non-annalistic one. But that does not, in fact, bring us any
farther away from myth, since the Fasti, as they have come
down to us, have evidently been doctored several times over, if
not repeatedly, and this process of forgery continued right down
until the time of Augustus (chapter 2, section 3). For retrospective jostling for places in the early Fasti, among rival political
groupings and competitive families, remained acute. It seemed
very important to project one's influence and genealogy as far
back as one possibly could.

Such widespread feelings, and all the imaginative activities
that stemmed from them, have had the somewhat ludicrous
result that no less than five consuls, instead of the required two,
are attributed to the first year of the Republic. It is not necessary
to repeat in detail the various subterfuges, comprising ingenious
and contradictory accounts of violent deaths and forced retirements, which Roman historians of various dates thought up in
order to explain this multiplicity. But one of those five names,
the one which emerges most strongly in this confused picture, is
that of Lucius Junius Brutus. In the last period of Tarquinius
Superbus' reign, as we have seen, he was believed to have
accompanied the king's sons on a mission to Apollo's oracle at
Delphi. Such a mission is a likely enough event in the later sixth
century B.C., when we know, for example, that neighbouring
Caere had close links with Delphi. But the details introduced
into the story make Brutus into a typical cunning hero of a folk-
tale. We are told that he was the only member of the deputation
who grasped the meaning of the oracle. For it declared that the
man who kissed his mother would reign at Rome: and so

Brutus, when they were back home, pretended to stumble, and kissed Mother Earth. 'Brutus' means stupid, but he is the folklore figure who is not as foolish as he seems. Moreover, his apparent crassness is somewhat at variance with the further assertion that before becoming consul he had been chief of the royal bodyguard or prefect of the city (a post that obviously did not exist at the time). Cicero, on the other hand, says he had not held either of these posts, but was out of a job.

At all events, after the Liberation Lucius Brutus was said to have behaved with the highest degree of rigorous Roman virtue. First he inflicted capital punishment upon his own sons for plotting to bring back the Tarquins. This was an edifying contrast between the austere father-son relationship of Roman tradition and the unpunished licence of Etruscan sons exemplified by Sextus Tarquinius. But at the same time this reference to a plot in favour of the Tarquins may well be one of a number of echoes of an authentic reaction in favour of the departed monarchy.[4] The movement probably arose among the common people, who had no doubt received better treatment from the Etruscan kings than they got from the aristocrats who had now taken charge (cf. chapter 5, section 2). Then Brutus performed a second and final sacrificial action. When an army from Veii and Tarquinii tried to restore the Etruscan royal house, he fought a duel against Tarquinius Superbus' son Arruns Tarquinius in which both he and his opponent were killed.[5]

Whether Lucius Junius Brutus ever existed can scarcely now be determined. If he did, however, he is unlikely to have possessed these three names, since surnames were a much later addition. But whether he was a real person or not, the formative age of Roman mythology provided extremely fertile ground for the evolution of his biography. For a Decimus Junius Brutus Scaeva was a successful consul in 325 B.C., and other Junii held consulships in abundance almost immediately afterwards; they were also thick on the ground once again during the following century. They and their relatives could not quite rise to the point of foisting a king into the antique list, but they did their best. And the best for a plebeian family like the Junii had to be more spectacular than anything the more relaxed patricians would need (cf. chapter 5, section 1).[6]

It was certainly spectacular to have one of the very first consuls as an ancestor. And so, not content with claiming that the family had arrived with Aeneas,[7] they arranged matters accordingly, transforming their real or hypothetical ancestor Lucius into the great Liberator of Rome. As such, he was honoured by a play, the *Brutus*, written by Accius (chapter 2, section 3; chapter 5, section 2), whose patron was an eminent member of the same family, Decimus Junius Brutus Callaicus (consul, 138 B.C.). Thereafter, like so many mythological figures, the Liberator Lucius Brutus became a highly topical talking-point, and never more so than in the disturbed decades which led to the dictatorship and murder of Julius Caesar. A vigorously programmatic silver coin, bearing the heads of Lucius Brutus and a certain Gaius Servilius Ahala (who was believed to have slain the would-be tyrant Spurius Maelius in 439 B.C.) cannot be exactly dated.[8] But it was probably issued by Marcus Junius (later Quintus Caepio) Brutus, the future assassin of Julius Caesar, when he was a young man serving as a moneyer or in some other official capacity; not only Lucius Brutus, but Ahala too (or perhaps his brother Servilius Structus), was among his alleged ancestors. The issue can be attributed either to the years of the dictatorial first triumvirate (Crassus, Pompey, Caesar), or to a date immediately preceding the Civil War between Pompey and Caesar; in the later event it is the illegalities of Caesar that the coin, by implication, denounces. In either case it belongs to the fifties B.C., and represents a powerful and open protest against contemporary tyranny. And then, after Marcus Brutus had murdered Caesar, he directly compared his own achievement with that of his revered ancestor by portraying himself in association with Lucius, who is described as first consul (PRIMus COS.).[9]

But meanwhile a school of thought hostile to these pretensions was awkwardly insisting that Lucius Brutus had never had a son at all, so that Marcus could not possibly be his descendant!

The first consuls of the Republic included another renowned

hero, Publius Valerius Poplicola. However, he is just as suspect as Brutus, though for a different reason : his family, from the earliest Republican times onwards, was so distinguished that the insertion of such a figure into the tradition was all too easy. Moreover the house of the Valerii, as we have seen, not only cherished, at various times, a powerful Sabine lobby to praise them (chapter 4, section 3), but possessed a loyal protégé among the historians of the first century B.C. – Valerius Antias, who made it his business to exalt the family right back into the dimmest past. There is a certain plausibility in the belief that an eminent Valerius helped to preside over the inauguration of the Republic, because of the leading part that this family, together with the Fabii, may authentically have played in the history of the early fifth century B.C. However, Publius Valerius Poplicola looks suspiciously like a reduplication of a consul of 449. And his anachronistic surname, derived from *populum colere*, 'favouring the ordinary people', is based on the supposition that he passed a law introducing the right of appeal : but the law seems foisted in here from much later events (chapter 5, note 52).[10] Poplicola's reported actions, too, are likewise anachronisms. Nevertheless, the highly influential Marcus Valerius Messalla Corvinus, who wrote a book *On Families* under Augustus (chapter 2, section 3), persisted in attributing the nobility of his own house to this alleged ancestor's consulship during the very first year of the Republic.[11]

Poplicola also owed much of his renown to his supposed share in the dedication of the national Temple of Jupiter, Juno and Minerva on the Capitol. For patriotic reasons, this great event had to be placed in the first year of the glorious Republic instead of under the alien kings to whom the completion of the building should, in fact, apparently be attributed (chapter 5, section 2). Some historians – those who liked the Valerii – gave Poplicola the main credit, whereas others ascribed it to a further hypothetical consul of this initial year, Marcus Horatius Pulvillus. There were also an idea, current in several different versions, that they were rivals for the honour.[12] Probably Pulvillus had been the first to figure in this capacity, because his family fell so far from eminence in later times that the insertion of his name must date from an early period. Yet, once inserted, it proved singularly hard to eradicate, surviving, for example, along with Brutus, in a reference during the second century B.C. by Polybius. This association of Marcus Horatius Pulvillus with the Capitoline temple persisted because his name was there for everyone to see, inscribed on the architrave of the temple itself, claiming the honour of the dedication. Moreover, it was believed that the inscription went right back to the time of the dedication itself – though, in fact, there is a suspicion that what people saw in historical times was an inscription by another Marcus Horatius, who may have restored the temple in 378 B.C.

Pulvillus, again with Brutus, is also credited with the first Roman treaty with Carthage.[13] This, in spite of much controversy, may conceivably be attributable to the late sixth or early fifth century B.C., when other places in this region, such as Caere, had close ties with Carthage – though, even so, there is no justification for ascribing the name of any particular Roman individual to the negotiation.

One of the other alleged inaugural consuls was Spurius Lucretius Tricipitinus. He owes this position to his fatherhood of Lucretia, who had played such an important part in the downfall of the monarchy. Some authorities, however, understandably thought that the list of consuls already looked quite full enough without him, and so they decided that he had not been consul at all but 'prefect of the city', having retained this office from the time of Tarquin (though others thought that Brutus had been Tarquin's city prefect). The interpolation of Lucretius' name in the list of the consuls for the first year of the Republic seems to date from about 200 B.C., since the first Lucretii to bear the first name 'Spurius' were members of the plebeian family of that name who held office as praetors in 205 and 172 (chapter 5, section 2, note 111).

The final candidate for the Republic's first consulships is Lucius Tarquinius of Collatia (Collatinus), the husband of Lucretia. Does he too owe his place in the list to his relationship with Lucretia, like her father? But the appearance of the name Tarquinius in this role of one of the Republic's founders is so unexpected that it looks authentic. The historians appreciated the anomaly, and Livy and Dionysius both go to great trouble to explain how Collatinus was forced to retire from the consulship because of the hated monarchic name. However, as we have seen, there was, in reality, no clean break with the Etruscans in *c.* 500, or at the beginning of the Republic (whenever that was). And when, in later Republican days, names were being interpolated into the Fasti the Tarquinian family had died out; so it was in nobody's interests to insert them at that subsequent stage. It is possible, therefore, that he had been there from the start, and that a Lucius Tarquinius from Collatia should be added to the other Tarquins who symbolized the Etruscan presence at Rome – the two kings of Roman tradition, and Cnaeus Tarquinius (not necessarily a king) of the Vulci tomb. Since Collatinus is described as a consul and not a king – though he cannot, in fact, have been known as a consul if he really existed at the end of the sixth century B.C. – his name may well represent some sort of a transitional period between monarchy and full Republic. Other such 'consuls' with Etruscan names continue to appear in the Fasti of these slightly later years, and again around 450 B.C.

The tradition maintains that early attempts to restore Tarquinius Superbus to the Roman throne were made, first by Veii and Tarquinii (the warfare in which Lucius Brutus and Arruns Tarquinius were killed), and then by Lars Porsenna (or Porsena), king of Clusium. Lars Porsenna, it was said, advanced as far as the Janiculum hill, just across the Tiber from the city: the hill that the Etruscans named after Aeneas (chapter 3, section 3). On the shield made for Aeneas, according to Virgil, by the god Vulcan, you could see Porsenna telling the Romans to take back the banished Tarquin, and laying strenuous siege to their city while its inhabitants took up the sword for freedom's sake.[14]

The story of their victory over Lars Porsenna goes back at least to Fabius Pictor, whose family was particularly well acquainted with the affairs of Etruria (note 76 below). But if there is any historical truth in the story the real nomenclature of the Etruscan leader does not appear to have come down to us, since the two names that are attributed to him are both titles: Lars is Laris or Larth, a great warrior or champion (chapter 5, section 2), and Porsenna comes from *purthna*, the title of an official, perhaps like the Greek *prytaneus* (president of the council) or Roman *praetor*. The tradition that Lars Porsenna was the ruler of Clusium (Chiusi) is also not unanimous; Pliny the Elder preferred Volsinii,[15] and modern scholars have proposed Veii or Vulci, both of which were so close to Rome. It has also been suggested that his home town was a hypothetical *second* Clusium on the coast, perhaps the modern Marsiliana d'Albegna or Orbetello. But the tradition favouring the famous inland Clusium may be tentatively accepted, since this city, following a path of independence from the maritime Etruscan powers, was strong and prosperous at the turn of the fifth century (chapter 1).

According to the accepted Roman canon, this Lars Porsenna was hurled back by the besieged Romans, and reeled away in defeat. But both Pliny and Tacitus had instead learnt somewhere or other that he was victorious: he actually conquered the city, and held it for a time.[16] This version should probably be accepted as historical truth, for it presents a typical example of an anti-Roman tradition, which originated among the Etruscans. The Romans did their best to suppress it, though in this case, as in others, their attempt to do so just failed to come off. It may have been the massive Etruscan studies of the emperor Claudius which enabled the dissident version to survive. In any case, it looks as if we have to make an addition to the Seven Kings of Rome – and surely, if we but knew, not the only possible addition, though other candidates, such as Mastarna and Cnaeus Tarquinius, look rather more uncertain (chapter 5, section 2).

Furthermore, the traditional supposition that Lars Porsenna was intervening on behalf of Tarquinius Superbus is open to considerable doubt. If that has been his purpose, why, since we now believe that Porsenna succeeded in taking Rome, was Tarquinius not restored after all?[17] Besides, there is a reliable report that the expelled Tarquins took refuge, not at Clusium or any other Etruscan city, but at Greek Cumae – whose chief Aristodemus was said to have joined the struggle, not on Porsenna's side, but against him. Probably the truth is that Porsenna was acting on his own account. Indeed, far from helping Tarquinius Superbus to re-establish himself at Rome, he may actually have helped to otherthrow Superbus; and for a time, it appears, Porsenna himself ruled the city. What is more, his rule was remembered by a statue near the senate-house.[18] Why he did not stay in Rome we cannot tell. But at all events we can be sure that, if thereafter he became the life-long friend of the Romans, as the myth suggests (and the statue seems to confirm), this was for some cogent political reason and not merely, as their own self-congratulatory tradition suggests, because of his admiration for their virtues.

These virtues proliferate in the canonical version which makes Porsenna's (allegedly unsuccessful) siege of Rome culminate in the heroic exploit of Horatius Cocles. The story went as follows:

On the approach of the Etruscan army, the Romans outside the city had to abandon their farms, and move within the walls. The invaders had to try to seize the Tiber's wooden bridge, the Pons Sublicius, and it was upon this that they concentrated their attack. The routed Romans fled before them onto the bridge. The soldier who was guarding it, Publius Horatius Cocles, tried to persuade them to stand and fight with him there, while his compatriots set about demolishing the bridge. Two comrades, Spurius Lartius and Titius Herminius, came to his help, and the three of them staved off the first onslaught. But soon, as the men who were hacking away at the timbers appealed to them to get away to safety, Horatius bade Lartius and Herminius leave him and save themselves. Now Horatius stood alone; and he held the Etruscans at bay. Before they could overcome his resistance, the bridge, safely demolished, crashed to its fall, and with a prayer to Father Tiber Horatius plunged fully armed into its stream and swam through a rain of missiles to safety.

This saga seems to have been recorded by Fabius Pictor and Ennius, and Polybius noted it as a typical specimen theme of Roman funeral oratory, a potent model of exemplary patriotic behaviour. Polybius preserves an earlier version of the story according to which Horatius was drowned. But this did not suit later historians, who were eager that his heroism should be rewarded, and consequently preserved the version that Livy, Dionysius and Plutarch helped to establish as canonical. It is also the most exciting of Thomas Babington Macaulay's *Lays* (1842), reconstructions of the banquet-ballads from which, unlike most scholars today (chapter 2, section 3), he believed that these national tales had evolved.

> But all Etruria's noblest
>   Felt their hearts sink to see
> On the earth the bloody corpses,
>   In the path the dauntless Three;
> And from the ghastly entrance
>   Where those bold Romans stood,
> All shrank, like boys who unaware,
>   Ranging the woods to start a hare,
> Come to the mouth of the dark lair
> Where, growling low, a fierce old bear
>   Lies amidst bones and blood.
> Was none who would be foremost
>   To lead such dire attack:
> But those behind cried 'Forward!'
>   And those before cried 'Back!'
> And backward now and forward
>   Wavers the deep array;
> And on the tossing sea of steel,
> To and fro the standards reel;
> And the victorious trumpet-peal
>   Dies fitfully away.
> Yet one man for one moment
>   Stood out before the crowd;
> Well known was he to all the Three,
>   And they gave him greeting loud,
> 'Now welcome, welcome, Sextus!
>   Now welcome to thy home!
> Why does thou stay, and turn away?
>   Here lies the road to Rome.'
> Thrice looked he at the city;
>   Thrice looked he at the dead;
> And thrice came on in fury,

And thrice turned back in dread:
And, white with fear and hatred,
    Scowled at the narrow way,
Where, wallowing in a pool of blood,
    The bravest Tuscans lay.

But meanwhile axe and lever
    Have manfully been plied;
And now the bridge hangs tottering
    Above the boiling tide.
'Come back, come back, Horatius!'
    Loud cried the Fathers all.
'Back, Lartius! back, Herminius!
    Back, ere the ruin fall!'

Back darted Spurius Lartius;
    Herminius darted back:
And, as they passed, beneath their feet
    They felt the timbers crack.
But when they turned their faces,
    And on the farther shore
Saw brave Horatius stand alone,
    They would have crossed once more.

But with a crash like thunder
    Fell every loosened beam,
And, like a dam, the mighty wreck
    Lay right athwart the stream.
And a long shout of triumph
    Rose from the walls of Rome,
As to the highest turret-tops
    Was splashed the yellow foam.

And, like a horse unbroken
    When first he feels the rein,
The furious river struggled hard,
    And tossed his tawny mane,
And burst the curb, and bounded,
    Rejoicing to be free,
And, whirling down, in fierce career,
Battlement, and plank, and pier,
    Rushed headlong to the sea.

Alone stood brave Horatius,
    But constant still in mind;
Thrice thirty thousand foes before,
    And the broad flood behind.

'Down with him!' cried false Sextus,
  With a smile on his pale face.
'Now yield thee,' cried Lars Porsena,
  'Now yield thee to our grace.'
Round turned he, as not deigning
  Those craven ranks to see;
Nought spake he to Lars Porsena,
  To Sextus nought spake he;
But he saw on Palatinus
  The white porch of his home;
And he spake to the noble river
  That rolls by the towers of Rome.
'Oh, Tiber! father Tiber!
  To whom the Romans pray,
A Roman's life, a Roman's arms,
  Take thou in charge this day!'
So he spake, and speaking sheathed
  The good sword by his side,
And with his harness on his back,
  Plunged headlong in the tide.[19]

And then, even the ranks of Tuscany could scarce forbear to cheer.

Florus, writing in the second century A.D., saw fit to remark that this was one of the stories which 'did they not appear in the annals, would today be thought of as fables'. True, but fables were as potent as history, or even more so. The myths reinforce the lessons and moral messages of history with a force to which history on its own account could hardly aspire.

Horatius Cocles, says Dionysius, was a nephew of the supposed first consul, Marcus Horatius Pulvillus, and a descendant of one of the triplets who fought the Curiatii (chapter 5, section 1).[20] Nothing else is recorded of him; he is a mysterious figure. Varro derives 'Cocles' from *oculus*, meaning one-eyed,[21] and that is the sense in which the word is used in Ennius and Plautus; it was supposed that Horatius bore the name because he lost an eye in battle. However, the whole story is likely to have arisen because opposite the old Sublician Bridge there stood an ancient statue of a one-eyed man. The figure also seemed to be lame – or perhaps the archaic sculptor could not represent legs

– and this was appropriate to the wounds that Cocles must have received on the bridge. However, the statue was also attributed, in historical times, to the fire-god Vulcan (Hephaestus), who, like Odin, Wotan and Varuna, was reputed to suffer from both these disabilities. And indeed, Vulcan possessed a connection with the Tiber, for at his festival on 23 August every year the heads of families took fishes that had been caught in the river, and threw them into a fire.[22]

In spite of the feat of Horatius Cocles, the tradition conceded that the blockade of the city by Porsenna went on. But another example of courage was exhibited by Gaius Mucius Scaevola. Scaevola, according to Plutarch,

> was a man endowed with every virtue, but most eminent in war; and, resolving to kill Porsenna, attired himself in the Tuscan habit, and using the Tuscan language, came to the camp, and approaching the seat where the king sat amongst his nobles, but not certainly knowing the king, and fearful to inquire, drew out his sword, and stabbed one who he thought had most the appearance of king. Mucius was taken in the act, and whilst he was under examination, a pan of fire was brought to the king, who intended to sacrifice, Mucius thrust his right hand into the flame, and whilst it burnt stood looking at Porsenna with a steadfast and undaunted countenance. Porsenna at last in admiration dismissed him, and returned his sword, reaching it from his seat. Mucius received it in his left hand, which occasioned the name of Scaevola, left-handed, and said, 'I have overcome the terrors of Porsenna, yet am vanquished by his generosity, and gratitude obliges me to disclose what no punishment could extort;' and assured him then that three hundred Romans, all of the same resolution, lurked about his camp, only waiting for an opportunity – he, by lot appointed to the enterprise, was not sorry that he had miscarried in it, because so brave and good a man deserved rather to be a friend to the Romans than an enemy.
>
> To this Porsenna gave credit, and thereupon expressed an inclination to a truce, not, I presume, so much out of fear of the three hundred Romans, as in admiration of the Roman courage.[23]

In the original version of the story, the hero's plunging of his right arm into the flame had evidently been a punishment for perjury, a familiar mythical theme. His heroic endurance was no doubt always stressed, but whether at the earliest stage there existed any connection with Porsenna is uncertain. The underlying idea is a widespread and ancient one, Scaevola being one-armed Thor, as Cocles is one-eyed Odin; and there are reasons for regarding the story of Scaevola as fairly antique.[24] However, his name is related to *scaevus*, the Greek *skaios*, left or left-handed. But this is not the only Greek element in the story, for there are also many signs that its final form, as we know it, has been augmented by borrowings from more than one Greek traditional tale. The killing of the king's secretary is Greek: it was only in Hellenistic states that kings had secretaries grand enough to be mistaken for themselves. But the most readily identifiable analogy relates to Codrus, a mythical king of Athens, who went among his Dorian enemies disguised as a wood-cutter and started a quarrel with them, in order to save his country.[25] The influence of this story on the tale of Scaevola is proved in a curious fashion by Dionysius' report that he 'possessed the surname of Cordus'.[26] This name, so closely resembling Codrus, has clearly entered into the story because of the latter's debt to the Codrus myth. And the Roman Cordi of historical times, some of whom belonged to the Mucian family, no doubt played their part in asserting that the hero generally known as Scaevola had been called Cordus. They were distinguished enough in late Republican times to have a moneyer;[27] and no doubt they encouraged this identification of Scaevola with one of their ancestors.

The saga of Scaevola, we are informed, was told by many people in many ways.[28] The final concoction had probably been assembled by the later third century B.C. It was then that the first historical Mucius Scaevola made his name – a praetor of 215 B.C., important enough to exercise his mite of influence upon the tradition. The earliest version which has come down to us, a fragmentary account, was written in the second century B.C. by Cassius Hemina. At this time the Scaevolae were becoming very influential. After a consul of 175, two eminent brothers became consuls in 133[29] – they backed the reformer Tiberius Gracchus and then prudently dropped him. One of them was the chief priest and jurist Publius Mucius Scaevola, who must have been interested in the patriotic mythology because it was he who published the *Annales Maximi* (chapter 2, section 3); and it was hardly to be expected that he would ignore myths relating to his own family. His son Quintus, who likewise became chief priest, had a daughter, Mucia, who married Pompey the Great. Moreover, the Mucii were still in the corridors of power under Augustus, when a Gaius Scaevola was a member of a religious board with antiquarian interests, and was therefore particularly likely to take a keen interest in the mythical past.[30] He must, therefore, have been annoyed when the Greek writer Athenodorus of Tarsus, in a book addressed to Augustus' sister Octavia, repeated a tradition that the hero had not been called Mucius Scaevola at all, but Postumus.

However, the Augustan writers adhered to the accepted identification and, in their different ways, tried to make the most of this classic tale of fanatical, patriotic endurance, inspired by indignation at Rome's shame. Dionysius prosaically tells how the whole plot was discussed and approved by the senate, while Livy, supplying three melodramatic tirades which he may, in part, have borrowed from one of his sources, brings the scene to a climax with Scaevola's dialogue with Porsenna – not forgetting, however, to provide an explanation for a field across the Tiber known as the Mucian Meadows, which he supposed to have been a gift made to Scaevola for his bravery.[31]

When Porsenna, deeply impressed by Scaevola's action, proposed peace, this was allegedly accepted, and four conditions were agreed upon. First the Tarquins were not to be restored to the throne of the Romans. Secondly, Veii was to receive some land back from Rome. Thirdly, the Janiculum hill was to be restored to the Romans. And fourthly they must provide hostages if they wished to have the hill back. One of the hostages, however, a girl called Cloelia, obtained permission to bathe in the river, but then, having told her guards to go away while she undressed and went into the water, proceeded to swim back across the river to Rome, accompanied by a band of her girl-friends. And, undeterred by a rain of Etruscan missiles, she brought them all in safety to their families in Rome. Lars Porsenna was angry. However (being apparently very long-suffering) he was so impressed by her feat that he supposedly not only agreed to let her and her friends stay in Rome, but also showed a very amenable attitude about returning the hostages who still remained in his hands.

Indeed, Dionysius reports that he sent every one of them back to their homes – and presented Cloelia with a finely-equipped war-horse as well. But Livy, though insistent on Porsenna's admiration of what she had achieved, felt that one should not overdo matters, and therefore said nothing about the gift, and indicated that only half the hostages were returned. This gives the opportunity for two moral points, for she was allowed to make her own choice of those who were to be released. 'She is said to have chosen the young boys, a choice in accordance with her maiden modesty: the other hostages, more-over, agreed that, in liberating them from the enemy, those should be first considered who were most subject to injurious treatment.' Yet even this unkind reference to the supposed pederastic tendencies of the Etruscans, whose enemies always stressed their corrupt habits, does not seem to have disturbed the equanimity of Porsenna, for friendly relations were now restored.

And, as usual, the opportunity was taken to bring in a topo-graphical explanation. For it was added that the Romans re-warded this new kind of valour with a new kind of honour, an equestrian statue, which represented the maiden riding on a horse. This statue, which stood at the summit of the Sacred Way, is believed to represent Cloelia by both Livy and Diony-sius, but it is hard to see why, since neither of them said anything about the maiden being on horseback when she crossed the river; though Livy (not Dionysius) specifies that the statue was equestrian. Yet clearly they had before them an alternative version which did record that this was how she crossed. Dionysius, to do him justice, also reports an attempt at archaeological research such as Livy would never have bothered or found the time to undertake. 'This statue I discovered to be no longer standing; it was said to have been destroyed when a fire broke out in the adjacent houses.'[32] The correct identification of the statue is no more practicable now than it was then.

Probably it represented a deity, perhaps Venus on Horseback (Equestris), of whom a Roman statue was known to have existed. Her cult was said to have been instituted by her son Aeneas, and the Cloelii claimed descent from one of Aeneas' comrades, by way of Alba Longa (chapter 4, section 1). There are many references to the importance of the family in early Republican days. In the last century B.C. one of the nastiest of Rome's second-rate political thugs was a Sextus Cloelius, though it is doubtful if he took much interest in these antique traditions.

Cloelia's escape across the river may have been an old story. It could even have been true. But it was still being doctored and amended, and disputed about, as late as the first century B.C. Dionysius gives a leading part in the story to the consuls, identified as Marcus Horatius Pulvillus and Publius Valerius Valerius Poplicola, who had contributed a son and a daughter respectively to the hostages. Poplicola, he says, defended the girls before Porsenna, and successfully persuaded him to make friends with Rome. This sort of high praise of Poplicola, as we have seen earlier in this section, is very likely to be due to the historian Valerius Antias, whom we may consequently assume that Dionysius is following at this point. Livy, on the other hand, says nothing about the role of Poplicola. So his source must be a different one.

Although Lars Porsenna had made peace, the tradition recounted that Tarquinius Superbus – or, some said, his son Sextus Tarquinius, who had not yet been assassinated – went on with the war against Rome. But, if so, their allies were henceforward no longer their fellow-Etruscans from Clusium, but the Latins, under their leader Octavius Mamilius of Tusculum, who was married to Tarquinius Superbus' daughter or granddaughter. These Latins and the troops of Superbus lay encamped near Lake Regillus (Panzano Secco) in the territory of Tusculum, and the Roman commander Aulus Postumius pitched his camp on a hill overlooking their position. There, according to Dionysius, he inflicted on his troops a speech of quite inordinate length. Then followed the battle; it took the form, according to the tradition, of a series of individual combats in the archaic, epic manner of the fight between the Horatii and Curiatii, or the duels depicted on the François Tomb (chapter 5, section 2).

The result was said to have been a great triumph for the Romans, in which the Latins suffered unprecedented losses. The Roman victory, however, was due to divine intervention; and this is how Dionysius described what happened.

It is said that in this battle two men on horseback, far excelling in both beauty and stature those our human stock produces, and just growing their first beard, appeared to Postumius the dictator, and to those arrayed about him, and charged at the head of the Roman horse, striking with their spears all the Latins they encountered and driving them headlong before them.

And after the flight of the Latins and the capture of their camp, the battle having come to an end in the late afternoon, two youths are said to have appeared in the same manner in the Roman Forum attired in military garb, very tall and beautiful and of the same age, themselves retaining on their countenances, as having come from a battle, the look of combatants, and the horses they led being all in a sweat. And when they had each of them watered their horses and washed them at the fountain which rises near the temple of Vesta and forms a small but deep pool [the Spring of Juturna], and many people stood about them and inquired if they brought any news from the camp, they related how the battle had gone and that the Romans were the victors. And it is said that after they left the Forum they were not seen again by anyone, though great search was made for them by the man who had been left in command of the city. The next day, when those at the head of affairs received the letters from the dictator, and besides the other particulars of the battle learned also of the appearance of the divinities, they concluded, as we may reasonably infer, that it was the same gods who had appeared in both places, and were convinced that the apparitions had been those of Castor and Pollux, the Dioscuri.

Of this extraordinary and wonderful appearance of these gods there are many monuments at Rome, not only the temple of Castor and Pollux which the city erected in the Forum at the place where their apparitions had been seen, and the adjacent fountain, which bears the names of these gods and is to this day regarded as holy, but also the costly sacrifices which the people perform each year through their chief priests in the month called Quintilis, on the day known as the Ides, the day on which they gained this victory.

But above all these things there is the procession performed after the sacrifice by those who have a public horse and who, being arrayed by tribes and centuries, ride in regular ranks on horseback, as if they came from battle, crowned with olive branches and attired in the purple robes with stripes of scarlet which they call *trabeae*. They begin their procession from a certain temple of Mars built outside the walls, and, going through several parts of the city and the Forum, they pass by the temple of Castor and Pollux, sometimes to the number even of five thousand, wearing whatever rewards for valour in battle they have received from their commanders, a fine sight and worthy of the greatness of the Roman dominion. These are the things I have found both related and performed by the Romans in commemoration of the appearance of Castor and Pollux. And from these, as well as from many other important instances, one may judge how dear to the gods were the men of those times.[33]

Should this battle of Lake Regillus be regarded as pure myth, or is there a touch of authentic history about it?

Ancient reports about Rome's early relations with the Latins are conflicting. Sometimes they are depicted as Rome's subjects right from the time of Romulus. And yet we are also shown continuous fighting until the final subjection of the Latins, which took place in 338.[34] It is after the latter date that the stories about prehistoric times, in which Rome is pitted against the whole of Latium, were concocted. However, it is probable enough that at the beginning of the fifth century B.C., the period to which the Battle of Regillus was ascribed, certain Latin towns were organized in a league from which Rome, itself the leader of a number of satellites though not yet a dominant power in the area, was excluded; so that the two groups came to blows.

Perhaps it is true, also, that Tusculum had recently succeeded Aricia as the leader of the Latin confederation opposed to Rome. Indeed, the battle of Lake Regillus is quite likely to have taken place. The prominence of the cavalry in the engagement, at a time when it might have been forecast that heavy infantry (hoplites) would predominate (chapter 5 and note 79),[35] is an unexpected touch which suggests a core of reality in the memory of a transitional period. Granted, however, that there may have been a Battle of Lake Regillus the subsequent course of history shows that it was not the decisive victory that the Romans claimed. Nevertheless the treaty with the Latins that resulted from it, the Foedus Cassianum, appears to have been authentic – a defensive alliance between two more or less equal Latin groups. Cicero saw the inscriptions on a plate of bronze – though what he saw, admittedly, may have been a copy rather than the original.[36]

There was a difference of opinion in later days whether the Roman general, Aulus Postumius, had been consul or had held the emergency office of dictator.[37] He was said to have celebrated his victory by founding the famous Temple of Castor and Pollux in the Forum. Temple-foundation was an activity in which his family was prominent during the early Republic, and the same man was believed to have founded the Temple of Ceres, which became a rallying point for the plebeian cause.[38] As for Lake Regillus itself, later Postumii were clearly glad to have this success in their archives, because their family's very long record of military command included not only some notable triumphs but a number of catastrophic defeats ranging all the way from the fourth down to the first century B.C. The Postumian family must have produced a succession of singularly boneheaded generals. However, some of these defeats were presented as victories. So it offered no great problem to present the engagement of Regillus, which was probably not even a Roman defeat but a drawn battle, as yet another triumphant success.

In these tasks of interpretation, contributing to the exaltation of their family, the Postumii had the assistance of a historian of the second century B.C., Aulus Postumius Albinus (consul 151), who was interested in the remote past (chapter 2, section 3; chapter 3, note 120). And they may also have had the help of another historian of the same century, Lucius Calpurnius Piso Frugi, since the Postumii helped the Calpurnii to gain the commanding political position they had now come to possess. An Aulus Postumius Albinus issued coins showing the Dioscuri,[39] and the same man (or someone else of the same name) adopted Caesar's protégé Decimus Junius Brutus Albinus, who subsequently, like the more famous Marcus Brutus, became one of his murderers – perhaps the most distinguished member of the group. He ensured that the Postumii remained in the public eye.

Livy agrees with Dionysius that after the battle of Regillus the dictator Aulus Postumius vowed a temple to Castor.[40] Yet this historian completely ignores the famous epiphany of the Dioscuri on the battlefield. Even such a rationalist as Licinius Macer had referred to their miraculous appearance, but Livy's rationalism goes further and prefers to omit such an un-Roman sort of phenomenon. For the miracle was obviously borrowed from a similar myth about Greek south Italy, recounting that the same sacred twins had appeared at the battle of the river Sagra (Allaro ?) (c. 540 B.C.) where they helped the army of Locri against the forces of Croton. There is many a passage in the *Iliad* to remind us that this was not the first time gods had appeared in battles, and similar interventions by the Dioscuri continued to be reported as late as the second century, when they were believed to have manifested themselves again in two different engagements.[41] In our own epoch, too, guardian angels were seen at the Battle of Mons in the First World War, and during the Second World War Greek soldiers saw the Virgin leading them into battle.

It was from Locri, or perhaps from the great city of Taras (Tarentum) which was of Spartan origin like the Dioscuri themselves (chapter 4, section 3), that the Brethren became known in non-Greek Italy. This link with Rome was familiar to the Greeks, for when Demetrius 1 Poliorcetes of Macedonia (d. 283 B.C.) sent the Romans back some of their prisoners of war because of 'the kinship between the Romans and Greeks', his grounds for this assertion were provided by the worship of the Dioscuri which they shared.[42]

The sacred twins were well enough known to the Etruscans, although the failure of the latter to understand heroes or sympathize with the concept (chapter 3, note 28) meant that works of art in Etruria tend to represent them not as heroes but rather as gods, sometimes winged. No doubt it was open to the people of Latium to learn about the Dioscuri from Etruria, but we happen to know that one Latin centre, Lavinium, chose to worship them in their Greek rather than their Etruscan guise. For an inscription of *c.* 500 on a bronze plate from this holy town describes them as *quroi*, which is the Greek word *kouroi*, youths; they were the *Dios kouroi*, or sons of Zeus.[43] Lavinium identified them with its deified ancestors or Penates (chapter 3, section 3), and this identification appears to have taken effect by at least 470 B.C.[44]

The same equation with the Penates took place at Rome as well, and it was no doubt from Lavinium that the worship of the Dioscuri came to the Romans. The intermediary, however, may have been Tusculum, which was fifteen miles to the north-east of Lavinium and the same distance south-east of Rome. For Tusculum was the main Latin centre of the cult of Castor and Pollux – and it was likewise the territory in which Lake Regillus was situated. Tusculum was also the first Latin city to obtain Roman citizenship, which was granted to its population in 381 B.C. And it provided Rome with a number of families which became influential,[45] including the Porcii whose scion Marcus Porcius Cato, the historian of the second century B.C., kept the memory of the past glories of the place well alive. So did his great grandson of the same name, who was Caesar's most determined enemy.

The Dioscuri were the divine twins who appear in many other mythologies – the equivalents of the Sanskrit Açvins. Castor and Polydeuces possessed various functions in Greece, but it was particularly as divine horsemen, 'riders on white steeds' (*leucopoloi*), that they came to be worshipped in Italy. At Rome, Dionysius is right to associate their cult with the ceremonial parade of the knights which took place every year on 15 July, the traditional date of the Battle of Lake Regillus; though the institution may have gone back, in primitive forms, to times when the Dioscuri had not yet been thought of (chapter 3, section 3). Indeed it may have been this pre-existing festival which their epiphany at Regillus, and their bringing of the news to Rome, were invented to explain. The traditional date for the introduction of the cult at Rome was in the first years of the fifth century B.C., and this cannot be far wrong, since fragments of archaic statues of the twin gods, more or less contemporary copies of a work from Greek south Italy, were found at a neighbouring site associated with the temple – the spring of the nymph Juturna, where the Dioscuri were believed to have watered and washed their horses after the battle. Dionysius says the pool bore the name of the gods.[46]

For more than two centuries at the beginning of the Republic, the Romans were locked in two grim, prolonged series of conflicts, one external and the other internal. The external wars were waged against all their various neighbours, Etrsucans, Latins, Sabines, Volscians and Aequi. When Florus declared that the Romans of the early Republic were constantly harrowed, 'since they possessed not a clod of soil of their own, but the land immediately outside their walls belonged to enemies',[47] he was exaggerating a little, but not too much, for the small Roman state was continually beset by its numerous enemies.

The internal struggle was the Conflict of the Orders between the patricians and plebeians. This gave rise to an infinite number of contradictory partisan myths among families of the second and first centuries B.C. who were themselves plunged in what was regarded (not very accurately) as an analogous sort of strife – the struggle between *optimates* who supported the senate and *populares* who sought to appeal over its head to the Assembly (chapter 1). This was the time when Valerius Antias and Licinius Macer, for example, are ranged on opposite sides and eagerly reinterpret the ancient conflict accordingly.[48] Sometimes even the names attributed to the heroes and villains of the early disputes are scarcely altered from those of historical figures of the second and first centuries B.C.

One of the principal myths emerging from the external warfare mysteriously introduces the Volsci, that people of hillmen who, migrating from the valley of the river Liris (Garigliano), had moved up to the edge of the Latian plain. Indeed, they went further, since over a considerable period – perhaps for nearly two centuries – they controlled the port of Antium (Anzio). This was a matter of particular interest to the historian who came from that town, Valerius Antias. And Virgil, eager to bring into his picture all the Italians who had played a part in Rome's history, invented the warlike Volscian heroine Camilla, adapted from the warrior-maidens of Greek mythology.[49]

But the chief mythological embodiment of Romano-Volscian relations was Coriolanus. His original name, the tradition indicated, was Cnaeus Marcius, and he supposedly acquired the surname Coriolanus because he captured the little town of Corioli (Monte Giove, between Ardea and Aricia) from the Volscians in 493 B.C. Later, however, accused of tyrannical conduct, and charged in particular with opposing the distribution of grain to the starving plebeians, he was condemned to perpetual banishment. And so he withdrew to Antium, where he went over to Rome's Volscian foes, became their general, and led a Volscian army almost to the gates of Rome. The Romans sent envoys and priests to dissuade him from making war against his own people, but in vain. Then, however, his mother Volumnia and his wife Vergilia went out of the city to appeal to him, taking with them his two little sons. Volumnia addressed her plea to Coriolanus; and at first he listened in silence. Whereupon, according to Plutarch, she and his wife and children all threw themselves down before his feet. 'O mother!' cried Coriolanus, 'What have you done to me?' And he raised her up from the ground, and earnestly pressed her hand. 'You have gained a victory', he declared, 'that is fortunate enough for the Romans. However, it has destroyed your own son. No one else has defeated him : but that is what you have achieved.'[50]

Next, according to Livy,

Coriolanus kissed his wife and the two boys, sent them home, and withdrew his army. There are various accounts of his ultimate fate : he is said by some to have sunk under the burden of resentment which his behaviour brought upon him, though the manner of his death is not known. I have read in Fabius Pictor, our oldest authority, that he survived to old age; Pictor states that Coriolanus used often to say, towards the end of his life, that exile was a more bitter thing when one was old. As for Rome, in those days it was free from petty jealousy of others' success, and the men of Rome did not grudge the women their triumph. To preserve the memory of it for ever, a temple was built and consecrated to Fortuna Muliebris, the Fortune of Women.[51]

Livy's story of Coriolanus is relatively short and sharp, and marked by the stock tragic themes of reversal and recognition as well as by echoes of specific Athenian tragedies. Characteristically, too, all geographical details and other technicalities which might impede the dramatic picture are omitted. Plutarch's version is an abbreviation and improvement of the interminable rendering of Dionysius. One of the latter's sources was Valerius Antias, whose origin from Antium, as we have seen, gave him special reason to be interested in the Volscians. His hand clearly appears at a number of different stages of the story. For example, he took the credit away from Coriolanus' wife and gave it to a woman of his own Valerian family. For the kinswoman of Coriolanus, he says, were instigated to undertake their mission of appeal by Valeria Luperca (note 11 above), the aged and legendary sister of the great Valerius Poplicola, one of the supposed first consuls of the Republic; she was impelled to take this initiative by divine inspiration. Livy,[52] too, is aware of a suggestion that the mother and wife acted under external persuasion. But he finds it preferable to suppress Valeria's name, presumably hoping, by this compromise solution, not to cause too much annoyance to the Volumnian house. For such efforts to push Coriolanus' mother and wife out of the centre of the picture cannot have pleased that family at all, and it was a family which was not only antique – it is mentioned in the ancient Hymn of the Salii[53] – but possessed several representatives at Rome in the first century B.C.[54] However, the unfortunate Volumnii, who possessed a large tomb at Perusia (Perugia), had to cope with a second attempt to deprive them of the credit as well, for there was also a version denying that Volumnia was the mother of Coriolanus at all, but indicating that she was his wife, who played a subordinate role in the action.[55]

At an earlier stage, Dionysius had listed Corioli as a Latin town,[56] but it could also, as a matter of historical fact, have represented one of the furthest points occupied by the Volscians.[57] However, its capture by Coriolanus was probably invented to justify a piece of sharp practice ascribed to Rome in 446 B.C. In the course of the border raiding which was characteristic of this period, Ardea and Aricia were quarrelling with one another about the possession of this little town that lay between them, and the Romans, called in to arbitrate, adjudged Corioli to themselves! This account of the 'arbitration' bears the stamp of truth, and the story of an earlier annexation of Corioli by Roman forces under Coriolanus may have been a way of suggesting that the adjudication in 446 was legitimized by past history.

Another reason why the capture of Corioli by Coriolanus established itself in the tradition was because it served to explain his surname. He was an enigmatic figure because in some sources his hostile action towards the Roman people – by opposing distributions of grain – had taken place while he was consul, whereas the Fasti, to which historians of the later Republic had access, failed to indicate that he ever held the consulship at all. Moreover, honorific surnames awarded for victories, such as 'Coriolanus' purported to be, were not a feature of Roman nomenclature until at least the third century B.C. Consequently, the personage later known by that name must have acquired it in some other way. In origin he was probably nothing more than a hero or god who was the mythical founder of Corioli.

But the main feature of the myth presumably took shape during the fourth century B.C., when the family of the Marcii became famous. They achieved renown, in the first place, through Gaius Marcius Rutilus, four times consul and the first plebeian dictator and censor (356, 351 B.C.; cf. chapter 5, section 1). Yet it is doubtful whether the career of Rutilus had much to do with this particular myth, since he encountered hostility from the patricians, whereas Coriolanus, on the other hand, was said to have been 'admired by the best men' but to have caused fury to the plebeians. Or were the enemies of Rutilus trying to say that the Marcii were not so pro-plebeian and popular as they pretended? At all events the alleged attitude of Corio-lanus, which is described as the first development in the struggle between the Orders, may reflect the peculiar and equivocal status of the Marcii as a great plebeian family with interests on the borderline between the one order and the other. They themselves apparently came from south Latium,⁵⁸ which no doubt explains why the hero of a town in that region bears their family name. Moreover, the whole story, implying concessions by Rome's enemies in the hour of their victory, may well be an anti-Roman, *Latin* version of the Romano-Latin treaty (Foedus Cassianum) which, as seen above, the Romans attributed to their triumph at Regillus. We do not know whether it was the Marcii, or someone else, who also used the story in order to explain (wrongly) the name of a Roman shrine, the Temple of Fortune of Women four miles outside Rome on the Via Latina.⁵⁹

Cicero realized that the story of Coriolanus had been affected by the experience of the Athenian Themistocles, a man of this same early fifth century B.C. who had likewise been rejected by his ungrateful country, so that he too fled as a suppliant to foreigners and turned against his own people.⁶⁰ It was also found possible, as Shakespeare discovered, to infuse a whole host of morals into the tale. For one thing, it gave an oppor-tunity to exalt female nobility and courage. And then Livy manages to convey, in incidental fashion, the message that a true Roman's love for his fatherland, in a crisis, outweighs everything else: confronted with the external peril of Corio-lanus, the groups of Romans who were at variance with one another patriotically forgot their quarrels and rallied round to meet the common danger. Plutarch adds the further point that even a good natural environment can bear evil fruit; and he utilizes the behaviour of Coriolanus as an illustration of a treatise he had written *On Anger*,⁶¹ in the spirit of the philo-sopher Heraclitus' declaration that anger 'buys what it wants even at the price of soul'.⁶²

It is not surprising that Livy feels doubtful about what hap-pened to Coriolanus during the years that followed his great renunciation, because the story does not look very plausible;

the Volscians were hardly likely to have remained quite passive and allowed him to rob them of the fruits of victory. But Pictor was right, Livy says, in denying the tradition that when Coriolanus returned to the Volscians they killed him; and Cicero, too, is aware of the tradition that he survived. Dionysius, followed by Plutarch, declares that he not only survived but was honoured by his Volscian hosts, who, after he was dead, gave him a fine tomb, and revered and celebrated his memory. This suggests that if (as we may suppose) he had been a local hero or god of Corioli, the Volscians, when they occupied that town, took him over and made him into their hero as well: he was only imported to Rome at a later stage, through the efforts of the Marcii who themselves came from these southern regions of Latium.

2 CAMILLUS

And so early Republican Rome went ahead with its two series of struggles against external enemies on all sides and between the patrician and plebeian orders at home; until finally the external conflicts, as far as the Etruscan front was concerned, attained a mortal climax in the siege of Veii by the Romans during the years just before and after 400 B.C.[63] For although the Etruscan cities were weakened by the loss of their Trans-Apennine and Campanian empires, Veii, with its salient across the Tiber at Fidenae, could still exercise a stranglehold on the river communications between Rome and the interior. And Naevius' tradition of the visit of a king of Veii, Viba (?), to Alba Longa (chapter 4, section 1, note 14), hints that Veii, as one would expect from this geographical position, played an especially important part in the Etruscan encroachment on Latium.

According to the version of the siege preserved by the Romans, a version which is thickly encrusted with myths, they besieged Veii for ten years. They did not incur much opposition from other Etruscan cities, but were unable, amid varying fortunes and constant anxiety, to bring matters to a conclusion until Marcus Furius Camillus was appointed dictator in 396.

The Delphic oracle confirmed a report by a captured sooth-sayer from Veii that the city would not fall until the waters of the Alban Lake, which had risen to an abnormal height, were drained; and so the Romans drained the lake. Then Camillus drove a tunnel under Veii, and the tunnelling party heard the king of the city, who was about to sacrifice to Juno in the temple above their heads, declare that whoever offered the sacrifice would be victorious. Erupting out of the ground into the shrine, the Romans performed the sacrifice – and Veii fell. Camillus transferred the Veientine image of Juno to Rome, and sent a tithe of his spoils to the god Apollo at Delphi. He was accused, however, of keeping back part of the loot for him-self, and was also charged with celebrating an excessively grandiose Triumph, in which his chariot was drawn by four white horses. And so he went into exile.

The siege of Veii, and the Gallic invasions that followed, are the subject of Livy's Book v. This part of his work represents one of his most impressive artistic achievements, romantic, mys-terious and magical, filled with a powerfully sustained religious atmosphere, infused with Augustan sentiment and style, and built up, as the historian himself states, by a lively element of myth; the period for which he will feel able to claim a surer historical basis has not quite arrived.[64] The ten-year duration of the siege of Veii (Diodorus says it lasted for twelve years) is manifestly owed to the ten-year siege of Troy. The story of the long tunnel driven into the centre of the city is influenced by the story of the Trojan Horse; and the whole fight for Veii was a struggle of signs, a duel of rites, as the fight for Troy had been. But this time the Roman descendants of Aeneas were on the winning side: and this was a point which, by implication, was driven home in the *Aeneid*, when the Etruscan Mezentius is defeated and killed by Aeneas. For Virgil's account is deliber-ately assimilated to the traditions about the siege of Veii – and was written only a few years after Livy had completed his account of that event (chapter 2, section 3).

Livy's description of the siege may owe part of its dramatic material to Valerius Antias, with additional debts to Licinius Macer. At an earlier date Ennius, too, had probably played an important role in framing the epic patterns of these events. But there is also ample evidence that Livy is making use of Etruscan sources. For the rich tradition about the siege includes items that obviously come from Etruria, notably the Roman capture of an Etruscan soothsayer, on the lines of the capture of Cacus by the Vibennas – a favourite artistic theme among the Etruscans (chapter 3, section 1). These Etruscan features suggest that Fabius Pictor is likely to have played a significant part in the establishment of the tradition. For he drew strongly on the literature of Etruria, with which his family possessed very intimate connections (see below, and note 76).

Another Etruscan ingredient in the story attracted special attention because of events in later Roman history. This was the 'summoning out' (*evocatio*) of Veii's city-goddess Juno to Rome – a ritual designed to persuade the protecting deity of an enemy city to leave it and accept a new domicile in Rome.[65] This *evocatio* at Veii was no doubt a historical event. But it received great retrospective prominence from Roman writers owing to the solemn and spectacular employment of the same rite by Scipio Africanus the younger (Aemilianus), after Carthage had finally fallen to Rome at the end of the Third Punic War (146 B.C.).[66] The parallel between the two occasions was deliberately emphasized by a further incident. Plutarch declared that, when the Romans took Veii by storm, Camillus, gazing on the scene from a lofty tower, wept for pity. But that was what Scipio did, too, at the fall of Carthage; and whether he really wept or not, the incident gained such wide currency that it was reported in no less than three divergent versions.[67] When historians wrote of Camillus, they were often thinking of one or other of the Scipios. For example his subsequent trial foreshadowed, and was meant to foreshadow, the persecutions that struck both Scipios in turn at the moments of their greatest fame, after the Second and Third Punic Wars respectively.

For Camillus, like them, was depicted not as a general of any ordinary kind, but as a man of destiny, a *dux fatalis*, the agent of numerous *fata* or prodigies, many of them Etruscan. His very name, too – possibly reminiscent of the Marce Camitlnas of Vulci from the François tomb (chapter 5, section 2) – shows he was set apart and associated with omens, for the *camillus* was a patrician child who served a most ancient corporation of priests, the *flamines*.

His downfall and exile were caused by two things, given varying weight by the historians: the political or financial issue of the distribution of the spoils, and the sacrilegious impiety of the four white horses at his too extravagant triumph.[68] This last point assumed new significance in the first century B.C., when Julius Caesar, too, triumphed with four white horses. It is quite possible that Camillus' horses (showing him in so very different a light from the man whom the sight of captured Veii had reduced to tears) were invented to discredit Caesar. If so, a similar triumph, said to have been celebrated by Romulus himself – the only earlier triumph, it was believed, which involved the use of four white horses – was probably invented as a counterblast by Caesar's friends, in order to provide a venerable precedent for this spectacular feature of his own procession.

Plutarch presents his *Life of Camillus* as a parallel to Themistocles. For he too had won a great victory in the Persian War, and he too, as we saw in connection with Coriolanus, was rejected by his country. As for Camillus, in the spirit of Greek tragedy his success had courted jealousy both from gods and men. The atmosphere that surrounds his doings is heavy and portentous. Sinister signs prepare us for the miasma and pollution he is to bear. For he is destined to suffer the ancient expulsion of the accursed.

Was his fate undeserved, or should we regard it as justified by his overweening pride after the capture of Veii?[69] Opinions differed. On the whole, in our surviving sources, there is much sympathy for so great a man, the forerunner of national heroes of the future – and not only of the Scipios, as will become clear later. Moreover, his generosity to Veii's defeated dependency Falerii (394) was acclaimed as a model and stock example of Roman good faith, fair play and clemency.[70] And yet Camillus was also considered to be a man who hated the common people; whose constant subservience to the senate was matched by his harsh acrimony towards the poor. No doubt this charge – one which was also made against Scipio Africanus – lost nothing in the telling by democratic, popular, pro-Gracchan historians; while their conservative counterparts stressed his deference to the senate.

After Camillus had gone into exile, the Gauls attacked Rome. The invading army belonged to the Senones, one of the Gaulish tribes which was settled in north Italy beyond the Apennines, the region known as Cisalpine Gaul. Under the leadership of their king Brennus, the Senonian Gauls appeared in Etruria, before the gates of Clusium, and then they marched on Rome. After overwhelming the Romans beside the stream of the Allia (Fosso Maestro), eleven miles north of the city – the date, 18 July, for ever afterwards remained a day of mourning at Rome – they captured and sacked the city: with the single exception (according to the traditional account) of the citadel on the Capitoline hill.

We have Livy's description of these terrible events. The ancient summary leads off as follows:

When the Gallic Senones were besieging Clusium in Etruria, and the envoys sent by the senate to arrange a peace between Rome and Clusium fought in the Clusian army, the Senones were angered and marched to attack Rome. Defeating the Romans on the River Allia, they captured the city, all but the Capitol, in which the Romans of fighting age had taken refuge, and slew the elders who, dressed in the insignia of the offices which they held, were sitting in the vestibules of their houses.[71]

According to Plutarch, on the other hand, the Forum was the place where these priests and senior senators sat waiting in their ivory chairs:

Brennus, having taken possession of Rome, set a strong guard about the Capitol, and, going himself down into the Forum, was there struck by amazement at the sight of so many men sitting in that order and silence, observing that they neither rose at his coming, nor so much as changed colour or countenance, but remained without fear or concern, leaning upon their staves, and sitting quietly, looking at each other. The Gauls, for a great while, stood wondering at the strangeness of the sight, not daring to approach or touch them, taking them for an assembly of superior beings. But when one, bolder than the rest, drew near to Marcus Papirius, and putting forth his hand, gently touched his chin and stroked his long beard, Papirius with his staff struck him a severe blow on the head; upon which the barbarian drew his sword and slew him. This was the introduction to the slaughter; for the rest, following his example, set upon them all and killed them.[72]

Camillus, still in exile, was in Ardea, and from this place of refuge he led a sortie against the Gauls. Its success gave the Romans much-needed encouragement, and their surviving army, which was at Veii, launched a move to secure his restoration and reappointment as Roman commander-in-chief. But Camillus, the tradition continued, was so anxious to maintain constitutional propriety that he declared he would only accept the command if the Romans besieged on the Capitoline hill agreed that he should do so. A certain Pontius Cominius succeeded in getting through to them in disguise, and Camillus was duly appointed dictator.

But meanwhile the Gauls had discovered the marks Cominius had made with his feet and hands as he climbed up to the Capitol, and their king Brennus directed that a party of Gauls should mount the cliff by the same route, and surprise the Roman garrison.

When the king had thus spoken [continued Plutarch], the Gauls cheerfully undertook to perform it, and in the dead of night a good party of them together, with great silence, began to climb the rock, clinging to the precipitous and difficult ascent, which yet upon trial offered a way to them, and proved less difficult than they had expected. So that the foremost of them having gained the top of all, and and put themselves into order, they all but surprised the outworks, and mastered the watch, who were fast asleep; for neither man nor dog perceived their coming.

But there were sacred geese kept near the temple of Juno Moneta, which at other times were plentifully fed, but now, by reason that corn and other provisions were grown scarce for all, were but in a poor condition. The creature is by nature of quick sense, and apprehensive of the least noise, so that these, being moreover watchful through hunger and restless, immediately discovered the coming of the Gauls, and, running up and down with their noise and cackling, they raised the whole camp, while the barbarians on the other side, perceiving themselves discovered, no longer endeavoured to conceal their attempt, but with shouting and violence advanced to the assault.

The Romans, every one in haste snatching up the next weapon that came to hand, did what they could on the sudden occasion. Manlius, a man of consular dignity, of strong body and great spirit, was the first that made head against them, and, engaging with two of the enemy at once, with his sword cut off the right arm of one just as he was lifting up his blade to strike, and, running his target full in the face of the other, tumbled him headlong down the steep rock. Then, mounting the rampart, and there standing with others that came running to his assistance, he drove down the rest of them, who, indeed, to begin, had not been many, and did nothing worthy of so bold an attempt. The Romans, having thus escaped this danger, early in the morning took the captain of the watch and flung him down the rock upon the heads of their enemies, and to Manlius for his victory voted a reward, intended more for honour than advantage, bringing him, each man of them, as much as he received for his daily allowance, which was half a pound of bread and one eighth of a pint of wine.

Later, the Romans were reduced so low by hunger as to offer a thousand pounds of gold and with this price to purchase an end of the siege. Marcus Furius Camillus, having been appointed dictator in his absence, came up with his army in the midst of this very conference about the terms of peace, and six months after their coming drove out the Gauls from Rome and cut them to pieces.

Men said they ought to remove to Veii because the city had been burned and overthrown, but this counsel was rejected, at the instance of Camillus.

For the sequel we may return to Livy, or rather to his summary. The Gauls had been gradually displacing the Etruscans in the Padus (Po) valley from about 500 B.C. onwards,[73] and were at this period, as the present events showed, in a position to launch raids into Etruria proper, and even beyond. Before marching on Rome, they had been engaged in besieging Clusium. 'There is a tradition', says Livy,

that it was the lure of Italian fruits and especially of wine, a pleasure then new to them, that drew the Gauls to cross the Alps and settle in regions previously cultivated by the Etruscans. Arruns of Clusium, the story goes, had sent wine into their country deliberately to entice them over, as he wanted his revenge for the seduction of his wife by his ward Lucumo, a man in too powerful a position to be punished except by the help of foreigners called in for the purpose.[74]

This is a typical Greek *cherchez la femme* story in the tradition of Herodotus. Consequently, the second-century historian Polybius, who was a serious man, toned the story down, merely saying that Arruns acted 'on a slight pretext'. But his contemporary Cato was familiar with the adulterous loves of Arruns' wife.[75] Hidden here, beneath the familiar and inexpressive designations Arruns and Lucumo (of which the latter, at least, is a title rather than a name), are the remains of Etruscan sagas, reflecting heaven knows what rivalries between city and city, or clan and clan. The Roman who got to know the Etruscan tale of Arruns of Clusium, and passed it on to Cato, is extremely likely to have been the historian Fabius Pictor, whose family possessed a particularly intimate connection with Etruria and most of all with Clusium, a connection proved by a good deal of archaeological and other evidence.[76] As for the story of the Gallic interest in Clusian wine, it is true that the wine of the region is very pleasant – nowadays it bears the name of neighbouring Montepulciano. But the tale itself is conventional and we find it repeated, to explain a migration, among the folk-lore of many different peoples.

If, however, we leave this myth aside, the part ascribed to Clusium in the prelude to the Gauls' attack on Rome may be authentic. It has been argued against this that Clusium was too far away from Rome for the latter to have much concern for the place at so early a date, and that the whole relationship between the two cities is fictitiously moved backward from a political situation which really developed in the following century. But the man known as Lars Porsenna who had attacked Rome a century earlier was already said to have come from Clusium, a tradition which, on the whole, is likely to be true (section 1 above), and in any case it was a major city-state at this time, at the height of its power (chapter 1). When the Gauls arrived before its gates, it was said that the reason why Roman envoys were there at that juncture was because the Clusians had appealed to Rome. We cannot tell whether that is true or not, for it is always possible, in such cases, that the envoys were sent at the initiative of the Romans, who like other imperial peoples, were very prone to justify their interventions on the grounds that they had received appeals from other states. But, however that may be, at a time when they were concerned about a Gallic invasion from the north, the key position that Clusium occupied in the middle of the Clanis valley (Val di Chiana), the principal inland invasion route, could not fail to be of interest to them.

And so a Roman delegation was visiting the authorities of Clusium; and while it was there, it got itself involved in hostile action against the Gauls. That, it was said, was why the Gauls became angry with the Romans and attacked their city. This was an oblique way of explaining away the Roman defeat at the Allia. For it could now be said that the disaster was due not to military failure or lack of bravery, but to inevitability, seeing that the Romans were fighting in a cause which, being unjust owing to the action of their envoys at Clusium, lacked the approval of the gods. The leader of the Roman mission there, who caused this unhappy result by charging and slaying a Gallic chief, was Quintus Fabius Ambustus, and one must suppose that whereas later enemies of his family, notably the Claudii, were glad to see all the blame descending upon him, this was by no means to the taste of the Fabii themselves. Nor would it appeal to their historian Fabius Pictor, who, drawing upon his family's intimate connection with Etruria and particularly Clusium (note 76), described a heroic career for Ambustus, in the course of which his duel with the Gallic chief became an act of glory rather than treachery.[77]

However, another equally non-military, and therefore equally acceptable, explanation of the Allia defeat was also at hand. During the siege of Veii, it was said, the Romans had refused a Veientine offer to come to terms, so that the débâcle at Allia was a divine punishment for this refusal.[78] Furthermore, the whole capture of Veii (and on doubt this was the version which the Etruscans favoured) was made to seem like a sin directly resulting in the occupation of Rome by the Gauls. And, as we shall see, some Romans also regarded the Gallic catastrophe as a judgement for the unjust exile inflicted upon Camillus. All these were methods of getting away from a historical fact, the most uncomfortable fact in Roman military history: for Rome did not fall to foreigners again for another eight hundred years.

This traumatic event, known to Aristotle and attributed to a variety of dates between 390 and 384–3,[79] was surrounded by as many myths as anything that had ever happened, or was supposed to have happened, during the preceding, prehistoric centuries of the city. One noteworthy mythical accretion seems to have been the story that the Romans, when they lost the rest of the city, nevertheless held out in the Capitol and never gave it up. However Ennius, as well as Lucan, who wrote his *Civil War* (Pharsalia) in the first century A.D., preserved an alternative tradition indicating that this was not true: the Capitol like the rest of the city fell to the Gauls.[80] The fact that such an unpalatable tradition survived at all, however successfully it was otherwise suppressed, suggests that it corresponded with what had actually happened. But the other version made infinitely better patriotic material, and most of the historians adopted this alternative so fervently that it passed without contradiction into the canon. If, as the Greek poet Simylus indicated, the story of Tarpeia's betrayal was originally associated with this event (chapter 4, section 3), it was an attempt to show that the loss of the Capitol (like the defeat on the Allia) was due to external causes and not to any failure of Roman courage.

Livy's picture of the entry of the Gauls into the city is based on the records of what took place after another, later, Roman disaster, the defeat by Hannibal at Cannae (216 B.C.). There are also certain echoes of Greece's Persian wars, with particular reference to Herodotus' account of the Persians' attempt on Delphi, followed by their occupations of Athens. And the account of the venerable Romans sitting in motionless solemnity to await the invaders recalls the Athenian priests on the Acropolis who waited in dignity for their Persian enemies to arrive.[81] The picture of what happened at Rome, with its stress on the intrepid Marcus (or he may have been called Manius) Papirius, was not at all likely to be given prominence by Fabius Pictor, because the greatest of all the members of the Papirian family, Lucius Papirius Cursor, five times consul and twice dictator in the later fourth century B.C., had wanted to execute a hero of the house of the Fabii, Quintus Fabius Maximus Rullianus, for disobedience of orders. But the heroism of Marcus or Manius Papirius was naturally presented in a vivid light by his own patrician family, which was in a singularly favourable position to influence the records both after and before 300 B.C. (chapter 4, section 3).[82] The anecdote was also, of course, highly flattering to the conservative senatorial cause as a whole, belonging to the same romantic category as the more authentic remark of king Pyrrhus' exasperated ambassador to his master, that the senate was an assembly of kings.

The catalogue of Examples of Virtue continues with the exploit of Marcus Manlius who, warned by the sacred geese, repulsed the night attack on the Capitol by the Gauls. Probably, as we have seen, there were really no Romans left in the Capitol to be attacked, since it had fallen with the rest of the city. But in any case the story served the useful purpose of explaining the surname borne by one of the branches of the Manlian family, Capitolinus. One of the six original noblest houses, with an alleged victorious consul, Cnaeus Manlius, as early as 480, the Manlii would have experienced little difficulty if they wanted to guide and adjust the patriotic canon. Besides, it was pleasant to make Marcus into a hero, since there was a rival tradition, disagreeably prominent in and after the Gracchan period, that Marcus Manlius, in spite of his patrician birth, later turned into a dangerous and revolutionary reformer. However, in the later Republic there were still a number of Manlii sufficiently prominent to sign their name on the coins. They achieved a consulate once again in 65 B.C., but its holder, Lucius Manlius Torquatus, may not have been the sort of man to make too much fuss about his ancestry, since he attracted pained comment by marrying a woman from a provincial Italian town.[83]

Marcus Manlius, as every Roman knew, was given the alarm by the geese kept on the Capitol. According to Virgil, Vulcan depicted the scene on the shield he forged for Aeneas.

Here too a silvery goose went fluttering through a golden
Colonnade, honking out an alarum, that the Gauls are on us:
Under the cover of a dark night, lucky for them, the Gauls
Creep closer through the brushwood, some have already scaled
The citadel's heights: their clothing and hair were done in gold;
The stripes on their cloaks are gleaming; about their fair skinned
    throats
Are necklaces fastened; each of them brandishes two Alpine
Spears in his hand, and carries a tall, narrow shield for
    protection.[84]

The Capitoline geese are described as sacred to Juno,[85] but it
does not, in fact, appear that this was the case. However, the
Capitol contained a place for divination (*auguraculum*), in
which hens were later kept; perhaps earlier there had been
geese, which may have given rise to the story. Plutarch recorded
that the Roman censors, after their appointment every five
years, traditionally made it one of their very first tasks to draw
up contracts for the food of the sacred geese: either because it
was a primary duty for vigilant men to tend the most vigilant of
creatures, or to show gratitude because they had saved Rome
from the Gauls.[86]

'The city,' declares Florus, 'was saved by Manlius and restored
by Camillus.'[87] The return of the national hero Camillus from
Ardea to revive his stricken country by taking command of
the Roman army, which had taken refuge at Veii, was directly
copied from an event during the Second Punic War when the
heroic Quintus Fabius Maximus Verrucosus Cunctator ('the Delayer') (much admired by the family historian Fabius Pictor,
who was his contemporary) returned to office in order to assume the emergency office of the dictatorship after a disastrous
defeat by Hannibal – not the battle of Cannae, to which reference was made above, but the catastrophe at Lake Trasimene
in the previous year (217 B.C.). But in the first century B.C.,
Camillus' recall also reminded many conservatives happily of
Sulla's return from the east to stamp out his Marian enemies.[88]
However, the eagle eyes of pro-Marian historians also lit upon
the incident, because Licinius Macer, for example, revolted
against Sulla's high-handed action in getting himself nominated

dictator in 82 B.C., and was consequently prepared to look critically upon appointments like that of Camillus.[89]

And so the perilous mission of Pontius Cominius, which had originally, perhaps, merely been ascribed to a desire to reopen communications between the besieged and the Roman army at Veii,[90] was endowed by later defenders of Camillus' memory with the further function of creating a constitutional justification for his appointment as dictator. But here again the traumatic events of 217 B.C., after the catastrophe at Trasimene, were still in people's minds. For democratically minded writers – this time, men eager to criticize Quintus Fabius Maximus the Delayer – wrote up the incident of Camillus' appointment as a precedent for the welcome fact that, when Fabius was appointed dictator, a co-dictator was appointed as well: for the particular point they wanted to bring out was that this colleague, Marcus Minucius, was not nominated by a consul on the senate's proposal, as dictators normally were, but elected by popular vote.[91]

When we come down to historical facts, however – or rather, when we get as close to them as we can – there are grave doubts whether Camillus had anything to do with the Gauls' withdrawal from Rome at all. Polybius knows nothing of any such intervention,[92] and R. M. Ogilvie sems to be right in describing it as 'one of the most daring fabrications in Roman history'.[93]

It was perpetrated because it seemed so urgently necessary to fabricate a military victory over the Gallic invaders. What actually happened was that, after occupying Rome for a number of months, they went away. But it was inglorious to say just that and no more: a Roman victory had to be invented. And so it was, with Camillus as its hero. The battle that consequently appears in the records was probably copied from another supposed success against the Gauls (perhaps authentic) attributed to Camillus' son Lucius in *c.* 349 B.C.[94] Yet in due course this fictitious victory of Marcus Camillus became a central feature of his saga. Indeed, in the eyes of Virgil, it was *the* central feature, since when he mentions Camillus it is only to portray him with the standards he was alleged to have recovered from the Gauls on this occasion. For it was Rome's psychologically necessary vengeance for the Allia.[95] And it was the mythical anticipation of the authentic final victories over the Cisalpine Gauls in 225–220 B.C., and the triumphs of Julius Caesar across the Alps, between 58 and 51.

It was all the more necessary to invent this military success of Marcus Camillus because of the real circumstances in which the Gauls departed from the city. Polybius believed that they were compelled to withdraw because their north Italian homes had been invaded by the neighbouring Veneti. This may have been part of the truth, but it was not very complimentary to Roman pride. Besides, the rest of the truth was much worse. For there was also the deeply embarrassing and no doubt historically accurate tradition that the Romans agreed to pay the Gauls a ransom, variously assessed at a thousand and two thousand pounds of gold.[96] It was impossible to deny the persistent report that such a ransom was offered. But Livy, although at one point he inadvertently assumes that the sum was actually handed over, is elsewhere at pains to stress that Marcus Camillus arrived in time to prevent the shameful action. Non-Roman sources are less accommodating. A Greek tradition, hardly likely to commend itself to patriotic Romans, asserted that the ransom was provided by Rome's Greek ally Massilia (Marseille). An Etruscan version claimed that the money was provided by Caere; but that, because of its source, was even more unflattering to the dignity of Rome. And so we have the much more comfortable Roman tradition that Camillus not only refused to pay after all, but also inflicted a resounding defeat on the invaders – and did so not once but twice.

For 'now the might of Heaven and human wisdom were engaged in the cause of Rome'.[97] The Gauls were driven away in disorder; and honour, after the fearful hazards to which it had been subjected, was fully restored once more.

The last act in Livy's drama is a remarkable speech attributed to Camillus. In this, he argues successfully against an attempt by certain Roman officials (tribunes of the people, who were appointed by the plebeians) to persuade the inhabitants of Rome to emigrate from their ruined city and go to live at Veii, where the remnants of the Roman army had gathered after the defeat of the Allia. Livy takes the opportunity to make Camillus utter a powerful eulogy of Rome. This is very much in the tradition of classical rhetoric, resembling praises of Athens and Boeotia delivered by Greek historians (Xenophon and Ephorus). But above all Livy's eulogy strongly echoes, indeed consciously imitates, a similar glorification of Rome by Cicero.[98]

It is a curious feature of Roman life that on quite a number of occasions throughout the centuries there were reports that the capital might be transferred to some other centre. Sometimes, no doubt, the rumours were authentic, either deliberately spread by hostile parties in order to embarrass the authorities, or arising in the natural course of events because gossip of all kinds spread so readily in the absence of reliable information. But in either case such reports were admirable fodder for moralizing historians, since they gave an opportunity to emphasize the superiority of the geographical site and bracing moral atmosphere of Rome.

After the sack of the city by the Gauls, it was perhaps not so unnatural to think of emigrating to Veii, a great city which its recent capture had not left so totally destroyed as our authorities suggest. But Camillus is made to declare the idea a grievous religious sin.[99] Similarly, in 122 B.C., the attempt of the reformer Gaius Gracchus to establish a pioneer overseas colony at Carthage foundered on powerful religious objections, based on the suspicion that once it was created he intended to make it the capital of the empire. Julius Caesar, too, it was fancifully said, thought of transferring his capital to the supposed cradle of the Roman race, Troy (Ilium), whose hero Aeneas he claimed as his ancestor – a point he emphasized by a widely publicized visit to the place (chapter 3, section 3). But what seemed more convincing to some people, in view of his evident distaste for Rome and its disaffected nobility, was a rumour (no doubt equally unfounded) that he harboured the desire to transfer the government to Alexandria where he had enjoyed himself with Cleopatra.

And then, after Caesar's death, the fact that Antony, whose share of the empire under the Second Triumvirate was the east, actually established himself at Alexandria, again with Cleopatra, revived the same sort of gossip. His enemy Octavian, the future Augustus, made the utmost use of these rumours, for propaganda purposes. And yet he too, after annexing Egypt and making himself sole ruler of the Roman empire, became subject to unfriendly reports of an extremely similar kind.

However, with his usual skill, Augustus turned this slander to his own advantage. All the poets who were sympathetic with his aims proceeded to stress that Troy must never be revived – by which they meant, not that the capital must never be moved (for another three hundred years there was no real question of this), but that eastern luxury and corruption must be shunned. Horace devoted stirring stanzas to the theme, and Virgil faced the special difficulty inherent in his own chosen thesis – namely that Augustan Rome *was* a reincarnation of Aenean Troy – by causing Juno to demand that Troy's successors shall not be exotic and Trojan, but native and Roman:

Do not command the indigenous Latins to change their ancient
Name, to become Trojans and to be called the Teucrians!
Allow them to keep the old language and their traditional dress:
Let it be Latium for ever, and the kings be Alban kings:
Let the line be Roman, the qualities making it great be Italian.
Troy is gone; may it be gone in name as well as reality.[100]

Livy wishes to put forward very much the same point of view. However he chooses as his text not the Troy of Aeneas but the Veii which had been overcome by that scarcely less glorious mythological figure, Camillus. Moreover, in the light of Augustan circumstances and sentiment, Livy rewrote the whole story in a way of his own choosing. In his pages Camillus, leader in war and then (less glamorously and in parts just as dubiously) leader in peace,[101] not only emerges as the 'Romulus and Father of his Country and a Second Founder of the City',[102] but also appears, like the hero of the *Aeneid*, as an obvious prefiguration of Augustus, who was already being informally hailed by the designation Father of his Country that he was later to assume as an official title.

But all this was relatively late in the mythology of Camillus; to earlier generations, he had already mirrored a lot of other national leaders of historical Rome. According to your political views, you could see him as a Sulla who had come back to preserve conservative institutions, or, if you preferred, as a dictator of an earlier brand who was elected by the will of the people (conveniently forgetting, if so, that according to other accounts he despised the lower orders). Or he could be thought of as a Scipio the younger, weeping over the ruins of the city he had captured; or he was whichever Scipio you liked, fatefully saving his country and then suffering its ingratitude in return. And meanwhile members of the ancient house of the Furii were always at hand to offer a stimulus to the reputation of their legendary ancestor. For example there was a consul of 196 B.C. – Lucius Furius Purpureo – likely to be particularly interested because he too had allegedly defeated the Gauls.[103] There was Lucius Furius Philus (consul, 136 B.C.) who was appropriately a friend of Scipio the younger; and there was a dependent of the family Aulus Furius Antias – a man from Antium like the historian Valerius Antias – who was, equally appropriately, an epic poet (*c.* 100 B.C.). And now, under Augustus himself, there was another man bearing the glorious names of Marcus Furius Camillus, who got himself launched, with imperial support, upon the traditional career of his ancestors. Later he was to become consul (in A.D. 8). But Augustus must have begun to encourage his promotion a good deal earlier. Indeed he had been continually pushing forward selected members of these ancient, legendary families from the time when Livy and Virgil were writing, early in his reign.

3 THE MYTHS OF LATER ROMAN TIMES

After the magical and fantastic excitements of the siege of Veii and the Gallic occupation of Rome, Livy insists that he is moving from mythology into history. Nevertheless, the story of Rome continued to produce a rich and ever renewed crop of myths. The Valerii let themselves go with the interminable exploits of their hero Marcus Valerius Corvus (see also note 94) who was supposed to have defeated Gauls, Volsci, Aequi, Samnites and Etruscans, and to have promulgated a law of appeal (300). And meanwhile the Decii (with a dissolute pro-Gracchan orator, Publius Decius Subulo, to keep them in the public eye) allegedly produced three successive generations of men called Publius Decius Mus, all of whom, by an antique, magical rite known as *devotio*, solemnly sacrificed themselves in battle to one enemy after another.[104]

Then in the First Punic War there was Marcus Atilius Regulus. After he had been captured by Carthage's Greek general Xanthippus in 255 B.C., he was sent back to Rome on the understanding that he would urge the Senate to make peace or at least to exchange prisoners. But it was said that he urged them to do neither, and returned to Carthage, where he was tortured to death. It made a great story which inspired generations of Romans. The historian Polybius does not know of it, only citing Regulus as a dramatic, tragic example of the mutability of Fortune.[105] As far as we are aware, the fuller version is first recorded by Gaius Sempronius Tuditanus (consul 129 B.C.). Cicero sees Regulus as a reliable, selfless public servant. By his time, and probably earlier, the rhetorical schools were full of the heroic tale. 'When his relatives and friends would have kept him back, he chose to return to a death by torture rather than prove false to his promise, though given to an enemy.'[106] And this moral tale was told again by Horace, in his most solemn vein.

> They say he drew back from the kiss his true wife
> And little children begged, and like a prisoner
>   Deprived of civil rights
> Bent an austere gaze grimly on the ground,
> Until his unexampled admonition
> Had fixed the wavering Senate in their purpose
>   And he could push through crowds
> Of grieving friends, exile- and glory-bound.
> And yet he knew what the barbarian torturer
> Had ready for him. Kinsmen blocked his passage,
>   The people held him back,
> But he returned as unconcernedly
> As if they were his clients and he'd settled
> Some lengthy lawsuits for them and was going

> On to Venafrum's fields
> Or to Tarentum, Sparta's colony.[107]

But Horace's contemporary, Diodorus (Chapter 2, section 1), happens to reveal that this noble myth conceals a startlingly different historical picture.[108] What Diodorus had learnt was that Regulus, having been defeated as a divine punishment for his arrogance in refusing peace terms, became a prisoner of war in Carthaginian Africa, where he died of neglect, poison or torture before an exchange of prisoners could be effected.[109] That is likely enough. However, Diodorus continues, the wife of Regulus back in Italy had been allotted two Carthaginian prisoners, Hamilcar and Bodostor, whom she was keeping in detention at her own Roman home. And on hearing of her husband's death, she maltreated them so savagely that Bodostor died of starvation, Hamilcar being saved from a similar fate by the intervention of Roman tribunes. (According to another version it was her sons who tortured the prisoners, putting them in a chest full of sharp spikes.)

It was to justify or palliate this action, taken by the widow or her sons, that the magnificent epic story, with its stress on the barbarity of the Carthaginians, was invented – no doubt under pressure from the family of the Atilii.[110]

One of them, named Marcus Atilius Regulus like the unsuccessful general, was a dramatist of the later third century B.C. He specialized in comedies, although they were rather savage ones. But other playwrights of the period were still busy converting contemporary events into myth. For example, Naevius wrote a patriotic play *Clastidium* about the Roman commander Marcus Claudius Marcellus who slew the Gallic enemy chieftain in a battle at that place (222 B.C.). The adaptation of historical events into dramatic, mythological form was by no means finished; and indeed it was destined to continue for many further years. Under Nero (A.D. 54–68), the poet Lucan chose to present the wars between Pompey and Caesar in this shape, and then in the latter part of the first century A.D. an unknown tragedian converted the story of Nero's wife Octavia into a tragic drama.[111] History had still not really taken over from myth. Portents and prodigies continued to be reported; and miracles, too, had a great vogue and a great future, often with official support – for example when the cult of the god Aesculapius (Asclepius) was imported into the city in 291 B.C. Much later, too, under the emperor Marcus Aurelius (A.D. 161–80), a miraculous shower of rain saved the imperial army from a military defeat – preparing the way for a host of Christian miracles under Constantine.

Aurelius and Constantine were quick to accord official recognition to these heavenly signs. For every emperor of Rome, like the Republican leaders before them, was eager to add new myths to old, if he saw any advantage in this. And they were also willing, of course, to exploit, interpret, expand and distort the traditional myths in any way that might prove valuable. We become particularly conscious of these processes under the founder of the imperial regime, Augustus, because we possess their incomparable (or, in the case of Dionysius, tedious) fruits in the writings of the poets and prose writers who were sympathetic to his regime. In the first place, their mythological transformations extend even to contemporary events, such as the defeat of Cleopatra; and, secondly, this was the period in which the entire mythical corpus, already quite a number of centuries old, received the last of its large-scale refurbishments, as we have seen on more than one occasion during the present study.[112] And this Augustan recapitulation and revision, by and large, is the rendering that has come down to us. It is from such material that we have to try to build up again, precariously, the prolonged, never ceasing, evolutions and transformations of the potent Roman myths.

7 THE CHARACTER OF ROMAN MYTHOLOGY

1 MYTH AS EXPLANATION AND PARA-HISTORY

Roman mythology, then, consists of a variety of ingredients. The external elements include, principally, importations from Greece and importations from Etruria. Both sets of importations are employed very frequently indeed for aetiological purposes, to explain some Roman institution or other when, in the course of time, its real explanation had been forgotten.[1]

Many stories too, and the names connected with them, are found to be anticipations of later historical events, cast back into remote antiquity in the interests of patriotic aggrandizement, political bias or family pride. Finally, there are traces of memories handed down locally, priestly and perhaps popular as well, though how far back they go on native Roman soil is questionable.

The imported Greek myths are innumerable. It is difficult for us, nowadays, to understand what a passion there was, throughout the Mediterranean world, for supplying every non-Greek nation with myths according to the Greek pattern. The writers of Greece got to work on the task in the most whole-hearted and light-hearted fashion, and the various 'barbarian' peoples – even those that hated the Greeks of their own time – accorded the keenest hospitality to this process of invention and adaptation, ruthlessly shelving their own relatively feeble local traditions in its favour. The Romans only drew the line by refusing to go the whole hog with the Greeks concerning divine interventions, which continued to seem un-Roman and were, therefore, reserved for very special and peculiarly solemn occasions.

It is a mistake, however, to draw too sharp and simple a contrast between what are interpreted as the fresh, living myths of Greece and the tired, late, artificial literary stories of Rome.[2] For even the first known writers about Greek mythology, Homer and Hesiod, come late in the development of the myths they describe – at a time when a long, selective and formalized tradition was already fully in existence. Homer's myths are already just as literary and artificial, in their way, as the Greek and Roman tales that were being told three or four centuries later.[3]

Furthermore, the whole current of modern research increasingly shows what a large number of Greek myths were adapted from the civilizations of the near east. Some of the stories had been learnt from the immigrants who in the course of the second millennium B.C. came to places in Greece such as Mycenae. But the Greeks had also, directly or indirectly, taken over a great many other stories, and parts of stories, from peoples in other parts of the Aegean and near east – Minoans, Syrians, Phoenicians, Hittites, Babylonians and Egyptians.[4] For these nations not only exchanged their myths with one another,[5] but transmitted them in considerable quantities to Greece. The fact that, when the authors of the Homeric and Hesiodic poems were writing, literacy was still a recent event in Greece, whereas it was quite old in Rome by the time of the first writers, does not establish an absolute contrast. For Homer and Hesiod, too, had an enormous period of literacy behind them – in the non-Greek near east.[6] And so the Greek borrowings from that source represent a comparable phenomenon to the subsequent borrowings of Rome from Greece.

Rome also imported many elements of its mythology from Etruria. And these debts, as the present study has attempted to indicate, were a good deal more important than has generally been supposed. Etruria consisted of a number of individualistic city-states, in varying relationships with each other and with Rome (chapter 1), and although it is only by gradual and continuing research that we are able to identify their individual characteristics, it can now be discerned that some of them, like the city-states of Greece, possessed distinctive local mythologies of their own. Sometimes these consisted of adaptations from the Greeks; but this was by no means always the case. Certain of the Etruscan mythologies left their impact on Rome. In addition to versions which the Romans eventually accepted as canonical, a number of very distinctive Etruscan tales that deviate markedly from the Roman canon have narrowly managed to avoid the unconscious, or more often conscious, censorship and suppression that this canon imposed.

How far do the surviving Roman myths reflect memories that were handed down locally in pre-literate times? This question has two aspects. First, there were undoubtedly Roman priests and priestly boards whose interest it was to hand down traditions relating to the cults and temples with which they were concerned. And there is no special reason, as we have seen, to suppose that all earlier records and memories were destroyed by the Gallic occupation early in the fourth century B.C. (chapter 2, section 3). Secondly, can we also detect traces of ancient folk-memories? Genuine Italian folklore has proved hard to lay hands upon. It is true that certain elements in our tradition, though not very extensive elements, seem to be of quite a different order from the priestly record, since they appear to go back to the more 'primitive' or magical rituals of the Bronze Age or even of Neolithic times.[7] But that does not, of course, mean that they necessarily go back to those times *on the spot*; they may only have arrived at Rome at a comparatively late date. And on more than one occasion a Roman ritual, custom or name shows signs of prehistoric antiquity, whereas the story introduced to explain belongs to a far later time.

The survival of these rituals, customs and names is a peculiar feature of Rome, where such remnants of early life are more readily identifiable than they were in Greece. For they remained right on the very surface of the religion of Rome: they were clearly visible to an ancient Roman every day. But their explanation had long since been forgotten. If Rome, in the dim past, had ever possessed a mythical imagination of its own, it had died ages ago – the primitive culture, in so far as it deserved the name, must have possessed a peculiar sort of aridity which repressed it. But then, in about the fourth (or conceivably to some extent the fifth) century B.C., this mythological faculty re-emerged, under Greek and Etruscan influences. And that is when the Romans began to feel the urge to elucidate these fascinating survivals: the urge for the aetiological explanations which play such a vast part in Roman mythology.

They extended to ceremonials and many other institutions, to the designations of places, geographical features, ancient monuments and tombs, and to the names of persons, heroes and gods. In very many cases the stories mobilized to explain these names had not actually been invented for this specific purpose but were taken over from other contexts altogether – often foreign contexts – and then adapted to meet these different circumstances. This is a common phenomenon in other parts of the world as well. It is how the Fijian myth of Mberewalaki came to be employed to explain the mountainous nature of an island, whereas it had originated in some quite different connection;[8] and there are many parallels in South America, Melanesia, Polynesia and Australia.[9] But aetiological myths also flourished in the near and middle east, among the peoples who bequeathed so many of their stories to Greece. The Babylonian myth of Adapa, for example, sought to explain why the priests of Eridu were exempted from feudal dues. And, long before that, a number of Sumerian myths had been designed or adapted for similar purposes.[10]

Among the Greeks, too, aetiology had been present in the myths of the country from the earliest known times. Early dwellers in Greece wondered why it was customary, at a sacrifice, for the best meat to be withheld from the god and eaten by the worshippers. To explain the custom, Hesiod explained how Prometheus had once wrapped up all the worst bits of meat in fat, and the best parts in another bundle: then he had told Zeus he could choose: and Zeus chose the inferior package.[11] But aetiological interpretations of this kind really only came into their own when antiquarianism became fashionable in Hellenistic times. Alexandrian writers of the third century B.C., such as Callimachus and Apollonius Rhodius, made great play with their ingenious explanations, pretending in their sophisticated, intellectual fashion that the quaint naïvetés of the old tales, and even their very implausibilities, have to be taken seriously. And then Roman antiquarians went ahead with the

same technique on an enormous scale – not always so patroniz-
ingly or playfully as the Hellenistic Greeks, since the learned
Varro or Verrius Flaccus, for example, were not famous for
their light touch; though Ovid and Propertius were thoroughly
Alexandrian in their attitudes, and Ovid outdid Alexandria at
its own flippant game.

Roman ritual provided a specially fertile field for this activity,
because the Romans were an obsessively ritualistic people, as
Livy, for one, was proud to proclaim.[12] It was by their rites that
they maintained their peace with the gods (*pax deorum*),
which practically amounted to a juridical covenant. It is obvious
that myth, although it need not invariably be associated with
religion, very frequently indeed possesses such a relation;[13] and
that applies strongly to Roman religion – to the ritual which
forms such a large part of it.[14]

One of the most amply discussed mythological problems
today relates to the question whether, when such a connection
does happen to exist between myth and ritual, the one or the
other came first.[15] But there is no need, in the present study, to
add to the vast literature on this subject, because at Rome, when
such a link existed, it often seems apparent that the ritual
came first and the myth was introduced later to explain it –
as in some other mythologies, though it would be incorrect to
generalize to all or even most of them. Or, to be more precise,
any given Roman myth may, in itself, have existed in some
other context from antique times, but *in relation to the ritual*
the myth was normally the later of the two.[16] In contrast to
other peoples (Greeks, Germans, Celts) whose myths were
stronger than their rites, the Roman rituals had survived wholly
or largely without any mythological accompaniment; and as
time went on an assortment of myths was brought in to 'explain'
them.

This is an important aspect of the Roman mythology. But
there is another which is more important still. This arises from
the peculiar, engrossed absorption of the Romans in the tem-
poral, chronological element in life. They possessed an abnormally developed sense of real and supposed past landmarks of

time, to which they felt bound by an unbroken chain of continuity.[17] 'The individual moment', rightly insisted Franz Altheim, 'was raised to an importance hitherto unknown. Everything is concentrated on single decisive acts; the special quality of the different moments of history is persistently felt.'[18]

But for 'history' read 'history and mythology', for the Romans showed the utmost determination to apply this obsession to both. Not only did they seek a chronological framework for all the events that had, in the historical sense, happened, but they were just as eager to fit their mythical stories into an equally firm, connected sequence of pseudo-historical, pseudo-chronological narrative – a pattern utterly different from, say, the cosmic pattern of Indian myths, since it provided a continuous, comforting, pride-inspiring series of fixed points extending between even the most legendary past and their own present day.

'The clumsy distinction,' writes Claude Lévi-Strauss, 'between "people without history" and others could with advantage be replaced by a distinction between what for convenience I would call "cold" and "hot" societies: the former seeking, by the institutions they give themselves, to annul the possible effects of historical factors on their equilibrium and continuity in a quasi-automatic manner; the latter resolutely internalizing the historical process and making it the moving power of their development.'[19] It is sometimes assumed that most myth-producing peoples have belonged to the former category, possessing a static, or cyclic, or at any rate non-historical, view of time. But that is very often not the case. For example, the Nupe of Nigeria clothe their accounts of the distant past 'in terms of a sober, pseudo-scientific history'.[20] And this is a very ancient and widespread practice indeed, founded upon a profound psychological need for a reference in time.[21] Even in the remotely ancient kingship lists of the Sumerians, it is carefully specified that the mythical Gilgamesh is the fifth king of the dynasty of Erech, the second dynasty after the Flood. And that is very much how the Romans liked to look at their own mythical past. According to the convenient distinction proposed by Lévi-Strauss, they were emphatically a 'hot', historically-minded society, and so they were determined to weld their myths into an ostensibly historical, chronological shape. That is why there emerged this great bulk of fictitious history or para-history or higher truth relating to Rome, which only occasionally coincides with that other kind of truth that we learn about from the archaeologists (chapter 1 init.).[22]

The Romans were abnormally single-minded in this conversion of their mythology into history. It was not entirely their own idea, for they had inherited from the Greeks a strong predisposition to proceed in this direction. Homer had encouraged the tendency by lavishing a careful orderliness upon his mythical patterns of chronology, and by investing genealogies and other time-sequences with a meticulous pseudo-precision. So convincingly was this done that in the fifth century B.C. the historian Thucydides, for all his revolutionary modernizations of historical thinking, fails to appreciate that the Homeric myths are wholly fictitious. On the contrary, he believes that the events recounted in them contain a nucleus of hard fact, and feels he has done enough to tidy them up when he eliminates obvious exaggerations and accretions: 'it is questionable whether we can have complete confidence in Homer's figures, which, since he was a poet, were probably exaggerated.'[23]

This attitude towards Homer, encouraged by a process of 'annalizing' the myths in anticipation of later Roman practice, continued among the Greeks for many hundreds of years. And that is how the Romans, too, came to adopt a similar attitude towards the myths they themselves had concocted. As the analyses attempted in the course of this book have suggested, the Roman writers are frequently and anxiously seeking to make distinctions between what is fabulous and what is not,[24] though they draw the line far too generously, classifying a great deal of fiction as fact, or at least as the product of fact. Very much the same sort of attempt to draw a distinction, with the same over-liberal result, is found among the Ibo and Yoruba societies of Nigeria, and among Indians of North America, and in communities of the South Pacific.[25]

We should not, however, blame the Romans and these other peoples because their attempts to delimit the two spheres were unsuccessful. For it is obvious enough that there can be no such thing as objective, wholly non-mythical history. Even in the unlikely event of a historical writer lacking the cruder biases, the 'facts', as he first receives them, are already so selective and incomplete that their very arbitrariness makes it impossible for him to be objective. And then when he casts them into literary form, he is setting a second perverting process of selection in motion.[26] Nevertheless, there still remains a type of fiction which, however much it may, by other means, enlighten us about the community who produced it, cannot claim to be any selection of historical truth whatever, even of the most incomplete and arbitrary kind. That, unquestionably, is myth. Yet a large part of their mythical corpus was not recognized by the ancients to be mythical at all – a situation which they share with many other peoples.

In other words, the Greeks and Romans, having carefully set aside the portions (too small portions) of the recorded past which they could not accept as historical truth, believed that the rest had really happened.[27] Or rather, most of them believed this. For there was also a good deal of deliberate invention and falsification, and it now remains to discuss this element, and assess the moving spirits behind it.

2   MORALS, POLITICS AND FAMILIES

Mythology has to select, just as much as history does. Its creators and narrators concentrate their attention upon the highlights in order to single out what is recognizable and significant. Avoiding psychological minutiae as unnecessarily distracting, the myths display what is typical in human behaviour. For they are exploring the permanent values of life.

This means that, if a people happens to be interested in morality, then it finds myths singularly well suited for the purveyance of moral truths. And no people has ever been more concerned about morality than the ancient Romans were. This sometimes causes irritation to a modern student, when he is reflecting upon some particularly high-handed and brutal piece of Roman behaviour. But this apparent disparity should not necessarily, or generally, lead to the conclusion that the Romans were hypocrites. True, they were sometimes compelled, by external circumstances or by flaws in their personal and national characters, to commit atrocities. But they remained profoundly conscious of the moral ideal – perhaps all the more so on that account.[28] Indeed, this ideal seemed to them quite indistinguishable from their political and social purposes: the latter without the former could not be imagined. Their insistence on the ethical basis of their whole lives and careers is the reason why they went to such tremendous pains to justify everything they did in ethical terms.

And so the Roman historians and mythologists, being more sensitive than their modern counterparts to common opinion and judgement, operated continually with moral aims in mind. Cicero pronounced that an important function of historiography is to be a guide to living, *magistra vitae*,[29] and Livy, in his preface, declared: 'History possesses the outstanding beneficial merit of setting all its varied lessons luminously on record for our attention, and from these one may select models for oneself and one's country.'[30] Dionysius, too, pronounced that Rome had provided infinite examples of all the virtues from its very beginnings – from the mythological age.[31] The virtues are clothed in human form; for it is characteristic of the ancients to be less aware of general movements and developments than we are, and more interested in human personages – they were inclined to telescope long drawn out, gradual tendencies into single human careers. Nevertheless, these human beings of the adjusted or imagined past are often scarcely more than embodiments of virtue and vice. The abstract moral qualities, *pietas*, *fides*, *pudicitia*, *frugalitas* and the rest, clothed in the accidental garb of the leaders of each generation, have been rightly identified as the true and enduring heroes of Livy's History.[32]

The moral approach, applied to historical and mythical events alike, possessed a Greek pedigree going back to Isocrates, who died in 338 B.C., and farther back still.[33] The Isocratean tendency to moralize was eagerly adopted by the Romans in the second century B.C., and the coming of Greek philosophy into their midst greatly accelerated its progress.[34] But it was above all the Romans themselves whose active and touchy national conscience provided the impetus, and impelled them to stuff the past full of their own moral paragons, to be revered continually as patriotic models or *exempla*. To Ennius these were the ancient ethical standards and heroes on which the prosperity of his own Rome depended.[35] Indeed, nearly six hundred years later, after every generation during the intervening centuries had never ceased to hear this same paean of praise in its schooldays,[36] St Augustine still felt that the great men of Roman history and myth had a great deal to offer, even in a Christian world.[37] Writers of much later times, men like Nathaniel Hawthorne (1851) and Charles Kingsley (1855), were only following the ancient standpoint when they saw the myths primarily as vehicles of didactic moral teaching.

The worship of the heroes of the past was encouraged by a profound attention to ancestors. They were as much part of the family as if they were still alive. As in Chinese tradition, the duty to pay them reverence was the core and nucleus of religious and social life.[38] One always had to try to live up to their demands. 'I won the praise of my ancestors,' announces a Scipio in his epitaph, 'so that they rejoiced that I had been born to them.'[39] The emperor Augustus, of course, displayed the same attitude because he possessed a keen appreciation of what was required of him, though he may have been acting from conviction as well. At any rate he took the trouble to make a collection of valuable *exempla* from the past.[40] And in the Hall of Fame in his Temple of Mars the Avenger, he lodged a portrait-gallery of his ancestors and of other great men, 'in order to require men and future rulers to live up to their standards'.[41]

Here lies one of the keys of Roman mythology. We have seen that the myths were intimately connected with Roman religion (section 1). But Roman religion was in the employment of the state. The historian Polybius, in the second century B.C., makes no bones about this. In Roman public and private life, he says, religion is dramatized and exploited to the highest possible degree; and he expresses the belief that the ruling class arranges matters in such a way on account of the masses, who need to be impressed and 'restrained'.[42] A few years later, the chief priest Quintus Mucius Scaevola put forward the view that 'it is expedient that populations should be deceived in the matter of religion'.[43] And no one was in a better position to arrange this 'opiate of the people' than the Scaevolas, since it was Quintus Scaevola's own father who sifted the pontifical chronicles and made them into the *Annales Maximi*, which included a great deal of suitably edited myth (chapter 2, section 3). In the next century, Varro and many others fully accepted the need for this sort of governmental manipulation. It is the kind of thing Cicero has in mind when he asserts that ' the people's constant need for the advice and authority of the conservative upper classes (*optimates*) is what holds the state together'.[44] Their advice and authority were meticulously directed towards the creation and adjustment of the national myths.

The writers who devoted themselves to this task were acquainted with a formula drawn up by the Stoic philosophers, who subdivided religion into three categories: natural (the sphere of the philosophers themselves), mythical (suitable for poets), and political (expedient in civil society, and devised by national leaders).[45] When one was thinking of the patriotic mythology, the second and third subdivisions went together. They represented two means of achieving the same end: the encouragement of the loyalist mystique, in the interests of the governing class and by their direction. It was in vain that the Epicureans attacked this conception of religion and mythology as an improper means of bolstering the power of priests and rulers.[46] The priests and rulers, and the imaginative writers who were their friends, knew just what they were doing.

Looking backwards into Roman history, as far back as the fourth and third centuries B.C. when the benefit of this Stoic advice had not yet been received, it must be concluded that the people who took the vital steps towards the formation of the mythology were already members of the ruling groups, or their spokesmen, and were already devising and slanting their stories in the patriotic interest. It is tantalizing that we do not know who these men were.[47]

But one thing that is quite certain is that the Roman stories, unlike, apparently, the mythologies of certain other parts of the world, did not just well up from the masses of the population as collective expressions of its will.[48] On the contrary, these sagas, even if they made use of a certain amount of folklore, were on the whole invented or adapted or adjusted at the top, and steps were then taken to ensure that they flowed downwards.

Moreover, the process was not unconscious but fully conscious. This is not, then, the right field for applying the assertion of Lévi-Strauss that 'myths think themselves out in men, and without men's knowledge[49] ... since myths are collective representations no particular "mind" can be said to be responsible for them'.[50] This would not, it seems, be true of Roman myths (at least in their creative phases at the top, though there may have been a flavour of the subliminal about their subsequent impact on the less educated classes). Perhaps Lévi-Strauss would say that this cerebral, conscious character of Roman myth means that it cannot be properly classified as myth at all; certainly he has said little about the subject. At all events, there were minds consciously at work concocting the Roman stories: not very many minds, perhaps, but strong and imaginative minds – or at any rate imaginative enough to pick out, by no means subliminally, what they needed for their purpose and what they thought would be good for their fellow-Romans.

We find this whole idea rather distasteful, because it reminds us of the myths about the German past so keenly propagated by the Nazi state. But since the thousand-year Reich only lasted twelve years, the Nazi myths failed to take root. A closer parallel, therefore is provided by the much more durable Japanese mythology, of which a large part was invented in the period around A.D. 700 for political purposes. The throne, which these myths were largely designed to serve, is still with us. Ancient Rome, too, though it did not last for quite so long, did continue for nearly a thousand years and its mythology, like Japan's, took very powerful roots indeed. It dramatically confirmed the Romans' high opinion of themselves, and their determination to vindicate it by their actions and their confidence in the destiny of their city and nation.

The Romans felt like T. S. Eliot:

> We will take heart for the future,
> Remembering the past.[51]

More specifically, the aim of the Roman myths, as compiled by these high authorities, was to justify the traditional Roman social institutions. More than half a century has now passed since Bronislaw Malinowski declared that myths are a charter for social action: that they come into play when a rite, a ceremony, or a social or moral rule demands a justification – a warrant of its antiquity, reality or sanctity. He should not, we now feel, have generalized by trying to apply his explanation to the whole of mythology, since the commonest of errors in regard to this Protean concept of myth is generalization.[52] Nevertheless, his theory is by no means only applicable to the Trobriand islanders who were the special subjects of his study. It applies also, for example, to the Nigerian Nupe, and to North American Indians. But it should not be thought that the same sort of interpretation can only be applied to non-literate societies. The Japanese *Nihongi* and *Kojiki* were recorded for the purpose of confirming the celestial origins of the Yamato court and population. In the same way the ancient Roman statesmen and thinkers sought to endow the elements in their national life with greater value, prestige and reverence by tracing them back to venerable and exalted origins: by arranging the mutual refraction of contemporary and ancient institutions.

However, the national leaders of Rome, the politicians and writers who organized these hand-outs, did not, at any given time, speak with a single voice. It is because of this diversity of opinion that so many of their myths have come down to us in a bewildering number of different forms.

Sometimes one hears the voice of the priests who wanted to boost a particular cult – and boost themselves at the same time – like the priests of Babylonian Eridu, millennia earlier, who had invented the myth of Adapa to justify their own tax-free condition. And then, in Republican Rome, there was also, as we have seen, frequent and highly acrimonious in-fighting between political groups, who have left their strong mark on the traditions about alleged events belonging even to the remotest mythological past. At any given moment of the Republic there were some twenty or thirty really important Romans: and the families to which they belonged numbered about a dozen. These families, including the six Great Houses and others equally indefatigable in self-aggrandizement, were continually building up and adjusting the national myths in the interests of their own houses and persons, with the aid of historians from their own ranks or under their patronage.

The strange thing, to us, is that it seemed important to people in each successive generation to edit and re-edit these tales for their own sectional purposes. One might have been tempted to regard the old myths as insubstantial antiquities irrelevant to present-day concerns. But that is clearly not how the Romans assessed them. The sagas had been created by their governing cliques, and for centuries the successive members of these cliques went back to them over and over again, and went to work on their reformulation afresh. 'When telling a tale,' remarked Aristotle, 'all men add something to it, because that increases the pleasure.'[53] And certainly everyone who got a chance added something to the Roman myths. Of course this was partly – and it is a factor we should never forget – because people like telling a good entertaining story: and a story gets changed in the process.[54] But, even more, it was for the sake of family prestige or political advantage.

And so the myths of the Romans, unlike the religious dogmas of later societies, were plastic and dynamic. They belonged, to an extent almost unimaginable in modern times, to the present as well as the past. They anchored the one to the other.[55] 'Mythical history', aptly observed Lévi-Strauss, 'is conjoined with the present because nothing has been going on since the appearance of the ancestors except events whose recurrence periodically effaces their particularity.'[56] Yet Lévi-Strauss bases his own general approach to mythology (if one may reproduce an elaborate theory in the shortest possible form) upon the assumption that every element in the structure or pattern of a myth, as it has come down to us, is a significant part of its meaning.[57] Sometimes he maintains this structuralist interpretation regardless of the date or stage at which the element in question became part of a pre-existing myth; though elsewhere he does note that a long process of evolution is a hindrance to the structuralist method.[58]

In the case of Roman myth (which, as suggested above, he may regard as irrelevant for this purpose), it is surely quite a substantial hindrance.[59] For this is a mythology in which, uniquely, we can detect many of the stages of the build-up, so that the eventual patterns are due rather to a series of successive hazards than to any overall plan. Other mythologies no doubt obey different rules. But the Roman myths can be more profitably regarded as the creation of a long sequence of different story-tellers, whose approximate dates, and (if possible) individual personalities and efforts need to be disentangled before we can understand much about what they were trying to say.[60]

A comparison with Japan has already been suggested. Japan's mythology arose later than Rome's. But if we also go back to much earlier times than either, the political character of Roman myths, imposed from above, does not set them apart from the rest of ancient mythology as much as is often thought. Chinese myths, with their Golden Age and 'sage kings', had an early political bias. Mesopotamian myths, of very much earlier date, had already been full of political preoccupations; and considerable sections of the Old Testament [61] and the *Iliad*[62] were intended to glorify tribal history and famous leaders.

From then onwards, even if Greek myths, taken as a whole, never became so overwhelmingly political as those of Rome,[63] nevertheless they were very frequently invented, adjusted and exploited for political purposes.[64] Long after their first formulation, for example, when the Athenian tragic dramatists of the fifth century B.C. found it more economically productive of dramatic situations to rewrite old myths than invent new ones, and when, in consequence, they recast a vast range of them quite as drastically as the Romans ever did later, a great many of their plays were directly related to political developments of their times.[65] And subsequent Greeks, too, remained active in converting their mythology to topical political uses.[66]

Moreover, the Greek myths were, at many epochs, just as sensitive and subject to family pressures as they were to other types of political interest. Indeed, family pretensions exercised scarcely less influence on the mythology of Greece than of Rome. Until only a few years before 400 B.C., until the time when the writing of history first began, the custody of the historical tradition at Greece was almost wholly in the hands of its leading families; and many a myth discloses their jostlings for position in this very family-minded nation, after a fashion that closely anticipates the later practice of the Romans.[67] Nor did the process come to an end after history started to take over, though the full story of Greek family and political myths still remains to be written.[68] This strong element of politics and family is paralleled in the mythologies of many other societies.

Roman myth, then, is not quite so unlike Greek myth as has been supposed – though certainly it contains very remarkable features of its own. For both these reasons, because of the similarities as well as the dissimilarities, the time has come for the habit, mentioned at the beginning of this chapter, of regarding the mythology of Rome as a fake sort of affair, an inconsiderable bastard of Greek myths, to be abandoned; and with it should go all the rest of the nineteenth-century romanticism which denied that the Romans are worth studying on their own account. Countless generations of Europeans, profoundly impressed by the Roman mythical tradition, knew much better.

NOTES

The following abbreviations are used: *BMC=Catalogues of Roman Coins in the British Museum*; DH=Dionysius of Halicarnassus; Ogilvie, *Comm.*=R. M. Ogilvie, *A Commentary of Livy, Books I–V.*

The fragments of the early Latin historians are quoted from H. Peter, *Historicorum Romanorum Reliquiae*, I² (Leipzig 1914), II (Leipzig 1906). The fragments of early Latin poets are given according to E. H. Warmington, *Remains of Old Latin* (Heinemann and Harvard U. P. 1935.)

INTRODUCTION

1. For the view that the term should be restricted to sacred tales, see chapter 7, note 13. For 'legends', chapter 7, note 24. For 'folk-tales', chapter 7, note 27.
2. cf. chapter 7, note 48.
3. Northrop Frye. 'The Archetypes of Literature', in *Myth and Literature*, ed. J. B. Vickery, p. 88.
4. H. J. Rose: cf. chapter 7 and note 2.
5. cf. the structuralist approach of C. Lévi-Strauss, chapter 7, notes 58 and 59.
6. For the 'foundation', see chapter 1 and chapter 4, section 1. For the Etruscans, chapter 1; chapter 2, section 2; chapter 3, section 3; chapter 5, section 2; chapter 6, section 2; etc. For the Sabines, chapter 4, section 3.
7. cf. chapter 7 and note 26.
8. cf. chapter 7 and notes 64–6.

1   ROME AND ETRURIA WITHOUT THEIR MYTHS

1. M. Grant, *The Ancient Mediterranean* (1969), p. 232.
2. E. Gjerstad, *Legends and Facts of Early Roman History*, pp. 7ff.
3. Merger of Bronze into Iron Age: e.g. Allumiere urnfield, in the

hills above Civitavecchia.

4. Sabine centres: Reate (Rieti), Amiternum.

5. D. H. Trump, *Central and Southern Italy Before Rome* (1966), pp. 126, 157.

6. The Septimontium (two villages on Palatine, four on Esquiline, one on Caelian).

7. M. Grant, *The Roman Forum* (1970), p. 14. Cf. coexistence at Caere, Falerii, Athens (Geometric period).

8. e.g. words *asinus, scrofa, bos, rufus, popina*.

9. Bronze figurines from Vetulonia (*c.* 675–650 B.C.) show orientalizing elements. Both Caere (Cerveteri: Regolini-Galassi Tomb in Vatican Museum) and Praeneste (Palestrina) provide Syrian bowls of *c.* 650.

10. H. Hencken, *American Journal of Archaeology*, LXII (1958), p. 272.

11. Strabo, V, 219C.

12. Probably the political league, on the model of the Ionian twelve cities, only dates from the mid sixth century B.C.

13. Especially by the battle of Alalia (Aleria) in 535 B.C. The Greeks were glad to suppose that the Phoenicians had founded the feud between Europe and Asia in mythical times by kidnapping Io from Argos (Herodotus, I, 1, 4–5).

14. Herodotus, I, 107.

15. Fidenae commanded the entrance to the Cremera valley on the opposite side.

16. One derivation of 'Tiber' was from Thebris chief of Veii, Varro, *On the Latin Language*, V, 30 (the derivation from Tiberinus, king of Alba, is wrong). A ruler of Caere was Thefarie (Tiberius) Velianas: see n. 20 below.

17. The tempo of Etruscanization at Satricum was somewhat similar; cf. also Tusculum (Frascati), Ardea, Velitrae (Velletri).

18. e.g. Temple at Vesta, and shrine in Comitium, and S. Omobono (?550–500).

19. Found beneath the Black Stone, *The Roman Forum*, pp. 51ff.: *rex* probably refers to a king rather than to a *rex sacrorum* (priest) of Republican times.

20. M. Pallottino, *Archaeologia Classica* (1964), pp. 49ff.; *Studi Romani* (1965), pp. 1ff.

21. cf. contemporary building activity (early fifth century) at Lanuvium and Falerii (Etruscan) and Satricum (Etrusco-Greek).

22. Their last stage was the destruction of Volsinii in 264. Caere re-

ceived a second-grade Roman franchise, perhaps after an attempted revolt in *c.* 273.

23. The date is variously estimated at 348, 332, 315 and 303.

2 SOURCES OF INFORMATION

1. An allegedly earlier Hippys of Rhegium is now reattributed to *c.* 300.
2. Lycophron, *Alexandra*, 1226–80. Variously attributed to early or late third century, or later.
3. Plutarch, *Camillus*, 22, 3.
4. Plutarch, *Romulus*, 3, 8.
5. cf. also the Troy romance of Hegesianax of the Troad.
6. DH, V, 77 4ff. Dionysius was under the patronage of Aelius Tubero, perhaps Quintus (consul 11 B.C.). See below, note 51.
7. DH, II, 19; V, 56, 1.
8. e.g. Gaius Julius Theopompus of Cnidus (a friend of Julius Caesar), Alexander of Myndus (time of Augustus and Tiberius).
9. e.g., the *Bibliotheca* which bears the name of Apollodorus of Athens (second century B.C.) but was written in the second or third century A.D.
10. Possibly his prehistoric material goes back to Posidonius of Apamea; but he also makes use of an earlier Roman historian.
11. J. Heurgon, *La vie quotidienne chez les Etrusques*, p. 307.
12. e.g. Ionian and other non-Attic vases, bronzes and gems.
13. Cicero, *On Divination*, I, 100; Livy, V, 15, 10.
14. e.g. Persius, *Satires*, III, 8.
15. Varro, *On the Latin Language*, V, 55.
16. P. Romanelli, *Notizie degli Scavi* (1948), pp. 260ff, U. Kahrstedt, *Symbolae Osloenses*, XXX (1953), pp. 68ff. But the *elogia* of Arretium (early first century B.C.) are purely Latin in content.
17. *Corpus Inscriptionum Etruscarum*, I, 272.
18. Horace, *Odes*, I, 1, 1; I, 29, 1.
19. As Suetonius, *Augustus*, 66, 3, suggests.
20. DH, I, 30, 4.
21. Suetonius, *Claudius*, 42, 2. For Plautia Urgulanilla, see W. V. Harris, *Rome in Etruria and Umbria*, pp. 27ff.
22. The oldest is the battered Calendar of Antium (first half of first century B.C.); we also have about forty copies of Caesar's calendar. The Roman calendar was attributed to Numa Pompilius, but probably, in its surviving form, goes back to the Etruscan monarchy (? sixth century B.C.), though it contains traces of an earlier

stratum. Changes were introduced by Cnaeus Flavius (aedile 304 B.C.).

23. F. Altheim, *History of Roman Religion* (1938), pp. 249ff.

24. Cicero, *On the Orator*, II, 52. The chief priest (replacing the king) was head of the *pontifices* who presided over the state cult. Other priestly boards had their Fasti also.

25. The material was still mainly sacral in the time of Cato, *Origins*, IV, fragment 77.

26. Against Clodius (unidentifiable; possibly Claudius Quadrigarius, n. 50), in Plutarch, *Numa*, 1.

27. Livy, X, 6, 6 (the Lex Ogulnia – were Quintus and Cnaeus Ogulnius Gallus tribunes then?).

28. DH, I, 73, 1.

29. Others accept all but the first sets of consuls.

30. e.g. Horace, *Odes*, III, 17, 2ff (Aelii Lamiae).

31. Cicero, *Brutus*, 16, 62; Livy, VIII, 40, 4; echoes by Plutarch.

32. Earliest inscription: *Corpus Inscriptionum Latinarum*, I², 9 (epitaph of Lucius Cornelius Scipio Barbatus, consul 298, *Corpus Inscriptionum Latinarum*, I², 7).

33. cf. D. R. Dudley, *The Romans* (1970), p. 44. Tacitus, *Annals*, III, 5, 6 and 49, 1 refers to poems.

34. DH, V, 17 (Publius Valerius Poplicola).

35. Cato, *Origins*, fragment 118; Cicero, *Tusculans*, IV, 2, 3; *Brutus*, 19, 75: did decemviral legislation cause the decline and end of such ballad poetry (A. Momigliano, *Journal of Roman Studies* (1957), p. 113, n. 61)?

36. M. I. Finley, *History and Theory* (Middletown), IV (1965), p. 297.

37. He wrote moral apophthegms, and may have helped his secretary, Cnaeus Flavius (note 22 above) to write the first book on law. Another 'proto-historian' was Publius Sempronius Sophus (consul, 283).

38. The Latin 'Annals of Fabius' may have been an adaptation by Fabius Pictor himself – or the work of another man, a Servius Fabius.

39. cf. Lucius Cincius Alimentus (praetor 210–209), likewise writing in Greek, who helped to fix the senatorial tradition for the Second Punic War (in which he was captured).

40. By A. Alföldi, *Early Roman and the Latins* (1965) pp. 123ff.

41. Polybius, I, 11–13.

42. M. Grant, *The Ancient Historians*, pp. 142f.

43. Also the *Ambracia*, about the capture of that town by Marcus Fulvius Nobilior in 189 B.C.

44. cf. also the *Amphitryo* of Plautus (*c.* 254–184 B.C.).

45. His political opponent Publius Cornelius Scipio Africanus the younger (Aemilianus) took the same line, notably in a speech in 142 B.C.

46. Lucius Valerius Flaccus was his fellow-consul in 195 and fellow-censor in 184. Cato had seen his first service in 214 (and again in 209) under the great Quintus Fabius Maximus Verrucosus Cunctator.

47. Gaius Acilius (a senator who served as interpreter for visiting Greek philosophers in 155) wrote a Roman history in Greek (*c.* 142) which showed a similar interest (e.g. fragment 2 on Rhegium), and revived the theory that Rome was a Greek city.

48. Gaius Sempronius Tuditanus' treatise on magistracies showed similar 'optimate' tendencies, Gaius Junius Congus contrary ones.

49. *Origin of the Roman Nation*, 17f.; see below n. 66.

50. His contemporary, Claudius Quadrigarius, began his history at 390 B.C., because he declined to deal with shadowy themes – and probably because he was embarrassed by the strong anti-Claudian tradition regarding earlier periods. He was uninterested in politics, and avoided the Conflict of the Orders. His worst fault was the patriotic exaggeration of enemy casualties.

51. DH, I, 80, 1. cf. Livy, IV, 23, 3 (reading 'Q' uncertain). Tubero seems to have read Antias but may have used Macer for the Linen Books. For Dionysius' patron of this name, perhaps Quintus, see above, note 6.

52. Cicero, *Orator*, 120.

53. Varro was inspired by Lucius Aelius Stilo Praeconinus of Lanuvium (*c.* 154–74 B.C.).

54. Verrius' fellow freedman of Augustus, Gaius Julius Hyginus (from Spain or Alexandria), a pupil of Alexander Polyhistor of Miletus, wrote *On Trojan Families* and *On the Origin and Site of Italian Cities* (lost).

55. Pliny the Elder, *Natural History*, XXXV, 2, 8.

56. cf. Horace, *Satires*, I, 10, 42f. reading *regum fata* not *facta*.

57. Livy I, preface, 11.

58. M. Grant, *The Ancient Historians*, p. 238.

59. The ambivalence was typical of Roman Stoicism: it found the interventions theoretically credible, but was sceptical about individual cases.

60. He was 'Pompeian', i.e. more sympathetic to Pompey than to Caesar in the Civil War, Tacitus, *Annals*, IV, 34.

61. Ogilvie, *Comm.*, p. 5.

62. There is no traceable *direct* influence of Ennius either, though there are deliberate echoes and borrowings of poetic colour. Livy follows Cato to some extent.

63. Livy, IV, 7, 12. Probably he only knew the Linen Books through Macer.

64. Livy may also have felt an urge to supplant Tubero's style.

65. Augustus' restoration of temples began in 28 B.C., a year or two before the publication of Livy's Book I, but most of the Augustan revivals were subsequent to Books I–X.

66. Horace sets the Greek and Roman myths opposite to one another, keeping away from Hellenistic prettiness and renewing the old seriousness in a manner of his own. Ovid (especially in the *Fasti*) and Propertius (especially in Book IV) lavish much attention upon the Roman mythology in their own distinctive fashions.

   In the 2nd century A.D., Publius Annius (?) Florus wrote an *Epitome of All Wars* (including mythical ones) which depended on Livy and others. *The Origin of the Roman Nation* (*Origo Gentis Romanae*), of the fourth century A.D., appears to be a free elaboration of a book written under Augustus or Tiberius, which may perhaps have been based, directly or indirectly, on Livy (or on Varro or others).

3 AENEAS

1. DH, I, 89, 2. The language is a difficulty : he describes it as 'neither absolutely barbarous nor completely Greek'.

2. For the obscure Pelasgi see H. H. Scullard, *The Etruscan Cities and Rome*, pp. 35ff. Dionysius, unlike others, regarded them as Greek. For the Aborigines see chapter 3, section 3.

3. DH, I, 31, 1, 32, 5. The sixtieth year before the Trojan War was supposedly *c.* 1243 B.C.

4. Virgil, *Aeneid*, VIII, 51–4 (trans. C. Day Lewis).

5. Varro, *On the Latin Language*, V, 53, etc. Is there a link with the pastoral god Pales, or with the Phoenician Baal, or with a pre-Indo-European word meaning rock or hill? See also note 9 below.

6. Plato, *Republic*, VIII, 565 D.

7. Aristotle, fragment 549, ed. V. Rose. Cf. Plutarch, Roman *Questions*, 76, 282A (he specifically relates the name to Evander's followers).

8. The Greek goddess Themis was originally akin to, or identical with, Ge or Gaia (Terra Mater, Earth), but became an abstraction of Right.

9. DH, I, 43, 1 : his sons Pallas (another possible etymological basis of

'Palatine') and Latinus. 1, 24, 1: the Greek followers of Hercules settled on the Capitoline hill.

10. Plutarch, *Roman Questions*, 59, 278, quoting King Juba II of Mauretania (died c. A.D. 23), author of many works including a history of Rome and a comparative study of antiquities.

11. Virgil, *Aeneid*, VIII, 184–272 (trans. C. Day Lewis).

12. Diodorus IV, 21; perhaps based on Timaeus. He says nothing of the combat with Hercules. Dionysius is the only Greek writer who does.

13. References in J. Heurgon, *La vie quotidienne chez les Etrusques*, p. 63 (fig. 11), p. 64, p. 335, n. 25, p. 283. According to a certain Dercyllus, Hercules killed not Cacus but Faunus (Pan).

14. Cnaeus Gellius, fragment 7.

15. The Greek Admetus is another mythical figure varying between good and bad.

16. Lactantius, *Divine Institutions*, 1, 20, 36.

17. More probably than with Cronos (Saturn), or Quirinus, as has also been suggested.

18. Propertius IV, 9, 9–12 (trans. S. G. Tremenheere).

19. They do not admit of any single explanation. According to Lévi-Strauss, the slaying of the monster by Oedipus denies the autochthonous nature of man.

20. Humbaba in Assyrian. The slaying of a dragon is also a central element in the Babylonian Myth of Creation.

21. e.g. Pisander of Rhodes (sixth century), Panyassis of Halicarnassus (fifth century). The story of Heracles' Labours may sometimes have contained an element of guilt and atonement.

22. Tibur (Tivoli) may have been an intermediary.

23. Propertius, IV, 9, 71ff., wrongly identified him with the god of oaths, Semo Sancus Dius Fidius (see below, chapter 5 and note 18).

24. Etruscan mirrors show Uni (Juno) suckling him, i.e. his mother (like his father) was divine, not the mortal Alcmena as supposed.

25. According to Hesiod, they had been one of the five Ages of Mankind. Some modern writers classify stories about the heroes as a distinct branch of mythology.

26. Plutarch, *Roman Questions*, 18, 267. Other reasons were also suggested, cf. chapter 3, section 3, and reference in note 80.

27. Sources given in Strabo, V, 230 C.

28. As Caere, Thefarie Velianas made a bilingual dedication to Uni-Astarte in c. 500 B.C.: for references see chapter 1, note 20.

29. *Origin of the Roman Nation*, 8, 5, is wrong to say that women were admitted in the fourth century B.C., since they were still ex-

cluded in the first century. There were also vetoes on flies and dogs.

30. A torso of Hercules was found on the early S. Omobono site.

31. Near the Porta Trigemina: Cnaeus Gellius, fragment 7.

32. Until Trajan (A.D. 98–117) at least (much later, according to *Origin of the Roman Nation*, 8, 2) – but not necessarily descended from the old Republican family.

33. *BMC, Empire*, I, p. CXXVI.

34. e.g. Temple of Zeus Ouranios, Baetocaece (near Apamea).

35. Horace, *Odes*, III, 3, 9f.

36. There was a second prophecy and portent too. Celaeno, harpy at the Strophades islands, had told Aeneas he would found a city when hunger made him and his men eat their plates: the prophecy was fulfilled when they ate the flat bread-cakes they had been using as plates.

37. cf. M. Grant, *Proceedings of the Virgil Society*, III (1963–4), pp. 1ff. Augustus was himself initiated into the Eleusinian Mysteries in 19 B.C., the year of Virgil's death.

38. cf. the ancient Sumerian myth of Dumuzi and Inanna.

39. Virgil, *Aeneid*, VI, 42–4 (trans. C. Day Lewis).

40. He returns through the Ivory Gate: for the significance cf. M. Grant, *Myths of the Greeks and Romans*, pp. 343ff., etc.

41. Perhaps Stesichorus. Aeneas was also believed to be the founder of Capua. So, alternatively, was his grandfather Capys, the father of Anchises.

42. Naevius, *Punic War*, fragments 13–15. Lycophron mentions the Sibyl in south Latium, but not in any relation to Aeneas.

43. Cicero, *On Divination*, I, 21, 43.

44. Cicero's *Dream of Scipio* (*On the State*, VI).

45. Virgil, *Aeneid*, VI, ed. F. Fletcher (1941), pp. ix ff. In the fifth century B.C. Polygnotus had painted the Underworld: Pausanias, X 28f.

46. There was believed to have been a Sibyl at Erythrae (Ildir) before the Trojan War. Aeneas was said to have consulted another at Marpessus near Troy (a prototype for the Cumae story). Heraclitus of Ephesus (*c.* 500) wrote of a Sibyl (fragment 248, Kirk and Raven).

47. *BMC, Empire*, I, p. 18, no. 95.

48. Thucydides, VI, 2, 3.

49. Through Achilles' son Neoptolemus, who was also called Pyrrhus.

50. Suetonius, *Claudius*, 25, 3 (Seleucus II Callinicus).

51. Justin, *Historiae Philippicae*, 28, 6 (against the Aetolians).

52. Or the identification may have come about partly because of the Charites (Gratiae, Graces).

53. e.g. Gaius Livius Salinator in 190 B.C. (L. 37.9).

54. Plutarch, *On the Pythian Oracles*, 11.

55. Plutarch, *Sulla*, 34, 4; Appian, *Civil War*, I, 97, 452

56. *BMC, Republic*, I, 1140 (Sextus Julius Caesar), I, 1405 (Lucius Julius Caesar).

57. e.g. funeral speech for his aunt Julia in 69 B.C., cf. chapter 5, section 2.

58. *BMC, Republic*, II, p. 469, no. 31.

59. *BMC, Republic*, I. 4257.

60. Ovid, *Fasti*, V, 563f.

61. Virgil, *Aeneid*, I, 257ff.

62. W. H. Auden, *Secondary Epic*.

63. V. Pöschl. *The Art of Virgil*, p. 7. The view that Virgil knew Homer through Naevius and Ennius is improbable, though Ennius begins with the fall of Troy.

64. Homer, *Iliad*, XX, 180f.

65. Homer, *Iliad*, XX, 307f.

66. cf. *Iliad*, 11, 557f., etc. For Pisistratus see Dieuchides of Megara in Diogenes Laertius, I, 57.

67. Strabo, XIII, 1, 53, 608 (*pantessin* for *Troessin*).

68. Menecrates of Xanthus (fourth century B.C. ?) in DH, I, 48, 3; cf. Alexander (Lychnus) of Ephesus (c. 60 B.C.), on the permission granted by Agamemnon.

69. *Origin of the Roman Nation*, 9, 2; cf; Servius, *Commentary on Virgil, Aeneid*, IX, 707.

70. The theory that the *Sack of Troy* was written by a second Stesichorus in the early fifth century is not very likely.

71. Cassius Hemina, fragment 7: Aeneas received the Palladium from Diomedes. Or had Aeneas himself brought it, or a follower Nautes? Or was it brought to Rome by Numa (chapter 5, section 1, note 2)? Or did it not exist (DH, I, 69, 11, 66, cf. Plutarch, *Camillus*, 20, etc).? Perhaps the old cult-image was taken from Troy to Rome in c. 85 B.C. by Gaius Flavius Fimbria.

72. Hesiod, *Theogony*, 1011–16. Cf. chapter 1, section 4 and note 4.

73. Odysseus also appeared on many seventh-century vases in Italy. Octavius Mamilius, ruler of Tusculum (chapter 6, section 1), traced his ancestry back to him. In south Italy, Lucius Livius Andronicus of Tarentum (third century B.C.) found a public for his *Odyssia Latina*.

74. F. Jacoby, *Fragmente der griechischen Historiker* (1923–), 4 F 84, reading 'with' not 'after'.

75. cf. Ambracia, Pallene, Zacynthus.

76. A recent theory not altogether convincingly attributes his intro-duction to the Phocaeans who tried to colonize Corsica.

77. Sometimes there are versions unknown (so far) in Greek art, e.g. Aeneas bearing gifts as Paris meets Helen, with Aphrodite (Venus) in attendance.

78. DH, I, 89, 2, envisages Trojan settlers at Rome before Aeneas.

79. Telephus; cf. Plutarch, *Romulus*, 2, 1. Telephus was also some-times considered the father of Tyrrhenus.

80. Cato, *Origins*, fragment 12. A somewhat similar story was cited as the origin of the Roman festival of the Vinalia; cf. also chapter 3, section 1 and note 26. According to Cato, fragment 10, after Aeneas' death, Ascanius defeated Mezentius in single combat. In one version or another the Mezentius story was known to Alcimus (and Lycophron), and may be much earlier. In Etruscan the name would have started Medi- or Mess-.

81. Livy, V, 1, 6.

82. Lycophron, *Alexandra*, 1242, 1248.

83. Virgil, *Aeneid*, X, 203.

84. Phocas, *Life of Virgil* (fifth century A.D.): *vates Etruscus*.

85. *Maru* was used for the office of the chief magistrates by Sabines and Umbrians also, instead of the usual Italian *meddix*.

86. Sallust, *Catiline*, 6, 1; he was joined by the Aborigines.

87. Virgil, *Aeneid*, VIII, 39–49.

88. DH, I, 56, 6, Diodorus, VII, 5, 4.

89. Lycophron, *Alexandra*, 1252. Later, towns of the empire, to advertise their 'Latin' rank, erected statues of the sow and piglets.

90. cf. other 'white cities' (Beograd, Szekes-Fehervar, Sar Kel). Dio-dorus VII, 5, 3, and 6, also introduces the old name of the Tiber, Alba (elsewhere Albula). Current research tends to prefer 'height' or 'mountain' as the original meaning.

91. Cassius Hemina, fragment 11 (Lares Grundules).

92. Varro, *On Agriculture* (*Res Rusticae*), II, 4, 18.

93. Cato, *Origins*, fragment 4; DH, I, 53, 3 etc.

94. The Tragliatelle *oenochoe*, G.Q. Giglioli, *Studi Etruschi*, III (1929), pp. 111ff.

95. DH, I, 72, 3.

96. Whether any statuettes or sacred objects actually passed from Lavinium to Rome cannot be said; but it is not improbable. The

opposite suggestion, that the cult passed from Rome to Lavinium, is less likely.

97. F. Jacoby, *Fragmente der griechischen Historiker*, 566 F 59.

98. The relics brought from Troy were much discussed and disputed; DH, I, 67, 4 etc.

99. Lycophron, *Alexandra*, 1259f.

100. e.g. Macer, fragments 3 (Alba Longa), 5 (Lavinium).

101. Rio Torto: or Canale dello Stagno, three miles south of Tiber mouth.

102. Thus translated *gerarches* in Diodorus, XXXVII, 11.

103. Fabius Pictor, fragment 4.

104. On the bronze casket from Praeneste, Latinus points to heaven to forecast the deification of Aeneas.

105. cf. Justin, XVIII, 6, 8.

106. Naevius, *Punic War*, fragments 19–20.

107. Ovid, *Fasti*, III, 607, makes Aeneas meet Anna on the banks of the Numicus. Anna is a Phoenician name (Hannah), perhaps of a goddess.

108. There were chronological objections because the traditional date of the foundation of Carthage was so much later than the supposed date of Aeneas.

109. Though Virgil's debt to Apollonius was not particularly extensive. Dido also owed something to Catullus' Ariadne.

110. Virgil, *Aeneid*, IV, 165–72.

111. ibid. 28–9, cf. Ovid, *Heroides*, VII, 93–6.

112. Justin, XVIII, 4, 3f. Cf. a foundation-myth which displayed Dido's cunning, again with reference to *Punica fides*. When she arrived in Africa, it was said that she was given as much land as she could cover with a cow-hide (*byrsa*), and she got more than her hosts reckoned by cutting it into strips. Not only is this a typical attempt to explain the name of the Byrsa Hill, which was the citadel of Carthage, but it also showed her Punic slyness. On their way from Phoenicia, her followers had seized ninety maidens in Cyprus, who became the ancestresses of the ninety greatest Carthaginian families. Cato said she founded 'Carthada' in the time of King Iapon (cf. Virgil's Iarbas) of Libya.

113. Virgil, *Aeneid*, IV, 261.

114. At first Virgil unfavourably compares the luxury of the Trojans, too, with Italian austerity.

115. Virgil, *Aeneid*, IV, 665.

116. *Corpus Inscriptionum Latinarum*, I², p. 50.

117. Homer, *Iliad*, XX, 347.

118. Naevius, *Punic War*, fragments 13–15, Ennius, *Annals*, fragments 16–17.
119. Virgil, *Aeneid*, II, 705–11.
120. Propertius, I, 61f. (trans. S. G. Tremeneheere). Ennius, too, had connected the foundation of the city with the flight of Aeneas from Troy. Accius' *Antenoridae* probably included the departure from Troy. Aulus Postumius Albinus wrote a Greek poem *On the Arrival of Aeneas*.
121. e.g. (Pseudo-?) Xenophon, *On Hunting*, I, 15, Lycophron, *Alexandra*, 1265, 1270.

4 ROMULUS

1. DH, I, 10, 13.
2. Cato in Servius, *Commentary* on Virgil, *Aeneid*, I, 36.
3. DH, I, 11, 1.
4. Hesiod, *Theogony*, 1011ff. (omitting the dubious reference to Telegonus).
5. Identified with Evander. But Latinus was also called the son of Evander's daughter Lavinia.
6. Ovid, *Metamorphoses*, XIV, 566–73 (trans. H. Gregory).
7. Cato, *Origins*, fragment 11, implies that Turnus with Mezentius are allied against Aeneas and Latinus.
8. There was a lake of Turnus near Aricia, Columella, X, 138, and a legendary Turnus Herdonius, either of Aricia or Corioli. Perhaps the family of the Herdonii took an interest in the memory of Turnus. See also note 105 below.
9. Cato, *Origins*, fragment 10 (though Aeneas does not appear personally in the battle).
10. Virgil, *Aeneid*, I, 257–71.
11. Cato, *Origins*, fragment 9.
12. Livy, I, 3, 2f.
13. One of the points at issue was whether Ascanius was the son of Aeneas by his Trojan wife Creusa – who had disappeared while she was fleeing with her husband from burning Troy – or of his subsequent wife Lavinia. The former version was sometimes accompanied by a story that the Alban kings were descended not from Ascanius but from his half-brother Silvius, Aeneas' son born to Lavinia after Aeneas' death. Virgil and the Julian coins, with their representations of Aeneas, Anchises and Ascanius, ignore this version (presumably relying on the alternative version that Silvius was Ascanius' son). The view that Ascanius was the son of Lavinia (referred to by Livy, who prefers not to commit himself), though it

had the advantage of deriving him from a union of Trojan and native Italian blood, has also been identified as Marian propaganda against Lucius Julius Caesar because it implies that Ascanius was not the same as Iulus at all, thus casting doubts on all the claims of the Julii to be descended from Venus and Aeneas through Iulus.

14. A fragment of Naevius tells of the visit of Viba (?), king of Veii, to Alba Longa; see n. 56 below.
15. In Livy, I, 30, 2, codices have 'Tullii' instead: an error or an attempt in one of Livy's sources (or copyists) to eliminate the Julii? For the Tullii, cf. chapter 5, n. 88.
16. O. Skutsch, *Studia Enniana* (1968), p. 12.
17. So called because he was born in the woods (*silvae*) Livy, I, 3, 6; did he or Rhea Silvia (chapter 4, section 2) come first? He may be the Agrios ('wild') referred to by Hesiod, *Theogony*, 1013.
18. Atys (variant of Epytus; Phrygian form; link with gens Atia, name of Augustus' mother. when Phrygian pedigrees were fashionable), Capys (relations with Capua important in third century B.C.), Tiberinus (said to have given his name to the river Tiber, where he was drowned and buried: but see chapter 1, n. 16), Agrippa (taken from a legendary hero of the Conflict of Orders – see chapter 6, n. 47 – at a time of party strife in the second or third century B.C.; interest revived when Marcus Vipsanius Agrippa was Augustus' chief minister).
19. DH, I, 70, 4. In *Aeneid*, I, Ascanius is founder of Alba Longa, in VI Silvius heads the royal pedigree.
20. DH, I, 74, 1. Ennius went back beyond Timaeus to *c*.900.
21. Her Greek name was no obstacle: cf. Andromache.
22. Melinno 1; or daughter of Asclepius (Aesculapius), or of Italus or Telephus.
23. Rome is written 'Ruma' on an archaic milestone from Vulci.
24. In Greek, foundation stories had been told in verse from the eighth and seventh centuries B.C. and in prose by Ion of Chios (born *c*.490), M. Grant, *The Ancient Historians*, pp. 16, 20.
25. According to Varro, *On the Latin Language*, VIII, 80, 'Roma' came from 'Romulus'. Romulus was claimed as ancestor by the early patrician family of the Romilii. The name of the Romilian tribe, across the Tiber on the edge of Etruscan territory, may have meant the 'Roman' tribe in Etruscan.
26. Ennius, *Annals*, fragments 32–48. The sister of the Volscian heroine Camilla was also called Acca.
27. There was also a story that she plunged into the Anio and be-

came a river goddess (*Rea* 'the dedicated', cf. *rea voti*). She was described as one of the Vestal Virgins (although their creation was attributed to Numa, chapter 5, section 1).

28. On this see G. S. Kirk, *Myth*, p. 192.

29. DH, I, 77.

30. Plutarch, *Romulus*, 2, 3ff. (trans. A. H. Clough).

31. Her son was Melicertes, who had sometimes been identified with Melqart.

32. cf. S. Eitrem, *Beiträge zur Religionsgeschichte*, pp. 152f.

33. M. Kontoleon, *Praktika Arkaiologikes Hetairias*, 1953 (published 1956), pp. 270f. (Chios).

34. Remona, Remuria or Remoria (part of Aventine Hill), ager Remurinus: fanciful link with *tarditas* (*remores*) in *Origin of the Roman Nation*, 21, 4.

35. Karl Gustav Jung interpreted such myths as imaginative transformations of personal inadequacies into great pretensions and powers.

36. Listed in H. J. Rose, *Handbook of Greek Mythology*, p. 289.

37. Livy, X, 23, 12.

38. *BMC*, *Republic*, II, p. 124, no. 28. For the woodpecker (*Picus*), which fed the infants, cf. chapter 5, note 34.

39. DH, I, 84, 5; they were not exposed, but Numitor gave them a good education at Gabii.

40. Varro, *On Agriculture* (*Res Rusticae*), II, 11, 5, etc. But the Ficus Ruminalis, surrounded by a bronze grating, may possibly have marked a spot struck by lightning. According to Tacitus, *Annals*, XIII, 58, the tree began to wither in A.D. 59 but recovered.

41. *The Roman Forum*, p. 214. Attus Navius, whose story was influenced by the Greek miracle-monger Epimenides, was supposed to have lived under the Tarquins.

42. DH, I, 79, 8.

43. *BMC*, *Republic*, I, 926 (Sextus Pompeius Fostlus).

44. M. Grant, *The Roman Forum*, p. 50; or the tomb of Romulus, or of Tullus Hostilius' father Hostus Hostilius.

45. Dessau, *Inscriptiones Latinae Selectae*, 5047–8. Varro attests the link, which may be authentic (see also note 51 below). She was also known as the mother of the Arval Brethren.

46. e.g. Tamar, Rahab, Ruth, Mary Magdalene, and the golden-hearted tart of the modern theatre.

47. Cato, *Origins*, fragment 16.

48. Macer, fragment 1.

49. Antias, fragment 1.

50. *BMC, Republic*, I, 4211 (Publius Accoleius Lariscolus).
51. *Fasti Praenestini*, x Kal. Jan., *Corpus Inscriptionum Latinarum*, I², p. 338 (from husband); Cato, fragment 16, Antias, fragment 1 (from prostitution).
52. One was attributed to the reign of Ancus Marcius: Macrobius, *Saturnalia*, I, 10, 12.
53. Livy, I, 7, 2.
54. According to another version, Remus was ambushed in a ravine at Caenina (Castel Giubbileo?), DH, I, 79, 13f.
55. Livy, I, 5, 7; cf. *Oxyrhynchus Papyri*, XI, 1379.
56. Naevius, *Praetextae*, fragments 2–3.
57 Livy, I, 85, 6: cf. n. 34 above.
58. Ennius, *Annals*, fragments 8off. (trans. W. A. Falconer).
59. cf. Censorinus, *On Birthdays* (*De Die Natali*, 17); reference was also made to the twelve sons of Acca Larentia.
60. Suetonius, *Augustus*, 95.
61. cf. G. S. Kirk, *Myth*, pp. 193f., etc.
62. Horace, *Epodes*, 7, 17–20.
63. cf. R. M. Ogilvie, *The Romans and their Gods*, p. 115.
64. e.g. Poemandrus and Leucippus, Oeneus and Toxeus. Cf. Plutarch, *Roman Questions*, 27, 271 etc.
65. DH, I, 87, 3f; cf. Ovid, *Fasti*, IV, 843.
66. Egnatius (unknown); cf. *Origin of the Roman Nation*, 23, 6.
67. DH, I, 4, 2f.
68. Cicero, *On the State*, III, 15.
69. DH, II, 12, 4.
70. The so-called Hut of Romulus (or Faustulus), burnt down in 38 B.C., was symbolically close to the house of Augustus on the Palatine Hill. There was also a hut similarly described on the Capitoline Hill.
71. He also promised deification to Scipio Africanus the elder.
72. Ovid, *Metamorphoses*, XIV, 818–28 (trans. H. Gregory).
73. Plutarch, *Romulus*, 27, 3ff. (trans. A. H. Clough). Plutarch in this *Life* employed Dionysius and probably Varro, but made little use of Livy or Cicero.
74. e.g. Aristeas of Proconnesus (Marmara) a servant of Apollo, who produced the semblance of death and appeared elsewhere.
75. Cicero, *On the State*, II, 15; I, 25; II, 17ff.
76. Livy, I, 16, 4.
77. DH, II, 56, 6, cf. 3.
78. Plutarch, *Romulus*, 28, 1ff. (trans. A. H. Clough).
79. Ennius, *Annals*, fragments 114–15. The name has not survived.

80. See above, n. 15, for a variant reading of the relevant passage.
81. Cicero, *On the State*, II, 20.
82. He treats Ascanius lightly (cf. note 13 above), and sometimes represents early Julii as insignificant or unpleasant.
83. But Tacitus, *Annals*, IV, 38, quotes a view that Tiberius' rejection of divine honours was degenerate because it showed he had no proper concern for his reputation.
84. Cicero, *On the Nature of the Gods*, III, 15, 39.
85. Virgil, *Georgics*, I, 498.
86. cf. O. Skutsch, *Studia Enniana*, pp. 130ff. And for the moneyer Numerius Fabius Pictor, *BMC, Republic*, I, 1172.
87. The etymology suggested by Kretschmer, *co-virium*, cf. H. J. Rose, *Oxford Classical Dictionary*, ed. 2, p. 908, is doubtful.
88. Livy, I, 9, 14–16 (trans. A de Selincourt).
89. cf. E. Leach, *Lévi-Strauss*, pp. 44, 104.
90. *Figaro*, 27 July 1961.
91. Plutarch, *Lycurgus*, 15. There were also warlike elements in Samnite marriages.
92. Plutarch, *Roman Questions*, 87, 285. Or, he asks, was this custom instituted because they were married to warlike men?
93. Cicero, *On the State*, II, 14.
94. DH, II, 38, 2–40, 3 (trans. E. Cary).
95. Livy, I, 11, 6–9. Probably from Valerius Antias.
96. Plutarch, *Romulus*, 17, 5, quoting Gaius Sulpicius Galba (the grandfather of the emperor Galba), from Juba II.
97. *BMC, Empire*, I, p. 6, no. 29 (Publius Petronius Turpilianus).
98. cf. Rumpf, *Journal of Hellenic Studies*, LXXI (1951) pp. 168ff. (fifth to third century). Cf. Ch. 6, n. 44.
99. Valerius Maximus, I, 1, 13, quotes a deviant (Etruscan?) tradition in which Tarpeia is connected with a betrayal under Titus Tarquinius or Tarpeius. The Spurius Tarpeius Capitolinus of the *Fasti*, alleged to have been consul in 454 B. C., may be fictitious.
100. Propertius, IV, 4, 87–92 (trans. E. A. Watts). On this poem see K. Wellesley, *Acta Cl. Univ. Scient. Debrecen*, V, (1969), pp. 93ff.
101. Plutarch, *Poplicola*, 8.
102. Festus, p. 363 M.
103. Ogilvie, *Comm.*, p. 74.
104. Livy, I, 11, 7. Or as another of his sources suggests to him, they wanted to make it appear that the citadel had been taken by assault.
105. This version may be prompted by another story (authentic? Or an early pro-Sabine, anti-Roman tradition?) that the Sabines under

Appius Herdonius (for the family, see note 8 above) occupied the Capitol briefly in 460 B.C.

106. Livy, I, 12, 8–10 (trans. A. de Selincourt).
107. M. Grant, *The Roman Forum*, p. 32.
108. Varro, *On the Latin Language*, v, 148–50 (trans. R. G. Kent).
109. Pindar, *Nemean Odes*, 24f.
110. Suetonius, *Augustus*, 57.
111. To counterbalance this, the Romans were to be called 'Quirites' collectively, DH, II, 46, 2.
112. Ogilvie, *Comm.*, p. 72.
113. *BMC, Republic*, I, 2355. The head of Tatius also appears on coins of Titus Vettius Sabinus, *BMC, Republic*, I, 3370.
114. Varro, *On the Latin Language*, v, 51.
115. On the more warlike Sabine tradition that their leader Appius Herdonius captured the Capitol, see above note 105.
116. DH, II, 46, 3 (Volesus Valerius): also Tallus Tyrannius.
117. Livy, v, 46, 1ff.
118. e.g. Kaeso Fabius in Etruria: others replaced him by a Gaius Claudius. Perhaps Claudius Quadrigarius (chapter 2, note 50) preferred to start his history after the Gallic sack because of the anti-Claudian nature of the early tradition. The Fabii were also sometimes at odds with the Cornelii Scipiones.
119. Livy, II, 16, 4.
120. Suetonius, *Tiberius*, 1. The Fabii also made play with the antique Luperci Fabiani, priests of the Lupercal (chapter 4, section 1).
121. e.g. the decemvir, see chapter 6, note 48. Appius Claudius the Blind was also denigrated, cf. chapter 2, section 3.
122. DH, II, 38, 3.
123. Nepos, *Cato*, 1, etc. cf. Horace, *Odes*, III, 6, 37–44, for the theme.

5 THE MYTHOLOGY OF THE ROMAN KINGS

1. Plutarch, *Numa* 1.
2. Florus, I, 2, 1–7 (trans. E. S. Forester).
3. Was it connected with the river Numicus?
4. *Corpus Inscriptionum Etruscarum*, 3335.
5. According to DH, II, 58, 1, it was a compromise appointment to satisfy both the old and the new senators.
6. Cicero, *On the State*, II, 24. According to DH, II, 62, 3f., Numa was very interested in class relations.
7. Florus, I, 8.

8. The picture of Numa may owe something to the *Sisyphus*, a tragic drama by the Athenian Critias (*c.* 460–403 B.C.).

9. Cicero, *On the State*, II, 29. The ostensible spokesmen are Publius Cornelius Scipio Africanus the younger (Aemilianus) and Manius Manilius.

10. Pliny the elder, *Natural History*, XXXIV, 12, 26. There was also a statue of Alcibiades.

11. Epicharmus, *Ad Antenorem*; cf. Plutarch, *Numa*, 8, 9.

12. Livy, XL, 29, 8.

13. cf. the burning of the mystery-books of Dionysus in Ptolemaic Egypt.

14. *BMC, Republic*, II, p. 311, no. 733 (Lucius Pomponius Molo).

15. *BMC, Republic*, II, p. 361, no. 62 (Cnaeus Calpurnius Piso, *c.* 49 B.C.).

16. Cassius Hemina, fragment 13. The law has a Pythagorean flavour.

17. Lydus, *De Ostentis*, 16, p. 27, 23W (Marcus Fulvius Nobilior).

18. The temple of Dius Fidius was attributed to 466 B.C. The cult appeared elsewhere in Italy as Jupiter Fisios or Fisovius. Dius Fidius was identified with the Sabine Semo Sancus.

19. e.g. coin of Locri (Greek inscriptions RHOME–PISTIS [=Fides]), time of Second Punic War, Mattingly, *Numismatic Chronicle* (1957), p. 288. Varro, *On the Latin Language*, V, 86, linked *foedus* and *fides*.

20. Virgil, *Aeneid*, VI, 810.

21. M. Grant, *The Six Main Aes Coinages of Augustus* (1953), pp. 104ff.

22. Lachmann, *Gromatici Veteres* (1848), I, 350.

23. Juvenal, *Satires*, III, 12.

24. Livius Andronicus, *Odyssia*, fragment 1.

25. Virgil, *Aeneid*, VII, 763.

26. Egerius Laevius, dictator of Tusculum. Did the name of the family or the goddess come first? The derivation offered by Q. Curtius Rufus, VII, 5, from water 'which is brought out (*egeritur*) from the earth' is very dubious.

27. Ovid, *Metamorphoses*, XV, 487ff.

28. Livy, I, 19, 4–5 (trans. A. de Selincourt).

29. A. de Selincourt, *Livy: The Early History of Rome* (London, 1960), p. 13.

30. cf. Varro, *On the Latin Language*, VII, 43.

31. Picenum, Ager Capenas, etc.

32. cf. Ogilvie, *Comm.*, p. 99.

33. Servius, *Commentary* on Virgil, *Aeneid*, VIII, 285.

34. cf. the Greek Proteus. Picus was originally the woodpecker, sacred to Mars, who watched over the infants Romulus and Remus, and guided the people of Picenum into new lands. He was rationalized into an early Italian king, who was turned into a woodpecker by Circe because he rejected her love.

35. He was so-called because celestial signs were 'elicited' from him.

36. Antias, fragment 6.

37. Ovid, *Fasti*, III, 339–44 (trans. L. P. Wilkinson).

38. Virgil, *Aeneid*, VI, 812–15 (trans. C. Day Lewis).

39. A recent theory, however, has dubiously interpreted his name as Germanic. He has also been compared to the Vedic warrior god Indra.

40. Hersilia. On this complex figure (identified with the divine Hora Quirini) see Ogilvie, *Comm.*, p. 73.

41. Cicero, *On the State*, II, 31.

42. The fact that such plebeian names appear at so early a stage has been found puzzling, but one and the same family could develop both patrician and plebeian branches. It is also possible that the creation of the patriciate was subsequent to the monarchic period. There are a number of plebeian names in the earliest Republican Fasti: cf. chapter 6, section 1.

43. Livy, I, 26, 5. Livy reshapes the reign into a series of distinct acts, in contrast to the more homogeneous and continuous treatment of DH.

44. Ennius, *Annals*, fragments 131–8.

45. DH, III, 22, 10.

46. The poet Horace's father was of slave descent.

47. *BMC, Republic*, I, 879, 942.

48. cf. G. Dumézil, *Horace at les Curiaces* (1942), pp. 11ff.

49. cf. Ogilvie, *Comm.*, p. 109.

50. DH, III, 22, 7.

51. But there also seems a possibility that 'Horatius' and 'Curiatius' were the same name: cf. the textual vagaries of DH, III, 13, 4.

52. A 'Valerian law' – as was the law of 300 (M. Valerius Corvus). For other Valerian legislation see chapter 6, notes 10, 12.

53. Though Ancus was also specially concerned with stabilizing war-like rituals (*bellicae caerimoniae*).

54. Ennius, *Annals*, fragments 145–7; cf. Cicero, *On the State*, III 5.

55. Cnaeus Marcius Coriolanus is not in the consular Fasti; cf. chapter 6, section 1.

56. The Marcii, too, were given a forebear in the time of Numa, Livy, I, 20–8 (Numa Marcius).

57. *BMC, Republic*, I, 2415.

58. Cicero, *On the State*, II, 33. For the new Tulli Cicerones see n. 88 and chapter 4, n. 15.

59. Virgil, *Aeneid*, v., 816f.

60. DH, III, 35, 3, etc.

61. Plutarch, *Numa*, 22, 6ff.

62. e.g. Capitoline temple, ambitious women, Latin wars, Circus Maximus, drainage.

63. e.g. the three oldest Roman tribes, the Ramnenses, Titienses and Luceres, names which (despite many other interpretations) the Etruscan writer Volnius was probably right in regarding as Etruscan (Varro, *On the Latin Language*, v, 55); i.e. Sabine attempts to connect Titienses with Titus Tatius were wrong (Chapter 4, section 3). Georges Dumézil's attempts to equate the tribes with the tripartite Indo-European class-division (*Jupiter Mars Quirinus*, IV, (1948) pp. 137ff; cf. other references in *Mythe et épopée*, p. 433, n. 1) are among the less acceptable features of his general thesis.

64. DH, III, 51, 4 (Clusium, Arretium, Volaterrae, Rusellae, Vetulonia).

65. Or, alternatively, 'Lucumo' may have been introduced because of some Lucius Tarquinius, for whom, as an Etruscan, the title seemed appropriate.

66. Pliny the elder, *Natural History*, XXXIV, 152; cf. Strabo, v, 219.

67. Cicero, *On the State*, II, 34. The Corinthians had also founded Syracuse.

68. Ogilvie, *Comm.*, p. 142.

69. Livy, I, 34f.

70. Ennius, *Annals*, fragments 150, 155; cf. also Polybius.

71. Cicero, *On the State*, III; DH, II, 37–2.

72. According to Plutarch, *Roman Questions*, 30, 271, Gaia Caecilia was the wife of one of Tarquinius Priscus's sons. She was also given the Alban name of Gegania.

73. The Temples of Semo Sancus Dius Fidius on the Quirinal end of Fortune in the Cattle Market (Forum Boarium). The toga was supposedly woven for Servius Tullius.

74. Regolini-Galassi tomb (Vatican Museum).

75. Pliny the Elder, *Natural History*, XXXV, 157.

76. Small cast bronze figurines had already been made in *c.* 700 (e.g. at Tarquinii).

77. Cicero, *On the State*, II, 38.

78. Livy, I, 48, 9; cf. 49, 7.

79. Heavy infantry (hoplite) tactics – and the bolstering of the middle class that they implied – were introduced to Rome, as to Greece and Etruria. The remains of armour and a chariot (before 600) have been found on the Esquiline, cf. chapter 1 above. Timaeus was aware of the reforms.

80. DH, IV, 21, 1 and 25, 1.

81. Cicero, *On the State*, II, 37 and 40.

82. Cicero, *For Sestius*, 58, 123.

83. Livy, I, 39, 5. DH, IV, 1, 2 does not say that she was royal, but that she excelled in beauty and modesty.

84. Livy, IV, 3, 13.

85. Pliny the Elder, *Natural History*, XXXIII, 13, 43. The first *aes signatum* was of the third century B.C. Timaeus was said to have attributed its introduction to Numa (F. Jacoby, *Fragmente der Griechischen Historiker*, 566, F. 61).

86. Dessau, *Inscriptiones Latinae Selectae*, 212 (trans. A. H. M. Jones) paraphrased (and altered) by Tacitus, *Annals*, XI, 23–35.

87. *BMC, Republic*, I, 3142, M. H. Crawford, *Numismatic Chronicle* (1964), p. 143 (81 B.C.); and *BMC, Republic*, I, 3154, D. Fishwick, *Journal of Roman Studies* (1967), p. 152, n. 74 (time of Sulla or *c.* 76 B.C.).

88. It has been argued that both of Servius Tullius' names are Etruscan. The suggestion that the Tullii came from Alba Longa (chapter 4, note 15) is unsupported. There was a Manius Tullius in the Fasti in *c.* 500 – from whom Marcus Tullius Cicero humorously refrained from claiming descent. Plutarch said that the Tullii Cicerones were also stated to go back to a Volscian who gave refuge to Coriolanus (chapter 6, section 1).

89. Unlike the other foes, Cnaeus Tarquinius has no red-bordered robe. Or does this only mean that he was surprised *en déshabille*? For modern studies of these paintings, see W. V. Harris, *Rome in Etruria and Umbria*, pp. 10ff.

90. Festus (W. M. Lindsay ed., 1913), p. 486.

91. Varro, *On the Latin Language*, v, 46.

92. Tacitus, *Annals*, IV, 65.

93. Red-figure imitating the school of the painter Duris. The earlier vase was black *bucchero*.

94. *Chronographia Urbis Romae* (A.D. 354).

95. DH, IV, 6f., 30, criticizes Fabius Pictor (on chronological grounds) for saying that Superbus was Priscus' son. The only historian to

get it right, he adds, was Lucius Calpurnius Piso Frugi. Claudius' speech (n. 86 above) suspends judgement on the point.

96. Livy, I, *Periochae* (trans. B. O. Foster).

97. Cicero, *On the State*, II, 49; cf. 43.

98. Herodotus V, 92, 6. There are also echoes of Zopyrus and the capture of Babylon, III, 154.

99. Livy, I, 53, 4 perhaps appreciates the point because he calls the war unexpectedly tedious.

100. Gaius Antistius Vetus (16 B.C.) and Gaius Antistius Reginus (13 B.C.), *BMC, Empire*, p. 19 no. 96, and p. 24 no. 118.

101. Livy, I, 46, 3.

102. Perhaps the first play in a trilogy of which the last play was his *Brutus*.

103. It is contrasted with the Vicus Cyprius, since Varro, *On the Latin Language*, V, 159, said that *cuprus* means 'good' in Sabine. There was a town Cupra in Picenum, and a goddess of that name in Picenum and Umbria.

104. Livy, I, 48, 3–7 (trans. A. de Selincourt). The reference to the Urbian slope (Clivus Urbius) recalled that a Clivus Virbius led up to the Temple of Diana at Aricia, and helped to guide the location of this Roman shrine.

105. Diodorus, X, 20, 1–21, 5 (trans. C. H. Oldfather).

106. Ovid, *Fasti*, II, 787–810 (trans. L. P. Wilkinson).

107. DH, IV, 67, 2.

108. Accius, *Praetextae* (*Brutus*), fragment 39.

109. Ennius, *Annals*, fragments 251–2.

110. cf. E. Pais, *Ancient Legends of Roman History*, p. 321 n. 5.

111. cf. the intrusion of a consul named Spurius into the very first years of the Republic (see chapter 6, section 1) – this *praenomen* was not found in the old family.

6 THE MYTHOLOGY OF THE ROMAN REPUBLIC

1. It was fixed when the aedile Cnaeus Flavius (304 B.C.) counted 204 nails (one fixed every year, i.e. since 509 or 508 or 507) in the Temple of Jupiter on the Capitol: cf. Etruscan Volsinii, which recorded years by nails in its Temple of Nortia (Fortune) – the purpose being to nail down the evil of the past year and make it harmless. But the fallacy was to suppose that the Republic must have been introduced in the same year in which the Capitoline temple was dedicated. For this complex question see A. Drummond, *Journal of Roman Studies* (1970), p. 201.

2. Livy, I, 59, 4.

3. cf. A. Alföldi, *Early Rome and the Latins*, p. 419.

4. cf. DH, v, 2.

5. DH, v, 15, 3.

6. For the early plebeian names, see also chapter 5, note 42. Some of the early Republican plebeians, if authentic, may have been pro-Etruscan nominees against the local aristocracy. Gjerstad, *Legends and Facts of Early Roman History*, pp. 44ff., conjectures that the Etruscan monarchy continued until the mid fifth century B.C.

7. DH, IV, 68, 1.

8. *BMC, Republic*, I, 3864.

9. *BMC, Republic*, II, p. 477 no. 57.

10. But Antias, fragment 17, gives it to another Valerius in 494 – to get it safely clear of the regal period.

11. His sister Valeria Luperca (or Cloelia) is a focus for many myths; cf. her introduction into the story of Coriolanus (below, same section).

12. For the date, see above, note 1. Livy's version is pro-Horatian, Dionysius' pro-Valerian. Anti-clerical touches go back to Macer. The Valerii was always connected by tradition with the Horatii, e.g. in the (dubious and obscure) joint legislation of 449 by L. Valerius Potitus and M. Horatius Barbatus, which was regarded as a landmark in the history of the Orders.

13. Polybius, III, 22ff. An alternative theory is that the first authentic treaty was in *c.* 348 B.C.

14. Virgil, *Aeneid*, VIII, 646–8 (trans. C. Day Lewis).

15. Pliny the Elder, *Natural History*, II, 140.

16. Pliny the Elder, *Natural History*, XXXIV, 139; Tacitus, *Histories*, III, 72.

17. DH, v, 34 (or his source), aware of the difficulty, reports that the two leaders quarrelled about their attitude to Cloelia.

18. Plutarch, *Poplicola*, 19, 11.

19. T. B. Macaulay, *Lays of Ancient Rome, Horatius*, LIII–LXIII.

20. DH, v, 23, 3.

21. Varro, *On the Latin Language*, VII, 71. Or 'Cocles' meant that his eyebrows were joined. The word was sometimes regarded as a corruption of 'Cyclops'.

22. Festus (W. M. Lindsay ed., 1913), p. 210 (*animalia*, according to Varro, *On the Latin Language*, VI, 20). The tale of Horatius Cocles has also been thought to be relevant to another festival on 15 May, when twenty-four or twenty-seven puppets of reed and straw known as Argei (the meaning of the name is unknown) were thrown into the Tiber from the Sublician Bridge, after being taken

in procession round the four antique regions of Rome (i.e. excluding the Capitoline and Aventine). This was a magical ceremony intended to gather up and throw away the uncleanness of the city (the Vestal Virgins conducted the rite), and the puppets may well stand for human victims, of whom Horatius, in an earlier version of his story, has been thought to have been one, sacrificing himself, or being sacrificed, to bless the bridge. But there may be no such connection. It has also been suggested that there is a reference to Horatius Cocles in Callimachus, *Aitia* (fragments 106, 107), who writes of a Roman mother consoling her lame son. But the identification is again dubious.

23. Plutarch, *Poplicola*, 17, 1ff.

24. Ogilvie, *Comm.*, p. 262; cf. Festus, 104.

25. Lycurgus, *Against Isocrates*, 84–7. The fall of Cynegirus at Marathon (Herodotus, VI, 114) also seems to have played a part.

26. DH, V, 25, 4.

27. *BMC, Republic*, I, 3358.

28. Plutarch, *Poplicola*, 17.

29. Publius Mucius Scaevola and Publius Licinius Crassus Mucianus.

30. The *quindecimviri sacris faciundis*, Dessau, *Inscriptiones Latinae Selectae*, 5050, line 150.

31. Livy, II, 13, 5. There were also Mucian Altars near Veii, perhaps marking the frontier between the two states.

32. DH, V, 35, 2.

33. DH VI, 13, 1–5 (trans. E. Cary).

34. Here, too, myth intervenes. The alleged Latin claim to independence or equality in 343 B.C. anticipates the Italian claims on the eve of Social (Marsian) War (91–87).

35. cf. the battle of the Cremera (attributed to 479 or 477 B.C.), fought by a non-hoplite feudal army of the Fabii, of whom only one survived; a familiar sort of tale ('the shipwrecked man'), obviously influenced by synchronization with Thermopylae. Ogilvie, *Comm.*, pp. 359f.

36. Cicero, *For Balbus*, 23, 53 (493 B.C.)

37. The date of the battle likewise fluctuates between 499 and 496 B.C.

38. DH, VI, 7, 12–14, (493 – when a Postumus Cominius was consul, Cicero, *For Balbus*, 53). Probably from Cumae or Sicily. Not in Livy.

39. *BMC, Republic*, II, p. 310; no. 718.

40. Livy, II, 20, 12.

41. Pydna (168 B.C.), Verona (101).

42. Strabo, v, 3, 5, 232.

43. S. Weinstock, *Journal of Roman Studies* (1960), pp. 112ff. The dative of Pollux (Latin *Polluci*) is rendered as *Podlouquei*. He was Pultuke at Perusia, Ptoloukes at Praeneste, Polluces (at first) in Latin.

44. Cassius Hemina, fragment 5, traced the Penates back to Samothrace (the Cabiri). For the containers (*doliola*) of the sacred objects of the Penates and Dioscuri, see Ogilvie, *Comm.*, pp. 723f.

45. Mamilii, Fulvii, Fonteii, Juventii. For the caps of the Dioscuri on the coins of Manius Fonteius see *BMC, Republic*, 1, 2476ff; the issue is datable to *c.* 85 B.C. For the antiquarian Gaius Fonteius Capito (consul, 33 B.C.) see chapter 2, section 3, and S. Weinstock, *Papers of the British School at Rome* (1950), pp. 44–9.

46. M. Grant, *The Roman Forum* (1970), pp. 85, 89. The statues were attributed to Pythagoras of Rhegium. A certain L. Domitius who saw the Dioscuri in the Forum was so shaken that his beard turned stiff like metal (Plutarch, *Aemilius Paullus*, 25), earning him and his descendants, who included the emperor Nero, the surname Ahenobarbus. The meaning 'ruddy-bearded' is less probable, cf. R. Syme, *Journal of Roman Studies* (1970), p 33. Domitius is a name of Balkan (Illyrian) type.

47. Florus, I, 3, 7.

48. Thus Valerius Antias stresses the Valerian-Horatian law of 449 (L. Valerius Potitus and M. Horatius Barbatus, see above n. 11), whereas Licinius Macer is more interested in the Licinian-Sextian law of 367 (C. Licinius Stolo and L. Sextius Lateranus). The conflict between the Orders, which began, according to tradition, early in the fifth century B.C. (it is doubtful if there was any sharp distinction between patricians and plebeians in the regal period, chapter 5, note 42) and ended in a sophisticated compromise in 287 (giving the force of law to the ordnances of the plebeians), consisted, on the plebeian side, of a search for more land and more liberal laws of debt and personal security, while wealthier plebeians (though evidence about their appearances in the early Republican Fasti is contradictory) were after political and social equality. Five times (reputedly) the plebeians wielded, or threatened to wield, the weapon of Secession – to the Aventine, or Sacred Mount beyond the River Anio on the road to Nomentum. Consequently Livy needs all his skill to avoid monotony. Yet DH, II, 11, 2, still felt able to claim that Rome had seen no internal bloodshed from Romulus for 630 years.

One of the plebeian heroes, whose story is based on Greek allegories and Indo-European folk-tales, was Menenius Agrippa, allegedly consul in 503 B.C. and conciliator after the alleged First Secession (494): but Antias suppressed him in favour of a Valerius.

Between the first alleged Secession and the second, just after the Board of Ten (decemvirs) had compiled the Twelve Tables which formed the basis of Roman law, comes the classic story of Verginia, slain by her father to save her from a fate worse than death at the hands of the wicked patrician decemvir Appius Claudius, who belonged to a family that the Fabii (represented by the historian Fabius Pictor) detested. The story, 'recorded in many of the greatest works of our literature' (Cicero, *On the State*, 11, 63) but of obscure origins, is markedly analogous to that of the equally chaste Lucretia (chapter 5, section 2: both outrages are the signals for uprisings and cause the supersession of a bad state of affairs), and may be taken from it or may have inspired it, though the lawyers of the second century B.C. added technical legal accretions. Indeed, it is possible that even the names (absent in Diodorus' tradition) were only introduced in the second century, Appius Claudius being invented from Appius Claudius Pulcher (consul, 143 B.C.) – the father-in-law of Tiberius Gracchus. The story of Verginia has close associations with Ardea (which also produced another saga of a Heroic Maid, E. Pais, *Ancient Legends of Roman History*, p. 187).

49. e.g. Harpalyce (warrior-daughter of Harpalycus of Thrace), Penthesilea (queen of the Amazons).

50. Plutarch, *Coriolanus*, 36, 4.

51. Livy, II, 40, 10–12 (trans. A. de Selincourt).

52. Livy, II, 40, 1f.

53. Varro, *On the Latin Language*, IX, 61.

54. Antony had an influential agent, of slave origin, named Publius Volumnius Eutrapelus, whose freedwoman the famous prostitute Cytheris (Antony's mistress) took the name Volumnia.

55. Livy and Dionysius called the mother Veturia; the Veturii had a moneyer, Ti. Veturius B(arrus?), of *c.* 149 B.C., R. Thomsen, *Numismatic Notes and Monographs* (1969), pp. 117–22, and a silver plate glorifies their family, B. Svoboda, *Journal of Roman Studies* (1968), pp. 124ff. The name Vergilius (*BMC, Republic*, 1, 2606f.) is often found, mostly in Etruscan territories (cf. chapter 3, section 3). Roman women of noble character appear as early as Callimachus, fragments 106–7 (identified as the mother of Horatius Cocles, but only conjecturally, n. 22 above).

56. DH, v, 61, 3.

57. Or has there been a confusion with Cora which was disputed between Latins and Volscians?

58. R. Syme, *The Roman Revolution* (1939), p. 85.

59. The temple was dedicated by women who had only had one husband, Ogilvie, *Comm.*, p. 336.

60. Cicero, *Brutus*, 43. Details also taken from the saga of Achilles.

61. Plutarch, *Coriolanus*, 22, 3; cf. *On Anger*, 457D.

62. Heraclitus, fragment 85 (Kirk and Raven 243).

63. According to Livy, v, 4, 13, it was the eighth war between the states: but this was an attempt to lend historic justification to the shocking destruction of a great Etruscan city.

64. Livy, vi, 1, 3; cf. v, 21, 8.

65. Ogilvie, *Comm.*, p. 674.

66. Scholiast on Virgil, *Aeneid*, xii, 841; cf. E. Fraenkel, *Horace* (Oxford, 1966 ed.), p. 238.

67. A. E. Astin, *Scipio Aemilianus* (1967), pp. 282ff.

68. Diodorus places the triumph not after the capture of Veii but after the liberation of Rome from the Gauls.

69. DH, xii, 13.

70. Livy, v, 27, 11ff.

71. Livy, v, *Periochae*.

72. Plutarch, *Camillus*, 22, 5.

73. The view that the attackers of Clusium at the beginning of the fourth century were the first Gauls to have crossed the Alps is contradicted by Livy, v, 33, 5.

74. Livy, v, 33, 2–4; cf. DH, xiii, 14f.

75. Cato, *Origins*, fragments 36.

76. Quintus Fabius Maximus Rullianus (consul 322 B.C. etc., a figure encrusted in anachronistic legend) was said to have a brother who was educated at Caere and knew the Etruscan language and literature well. Cf. Etruscan inscriptions of Au. Fabi. Larthial, A. Fabi. Iucnus. Curce (twice) at Clusium recalls Quintus Fabius Maximus Gurges, conqueror of Volsinii in 266. For the myth of the Fabii at the Cremera, see above, n. 35.

77. They were needed, *inter alia*, to compensate for hostile accounts of the defeat of Marcus Fabius Ambustus by Tarquinii (356–5 B.C.: Livy, vii, 17, 2ff.).

78. DH, xii, 13. The captured soothsayer had prophesied the early fall of Rome to the Gauls, Cicero, *On Divination*, I, 44, 100.

79. 387 B.C. is 'the agreed date' according to DH, I, 74, 4; but Livy's date was 390 and Pictor's 384.

80. Ennius, *Annals*, fragments 251–2; Lucan, fragment 16.

81. Nepos, *Themistocles*, II, 4, 1.

82. Lucius Papirius Cursor (consul 326 etc.) and his son of the same name (consul 293 and 272). The extreme democrat Gnaeus Papirius Carbo (consul 85) is likely to have been less interested (his branch of the family did not go back beyond the Gracchi).

83. Cicero, *For Sulla*, 25 (Asculum; Ascoli Piceno).

84. Virgil, *Aeneid*, VIII, 655–62 (trans. C. Day Lewis).

85. Livy, V, 47, 4.

86. Plutarch, *Roman Questions*, 98, 287.

87. Florus, I, 7, 13–19.

88. The prolongation of Camillus' dictatorship after the withdrawal of the Gauls was also taken from Sulla.

89. Livy, V, 46, 10, carefully prefers to think that Camillus did not leave Ardea for Veii until he had learnt of his appointment by the Assembly (Comitia Curiata).

90. Diodorus, XIV, 116.

91. On the other side, Camillus' praiseworthy rivalry with Lucius Furius Medullinus was inspired by the action of Quintus Fabius Maximus Verrucosus Cunctator in rescuing Marcus Minucius Rufus from disaster.

    The same theme was revived in honour of another classic hero assigned to a date earlier than Camillus, namely the homespun, frugal Lucius Quinctius Cincinnatus, who owed his fame to his call from the plough to save his fatherland (460 or 458 B.C.). For Cincinnatus, too, on appointment as dictator, was said to have rescued and rebuked a Lucius Minucius Esquilinus Augurinus in similar circumstances. If Cincinnatus ever existed, which is doubtful (an equally dubious Titus Quinctius, again a farmer, was appointed general in 342 B.C.), his career is buried beneath a diversified heap of topical quarrels injected from the second century B.C. Cincinnatus, legendary ancestor of a family who were regarded as patrons of letters, was a favourite figure of the plebeians (DH, X, 6, 1), a foil to the decadent Appius Claudius who wanted to seduce Verginia (see note 47 above).

92. Polybius, II, 18, 2–6, 22–5.

93. Ogilvie, *Comm.*, p. 727.

94. Though the Valerii took the credit for the victory of *c.* 349 for their legendary hero Marcus Valerius Corvus.

95. Virgil, *Aeneid*, VI, 826.

96. For the calculation that the former version (Livy) must date from before 52 B.C. and the latter (DH) from after that date, see Ogilvie, *Comm.*, p. 738.

97. Livy, V, 49, 5.

98. Cicero, *On the State*, II, 5, 10.

99. Livy, V, 52, 1. Perhaps the plebeians found Veii a more attractive prospect than patrician-controlled Rome.

100. Virgil, *Aeneid*, XII, 823–8 (trans. C. Day Lewis).

101. For Camillus was ascribed a further career of twenty-five years, active but not very dramatic. His part in the settlement of 367 B.C., introducing the plebeians to the consulship, and in the subsequent dedication of the Temple of Concordia, may be mythical. But Camillus may well have reorganized the Roman army (cf. Plutarch, not Livy) and helped Rome's long, hard and complete recovery from the Gallic disaster – during a period when Fabii and Licinii mainly governed the city, in alliance with Caere.

102. Livy, V, 49, 7; VII, 1, 10.

103. Though Livy's accounts (XXXI, 10, 21f, 47f.) suspiciously duplicate his victory and the subsequent success of Gaius Cornelius Cethegus (consul 197).

104. 340, 295 (the most likely to be authentic, if any of them are) and 279 B.C.

105. Polybius, I, 35.

106. Cicero, *On Duties*, I, 13, 39; cf. Tubero, fragment 9. Florus, I, 18, 2, 25 : prison or torture.

107. Horace, *Odes*, III, 5, 41–56 (trans. James Michie). Venafrum, on the border between Latium and Campania, was famous for its olives. For Spartan Tarentum see chapter 4 section 3.

108. Diodorus, XXIII, 15, 1–6. Probably from the pro-Carthaginian Philinus of Acragas (Agrigentum).

109. Cicero, *Against Piso*, 43, etc.

110. Another Marcus Atilius Regulus was consul in 227 B.C., and a Gaius in 225; in the second century the family produced several moneyers. The family was probably Campanian.

111. M. Grant, *Nero* (1970), p. 145.

112. He also, notoriously, gave a false piece of archaeological information to Livy (about Aulus Cornelius Cossus), for topical reasons of contemporary politics (Ogilvie, *Comm.*, pp. 72, 557f., 563ff.) : though it is possible that the mistake was due to a genuine misinterpretation rather than a deliberate falsification.

7 THE CHARACTER OF ROMAN MYTHOLOGY

1. M. Grant, *Myths of the Greeks and Romans*, pp. 121ff.

2. H. J. Rose, *A Handbook of Greek Mythology*, p. 305.

3. G. S. Kirk, *Myth*, p. 174; cf. A. M. Hocart, *The Life-giving Myth*

(London 1952), p. 10: 'It is as vain to look to Homer for the primitive significance of the myth as it would be to seek it in Malory.'

4. M. Grant, *History Today* (1969), pp. 93ff.; cf. P. Walcot, *Hesiod and the Near East* (1966) etc. Often the transmission process is complex, e.g. the Kumarbi story, G. S. Kirk, *Myth*, p. 219.

5. e.g. a fragment of the Gilgamesh myth has been found at Megiddo in Palestine; and the Babylonian myth of Adapa has turned up in Egypt. Hebrew writers adapted Canaanite myths to describe the deeds of Yahweh.

6. The same even applies to the Sumerian myths, which were already highly literate, philosophizing products of scribal schools.

7. It has been conjectured that the world's mythical corpus goes back to a common origin in *c.* 7,500–5,500 B.C., possibly in the middle east.

8. cf. M. Grant, *Myths of the Greeks and Romans*, p. 122; and for aetiological myths in general, ibid., index, s.v. methods (aetiological).

9. G .S. Kirk, *Myth*, p. 77 etc.

10. G. S. Kirk, *Myth*, pp. 115ff.

11. H. J. Rose – C. M. Robertson, *Oxford Classical Dictionary*, 2nd ed., p. 883; cf. the Pandora story, to explain evil. In the *Odyssey*, the 350 cattle of the Sun explain the days of the year, but the poet has inherited the story without taking note of the correspondence.

12. Livy, XLIV, I, II (Quintus Marcius Philippus). We know more about the rituals of the Romans than about their myths; cf. many North American Indian tribes, in contrast to the Greeks and the Bushmen.

13. Very often, especially by anthropologists and theologians, no myth is described as a myth unless it is a religious or sacred tale: 'the narrative has a sacred quality; the sacred communication is made in symbolic form' (P. S. Cohen, *Man*, n.s., IV (1969), p. 337). The present book does not narrow down the meaning of the term in this way (see Introduction; cf. G. S. Kirk, *Myth*, pp. 8f.; M. Grant, *Myths of the Greeks and Romans*, p. xix), but the divergence between the two definitions is a fruitful cause of misunderstandings: cf. E. R. Leach, *Lévi-Strauss*, p. 54; *Times Literary Supplement* (1970), p. 889. Moreover, there are also a great many other quite different definitions of the word 'myth'; some of them are collected by W. W. Douglas in *Myth and Literature*, ed. J. B. Vickery, pp. 119ff. (The word 'mythology', incidentally, gives rise to another sort of misunderstanding, because it can mean

either the study of myths, or their content, or a particular set of myths.)

14. For a summary of the present writer's views on Roman religion see forthcoming ed. of *Encyclopaedia Britannica*, s.v.

15. The most recent arguments are discussed by G. S. Kirk, *Myth*, pp. 8ff., 23ff., 115, 225.

16. J. Fontenrose, *Python*, p. 461: 'It is simpler to suppose that a well-known type of story was introduced in many places to serve as the primeval precedent of the rituals than to believe that in so many places the rituals spontaneously generated a uniform pattern of myth.'

17. M. Grant, *Roman Anniversary Issues* (1950), p. xii.

18. F. Altheim, *History of Roman Religion*, pp. 190f.

19. C. Lévi-Strauss, *Leçon inaugurale au Collège de France*, Paris (1960), pp. 41ff; cf. *The Savage Mind*, pp. 233f. But I owe to G. W. Robinson the comment that it is oddly hard to place the Japanese or Chinese firmly in one or other of these categories.

20. S. F. Nadel, *A Black Byzantium*, London, (1942), p. 72.

21. Possibly myths largely originate from narrative structures of this kind; cf. G. S. Kirk, *Myth*, p. 280. They 'link the moral affirmation with an earlier, original, childhood state' (P. S. Cohen, *Man*, n.s., IV (1969), p. 343).

22. The answer to the question whether we can learn more about ancient Rome from its archaeology (chapter I) or its myths is that we need both. Their coexistence makes Rome the ideal school of historical method (A. Momigliano, *Journal of Roman Studies* (1963), p. 108).

23. Thucydides, I, 10; cf. II, 29.

24. A useful modern distinction (though its systematic employment with regard to Roman mythology would be impracticable) is between 'myth', that is to say thoroughgoing fiction, and 'legend' (H. J. Rose called it pseudosaga), represented by stories based, however remotely, on historical fact; cf. M. Grant, *Myths of the Greeks and Romans*, p. 34. (*The Ballad of Chevy Chase*, and the Serbian epic on the battle of Kossovo, are examples of legend which contain so little historical fact that they have gone almost all the way towards myth.) Strabo, I, 2, 9, seems to be drawing a less usual distinction when he declares that the wanderings of Odysseus, Menelaus and Jason 'make no contribution to knowledge, which is the aim of the practical man'; but what he is virtually saying is that these stories are myth and not legend.

25. Often a chronological dividing-line is drawn, between remoter,

mythical epochs and more recent, ostensibly credible times, cf. W. Bascom, *Journal of American Folk-lore*, LXXVIII (1965), pp. 10f. Among the Crowe Indians, for example, marvellous happenings are thought to have been a matter of daily routine until a few decades ago. The Tsimshian Indians believe that the transition occurred when animals and human beings stopped exchanging shapes.

26. This familiar situation is forcibly restated by C. Lévi-Strauss, *The Savage Mind*, pp. 257–62: 'History is never history, but history-for ... As we say of certain careers, history may lead to anything provided you get out of it.' For ordinary men, he continues, as opposed to professional scholars, the importance of history lies in what is believed to have happened. It is doubtful if either history or myth could exist without the other (P. Munz, *Philosophical Quarterly* (1956), p. 9).

27. Belief or non-belief, on the part of those who told and listened to the stories, is one criterion employed in the distinction between the terms 'myth' and 'folk-tale'. Stories of these two categories are distinguished by the Trobrianders, Oglala Dakota (Sioux) Indians, and Haussa of Northern Nigeria, cf. R. Pettazzoni, *Essays on the Histories of Religions* (Leiden 1954), pp. 12f. But many other distinctions between the terms 'myth' and 'folk-tale' (or *märchen*) have also been attempted, cf. G. S. Kirk, *Myth*, pp. 34ff. In the present book I have occasionally used the words 'folk-tale', 'folklore', loosely to describe the less sophisticated type of story, but no distinction between these terms and 'myth' existed in the languages of the Greeks or the Romans, and the differentiation has been dismissed as a nineteenth-century invention (as E. W. Count in *Culture in History*, ed. S. Diamond, pp. 596f.); it can only justify the conclusion that the folk-tale is a species of myth, not a separate category altogether (cf. Kirk, *Myth*, p. 37).

28. This might, perhaps, be used as a text for the theory (to put it all too briefly) that myths are unconsciously designed to provide a mediation of insoluble problems and, in particular, to mask contradictions between morality and the facts of experience (Lévi-Strauss, *Structural Anthropology*, New York, 1963 (London 1968), p. 229; cf. *The Raw and the Cooked: Introduction to a Science of Mythology*, discussed by G. S. Kirk, *Myth*, see index, s.v. polarities). E. R. Leach has worked out a comparable thesis in 'The Legitimacy' of Solomon in *Genesis as Myth and Other Essays*, pp. 25ff. P. S. Cohen, *Man*, n.s., iv (1969), pp. 337f., prefers to see this tendency to polarization as a narrative device due to people's unease in reconciling different ideas to one another. G. E. R. Lloyd, *Polarity and*

Analogy (Cambridge 1966), recalled the importance of opposites in Greek pre-Socratic philosophy.

29. Cicero, *On the Orator*, II, 36.

30. Livy, I, preface, 10.

31. DH, I, 5, 3. cf. Florus, I, 17, 25, 5.

32. P. G. Walsh, *Livy*, p. 66.

33. M. Grant, *The Ancient Historians*, pp. 137ff. At the same time Plato (*Republic*, II, 378 B–C) was stressing that a person listening to myths will deduce moral principles from them. But centuries earlier Hesiod (perhaps nearly contemporary to the Hebrew prophet Amos) was already employing his myths to edify.

34. Especially the neo-Stoicism of Panaetius. Influenced by such approaches, DH, II, 20, 1f., is severely critical of Greek myths that do not toe the ethical line (but already in the sixth century Xenophanes, fragment 169 Kirk and Raven, had refused to believe in sordid action by the gods). The funeral oration for Lucius Caecilius Metellus (died 221 B.C.) is untouched by Greek ethics, but probably not the epitaph written at the end of the same century which describes Lucius Cornelius Scipio (consul, 259 B.C.) as 'the best of good men' (*Corpus Inscriptionum Latinarum*, I², 9).

35. Ennius, *Annals*, fragment 467.

36. Juvenal, *Satires*, VII, 233ff., complained that a schoolmaster was supposed to know every mythological detail, for example the family relationships of an obscure figure mentioned once in Virgil, or the name of Anchises' nurse.

37. Augustine, *City of God*, V, 18.

38. Herbert Spencer (1820–1903) explained myths as mainly consisting of glorified ancestral legends.

39. *Cirpus Inscriptionum Latinarum*, I², 15.

40. Suetonius, *Augustus*, 89, 2.

41. Suetonius, *Augustus*, 3, 5.

42. Polybius, VI, 56. Polybius, IX, 1 (4), cf. VII, 8 (7), maintained that historians ought to avoid myths – though miracle tales and the like were permissible if they did not go too far!

43. Quintus Mucius Scaevola, quoted by Varro in Augustine, *City of God*, VI, 27.

44. Cicero, *On Laws*, II, 12. This downward propagation was more far-seeing than the practice of the Ashantis etc. who only tell their myths for instruction within the in-group: W. Bascom, *Journal of American Folk-lore*, LXXVIII (1965), p. 12.

45. There is no place for personal religion: the social tradition was always hostile to the cultivation of purely private concerns.

46. The idea may go back to the fifth-century philosopher Democritus, who seems to have conceded no Justice, no irrational sanctions of behaviour, that could not be resolved into the interplay of atoms and void, cf. G. S. Kirk and J. E. Raven, *The Presocratic Philosophers* (Cambridge; paperback ed. 1966), p. 425.

47. We cannot, therefore, satisfy the very reasonable requirements of K. O. Müller (1797–1840), who stressed the importance of knowing the time and place when the earliest form of each tale appeared.

48. cf. H. J. Rose, *Handbook of Greek Mythology*, p. 306. In origin, therefore, Roman myth has little in common with the theories of Otto Rank ('a dream of the masses of the people', 1909), or Sigmund Freud ('the distorted vestige of the wish-phantasies of whole nations'); though owing to the cleverness of the Roman governing class the mythology caught on to such an extent that, in due course, such descriptions almost became applicable.

49. C. Lévi-Strauss, *The Raw and the Cooked*.

50. C. Lévi-Strauss, *Esprit*, n.s. x (1963), pp. 630ff.

51. T. S. Eliot, *The Rock*.

52. P. S. Cohen, *Man*, n.s., iv (1969), p. 351; M. Grant, *Myths of the Greeks and Romans*, p. xix; G. S. Kirk, *Myth*, pp. 7, 83, whose reviewer in the *Times Literary Supplement* (1970), p. 889, strongly objects to this conclusion, because, as he realizes, they are defining 'myth' in different senses: the reviewer himself prefers to follow the practice indicated in note 13 above.

53. Aristotle, *Poetics*, 24, 8.

54. Livy, i, preface, 5, makes the unusual admission that he enjoys writing about the remote past because it distracts attention from the anxious present. But this is partly a rhetorical commonplace deploring the deterioration from the Good Old Days, cf. chapter 2, section 3.

55. H. Meyerhoff, *Time in Literature* (Berkeley 1955), p. 109, points out that although the ancients *knew* much less about the past than we do, they *felt* a much greater sense of identification with it.

56. C. Lévi-Strauss, *The Savage Mind*, p. 236.

57. C. Lévi-Strauss, *Structural Anthropology*, p. 217, summarized by E. R. Leach, *Lévi-Strauss*, pp. 54–82; G. S. Kirk, *Myth*, pp. 42–83. Lévi-Strauss even feels, for example, that in considering the myth of Oedipus it is desirable to include Freud's interpretation when one is studying the structural pattern since the Freudian theory brings out additional meanings latent in the myth.

58. e.g. in the case of Jewish myths, *Esprit*, n.s., XI (1963), p. 632; though perhaps he might withdraw the reservation in the light of E. R. Leach's structuralist approaches to the Old Testament in *Genesis as Myth and other Essays*.

59. cf. G. S. Kirk, *Myth*, pp. 74, 82. This is denied, however, by the reviewer mentioned in note 52 above, who maintains that Lévi-Strauss is referring to another conception of 'structure, not closely linked with manifest content' but an 'algebra of relations between relations'. (Lately, however, W. G. Runciman, *British Journal of Sociology*, XX (1969), pp. 253–65 [cf. Mary Douglas, *The Structural Study of Myth and Totemism*, ed. E. R. Leach] has called this whole approach into question.) Lévi-Strauss himself compares South American myths to instrumental parts of a single musical work, to be studied in respect of their reciprocal interrelations, the last 'movement presupposed by its beginners': but he is accused of selecting the 'themes' arbitrarily, and in any case the Roman myths were often composed centuries apart. However, Lévi-Strauss, apart from incursions into Greek myth (e.g. Oedipus, cf. note 57 and chapter 3, note 19: *Structural Anthropology*, pp. 213ff., doubted by G. S. Kirk, *Myth*, pp. 49f, and 83, and E. R. Leach, *Lévi-Strauss*, p. 67) has largely concentrated on systems in which the historical record is virtually non-existent. According to P. Ricoeur, *Esprit*, n.s., XI (1963), p. 607, this is because all other sorts of society would be recalcitrant to any such attempts.

60. G. S. Kirk, *Myth*, p. 50; cf. p. 285; 'in the end the firmest part of our study will continue to be the careful and sympathetic documents, surviving myths themselves;' and A. M. Hocart, *The Life-giving Myth* (London 1952), p. 184, who praises an article because 'it gives us the Azande point of view in their own words and actions, and does not romance about what is going on inside their minds'.

61. cf. E. R. Leach, *Genesis as Myth and other Essays*, p. 64, cf. 56: Solomon is 'directly descended' from Esau the Edomite and Heth the Canaanite because he wants to claim their lands.

62. cf. Lord Raglan, *The Hero* (London 1949), p. 114. The wealth of Greek mythical personnel is due to the number of distinct regions involved. No doubt the equally individual regions and city-state areas of Etruria likewise each possessed their own distinct mythological personages.

63. Their origins probably had more to do with enquiry and curiosity regarding human behaviour.

64. e.g. Stesichorus (C. M. Bowra, *Classical Quarterly*, XXVIII (1934),

pp. 115ff.). The Dorians (who like the Romans had few myths of their own) adopted Heracles in order, through his sons, to legitimize their conquest of the Peloponnese, and the Macedonians did likewise to make themselves seem Greeks. Athens also doctored the myths, for example to support its claim to be the mother-city of Ionia, and Solon and Pisistratus were accused of tampering with the *Iliad* (chapter 3, section 3). Thucydides, 1, 20, was annoyed with falsifications of the story of the assassination of Hipparchus of Athens by Harmodius and Aristogeiton.

65. cf. A. J. Podlecki, *The Political Background of Aeschylean Tragedy* (Ann Arbor 1966); V. Ehrenberg, *Pericles and Sophocles* (Oxford 1954); G. Zunz, *The Political Plays of Euripides* (Oxford 1955) and others.

66. After Thucydides, the historians quickly went back to accepting as history a great many more myths than he had cared to admit. Orators of the fourth century B.C., too, wholly ignored the new rationalizing spirit; Isocrates and others deliberately glorified the Athenian mythological past. Alexander the Great claimed Zeus as his father (*vanitas*, according to Livy, IX, 18, 4). The kings who succeeded him developed ancestral mythologies of their own (for the Ptolemies cf. E. Bevan, *History of Egypt under the Ptolemaic Dynasty*, 1927, p. 120 and note 2), and respected local myths when they had to adjudicate the claims of rival Greek cities; cf. the mythical assertions of Acarnania to Rome in order to justify themselves on a current political issue, chapter 3, section 2.

67. One of the principal divergences of Greek myths from those of Mesopotamia consisted in their preoccupation with family affairs (including also a strong concern with tensions *within* the family).

68. The basis exists in M. P. Nilsson's *Cults, Myths, Oracles and Politics in Ancient Greece* (Athens 1951).

BIBLIOGRAPHY

I. MYTHICAL ROME

a Ancient Sources

These are discussed in chapter 2; the archaeological evidence, briefly, in chapter 1. The coins are also important: H. A. Grueber, *Catalogue of Roman Coins in the British Museum (Republic)* (*BMC, Republic*) (:910) has the fullest discussion of their designs (though it is by no means conclusive), but Michael Crawford, *Roman Republican Coinage* (O.U.P., 1973), is more up-to-date.

b Modern Sources

Alföldi, A., *Early Rome and the Latins* (Ann Arbor 1965) (principal conclusions unconvincing but much useful material).

    Die Trojanischen Urahnen der Römer (Basel 1957).

Badian, E., 'The early Historians', in *Latin Historians*, ed. T. A. Dorey (London 1966), ch. 1.

Barrow, R. H. *Plutarch and his Times* (London 1967).

Bayet, J., *Histoire politique et psychologique de la réligion romaine*, 2nd ed. (Paris 1969).

    Tite-Live: Histoire romaine, vol. 1 (Paris, from 1940).

Bloch, R., *The Etruscans*, 2nd ed. (London 1961; French ed. 1956).

    The Origins of Rome, 2nd ed. (London 1964; French ed. 1959).

    Tite-Live et les premiers siècles de Rome (Paris 1965) (also in J. Bayet, *Tite-Live*, 1, pp. 99ff.).

Bowersock, G. W., *Augustus and the Greek World* (Oxford 1965) (on Dionysius of Halicarnassus).

Boyancé, P., *La Religion de Virgile* (Paris 1963).

Camps, W. A., ed., *Propertius, Book IV* (Cambridge 1965).

Dumézil, G., *Archaic Roman Religion* (London 1971).

Fabre, P., *La Réligion romaine* (Paris 1955).

Fraenkel, E., *Horace* (Oxford 1957; paperback ed. 1966).

Galinsky, G. K., *Aeneas, Sicily and Rome* (Princeton 1969).

Gjerstad, E., *Legends and Facts of Early Roman History* (Lund 1962).

Gossage, A. J., 'Plutarch', in *Latin Biography*, ed. T. A. Dorey (London 1967), ch. 3.

Grant, M., *The Ancient Historians* (London and New York 1970).
   Myths of the Greeks and Romans (London and Ohio 1962, New York 1964).

Griffith, G. T. Bibliographical notes on Diodorus Siculus and Plutarch, in *Fifty Years (and Twelve) of Classical Scholarship* (Oxford 1958), pp. 237f.

Hampe, R., and Simon, E., *Griechische Sagen in der frühen Etruskischen Kunst* (Mainz 1964).

Hanell, K., 'Zur Problematik der älteren römischen Geschichtsschreibung', in *Entretiens de la Fondation Hardt*, IV, pp. 147ff. (Geneva 1956).

Harris, W. V., *Rome in Etruria and Umbria* (Oxford 1971).

Heurgon, J., *La vie quotidienne chez les Etrusques* (Paris 1961).

Hubaux, J., *Les grandes mythes de Rome* (Paris 1945).
   Rome et Véies (Louvain 1958).

Jones, C. P., *Plutarch and Rome* (Oxford 1971).

Kluckhohn, C., *Anthropology and the Classics* (Rhode Island 1961).

Latte, K., *Römische Religionsgeschichte* (Munich 1960).
   Les Origines de la République romaine, Entretiens de la Fondation Hardt, XIII (Geneva 1967).

McKay, A. G., *Vergil's Italy* (New York and Bath 1971).

Michels, A. K., *The Calendar of the Roman Republic* (Princeton 1967).

Mix, E. R., *Marcus Atilius Regulus* (Hague–Paris 1970).

Momigliano, A., *Studies in Historiography* (London 1966).

Münzer, F., *The Roman Nobility* (Blackwell, Oxford, 1969) (translation of *Römische Adelsparteien und Adelsfamilien*, Stuttgart 1920).

Ogilvie, R. M., *Commentary on Livy, Books I-V* (Oxford 1965), abbreviated as *Comm.*; invaluable: repays constant reference.
   The Romans and their Gods (London 1969).

Oswalt, S. G., *Concise Encyclopaedia of Greek and Roman Myth* (London 1969).

Pais, E., *Ancient Legends of Roman History* (New York and London 1906).

Pallottino, M., *The Etruscans* (London 1955), and new editions.

Palmer, R., *The Archaic Community of the Romans* (Cambridge 1970).

Perowne, S., *Roman Mythology* (London 1969), an illustrated survey of the religious beliefs of the Romans.

Perret, J., *Les Origines de la légende troyenne* (Paris 1942), main thesis unacceptable, but valuable collection of evidence.

Pöschl, V., *The Art of Vergil* (Ann Arbor 1962; German ed. 1950.)

Pouchet, J., 'Les origines mythiques des Sabins', *Recueil des travaux historiques et philosophiques*, Université de Louvain, sér. 4, fasc. 31–2 (Louvain 1963).

Quinn, K., *Virgil's Aeneid* (London 1968).

Rose, H. J., *Gods and Heroes of the Greeks* (London 1957). Chapter 6 on Roman myths.

Handbook of Greek Mythology: including its Extension to Rome (London 1928), and new eds.

Modern Methods in Classical Mythology (London 1930).

Rostagni, A., *Da Livio a Virgilio* (Padua 1942).

Scherer, M., *The Legends of Troy in Art and Literature* (London 1963).

Scullard, H. H., *The Etruscan Cities and Rome* (London 1967).

Strasburger, H., 'Zur Sage von der Gründung Roms' in *Sitzungsberichte der Heidelberger Akademie der Wissenschaften, Philosophisch-historische Klasse*, v (Heidelberg 1958).

Strong, D., *The Early Etruscans* (London 1968).

Walsh, P. G., *Livy: His Historical Aims and Methods* (Cambridge 1967).

Werner, R., *Der Beginn der römischen Republik* (Munich 1953).

II. MYTHOLOGY IN GENERAL

A brief bibliography was given in my *Myths of the Greeks and Romans* (1962), pp. 445ff. Out of the immense amount that has been published since that book went to press, the following may be found interesting. Some of these subjects are discussed in chapter 7 above.

Diamond, S., ed., *Culture in History* (New York 1960).

Dillistone, F. W., ed., *Myth and Symbol* (London 1966).

Dumézil, G., *Mythe et épopée* (Paris 1968). See also below s.v. Littleton.

Kirk, G. S., *Myth* (Cambridge and California 1970), with detailed references to articles in journals.

Leach, E. R., *Genesis as Myth and other Essays* (London 1969).
  Lévi-Strauss (London 1970).
  ed., *The Structural Study of Myth and Totemism* (London 1967).
Lévi-Strauss, C., *The Raw and the Cooked* (London and New York
    1970) (French ed., vol. 1 of *Mythologiques*, 1964).
  The Savage Mind (London 1966; French ed. 1962).
Littleton, C. Scott, *The New Comparative Mythology* (Cambridge
    1967), on the theories of G. Dumézil.
Murray, H. A., ed., *Myth and Mythmaking*, new ed. (Boston 1968).
Paz, O., *Claude Lévi-Strauss* (Ithaca 1970).
Robinson, G. W., 'Early Japanese Chronicles: The Six National
    Histories' in *Historians of China and Japan* (Oxford 1961).
Slote, B., ed., *Myth and Symbol* (Lincoln 1963).
Vickery, J., ed., *Myth and Literature* (Lincoln 1966; Bison ed. 1969).
Watts, A., ed., *Patterns of Myth* (New York 1969).

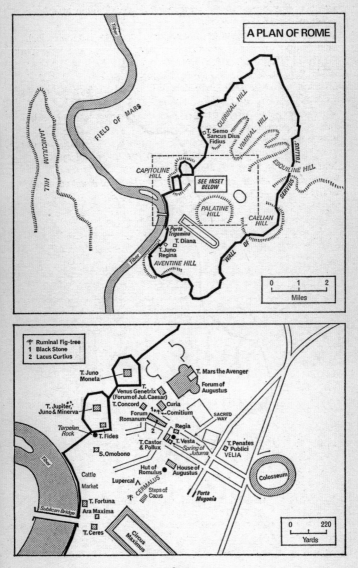

A PLAN OF ROME

Tiber

JANICULUM HILL

FIELD OF MARS

QUIRINAL HILL

VIMINAL HILL

T. Semo Sancus Dius Fidius

CAPITOLINE HILL

SEE INSET BELOW

ESQUILINE HILL

SERVIUS

PALATINE HILL

CAELIAN HILL

Porta Trigemina
T. Diana
T. Juno Regina

WALL OF

Tiber

AVENTINE HILL

| 0 | 1 | 2 |

Miles

🌳 Ruminal Fig-tree
1 Black Stone
2 Lacus Curtius

T. Juno Moneta

T. Mars the Avenger

T. Venus Genetrix (Forum of Jul. Caesar)

Forum of Augustus

T. Jupiter, Juno & Minerva

T. Concord

Curia
Comitium

SACRED WAY

Tarpeian Rock

Forum Romanum

Regia

T. Fides

S. Omobono

T. Castor & Pollux

T. Vesta
Spring of Juturna

T. Penates Publici
VELIA

Tiber

Cattle Market

Lupercal

Hut of Romulus

House of Augustus

Colosseum

Sublican bridge

T. Fortuna

CERMALUS
Steps of Cacus

Porta Mugonia

Ara Maxima

Circus Maximus

T. Ceres

| 0 | 220 |

Yards

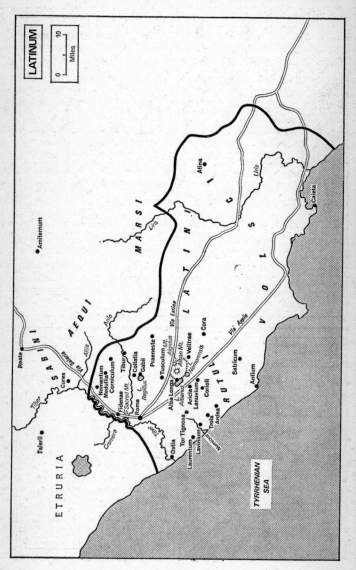

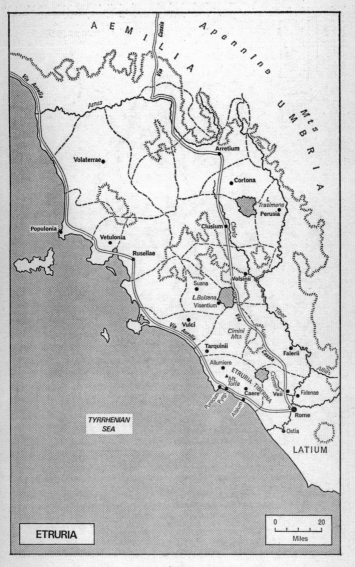

ETRURIA

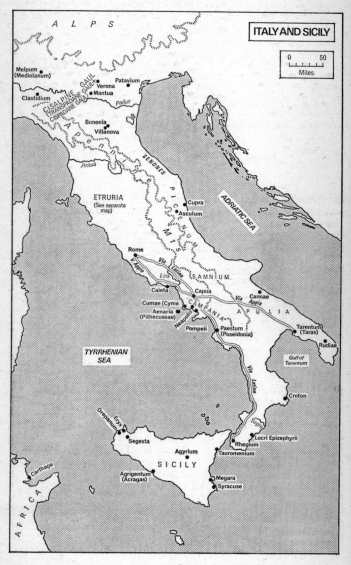

ITALY AND SICILY

0   50
Miles

ALPS

Melpum
(Mediolanum)

CISALPINE GAUL

Clastidium

TRANSPADANE GAUL

CISPADANE GAUL

Verona   Patavium

Mantua

Padus

Bononia

Villanova

Apennines

Arnus

ETRURIA
(See separate
map)

SENONES

PICENUM

Cupra

Asculum

ADRIATIC SEA

Mts

Rome

Via Latina

Via Appia

Liris

Caieta

Capua

Cumae (Cyme)

Aenaria
(Pithecussae)

Neapolis

Pompeii

Paestum
(Poseidonia)

SAMNIUM

CAMPANIA

Cannae

Via Appia

APULIA

Tarentum
(Taras)

Rudiae

TYRRHENIAN
SEA

Gulf of
Tarentum

Via Latina

Croton

Drepanum

Eryx

Segesta

Agyrium

Sagra

Rhegium

Locri Epizephyrii

Tauromenium

SICILY

Carthage

Agrigentum
(Acragas)

Megara

Syracuse

AFRICA

298

INDEX